Countryside Character

Volume 7:
South East & London

The character of

England's natural and

man-made landscape

The
Countryside
Agency

Contents

	page
Chairman's Foreword	4
Introduction	5
The character of England	5
The Countryside Agency and countryside character	8
How we have defined the character of England's countryside	8
– *The National Mapping project*	8
– *Character of England map: a joint approach*	11
– *Describing the character of England*	11
The character of England: shaping the future	11

Areas covered by more than one volume are shown hatched

This is volume 7 of 8 covering the character of England

Character Areas

		page
81	Greater Thames Estuary	13
88	Bedfordshire and Cambridgeshire Claylands	18
90	Bedfordshire Greensand Ridge	25
91	Yardley–Whittlewood Ridge	30
95	Northamptonshire Uplands	35
107	Cotswolds	40
108	Upper Thames Clay Vales	45
109	Midvale Ridge	52
110	Chilterns	56
111	Northern Thames Basin	62
112	Inner London	73
113	North Kent Plain	76
114	Thames Basin Lowlands	80
115	Thames Valley	84
116	Berkshire and Marlborough Downs	89

		page
119	North Downs	94
120	Wealden Greensand	99
121	Low Weald	106
122	High Weald	111
123	Romney Marshes	116
124	Pevensey Levels	121
125	South Downs	125
126	South Coast Plain	131
127	Isle of Wight	137
128	South Hampshire Lowlands	142
129	Thames Basin Heaths	146
130	Hampshire Downs	152
131	New Forest	156
132	Salisbury Plain and West Wiltshire Downs	162
134	Dorset Downs and Cranborne Chase	167
135	Dorset Heaths	172

JOHN DYKE

Acknowledgements

The Countryside Agency acknowledges the contribution to this publication of a great many individuals, partners and organisations without which it would not have been possible. We also wish to thank Chris Blandford Associates, the lead consultants on this project.

View of the wooded Weald from the Surrey Hills. The South Downs can be seen on the horizon, across the extensive patchwork landscape of woods, hedgerows, sunken lanes and enclosed fields.

Foreword

As soon as I saw the Character Map of England I realised that it should have been one of the front pages of my school atlas. Not only does it reflect influences such as geology and landform, but it also records the effect of thousands of years of human activity within an ever-evolving natural world. Thus it, and the supporting descriptive documents, are not merely a celebration of the diversity of our country but they are also an important educational and planning tool – for today and tomorrow.

For unless we recognise and understand the special and local nature of the variety of character within England, we can never hope to protect it, conserve it or even put right some of the damage we have done to it.

A better understanding of what we have now is at the heart of achieving sustainable development in the future.

The landscape descriptions and maps presented here, set out the qualities of today's countryside. They do not ascribe values to particular aspects of the countryside. That is for others to do in a way which is appropriate to the particular purpose for which they want the information. The Countryside Agency will use it to inspire its work.

We have a unique legacy to bequeath to our children – a legacy not just of biodiversity; not just about landscape or history. It is the juxtaposition of town, country and coast; of land form and land use; of history and modern progress; it is, in two words, England's Character; and this book, along with its companion volumes, will tell you what that means.

Richard Simmonds

Richard Simmonds
Chairman, Countryside Commission, 1996-1999

Introduction

The character of England

Think of England and the chances are that you will conjure up an image of the countryside.

That image might be of a willow lined river, quietly meandering through pastures, where cows graze. It might be of a windswept fell, cloaked in purple heather and bounded by crumbling grey stone walls. It might equally be of pylons marching across fields of yellow rape set against a steel grey sky. Or perhaps of dark sunken lanes cutting through chalk ridges crowned with beech and ash woodland. Your image, whatever it is, will grow in your mind as you begin to add in other things you associate with it - a distant church spire, the song of skylarks, the angular horizon of slag heaps, the sudden view across open downland to a hidden vale below.

This is the character of England's countryside. This and much more. We may each have our own particular image, a personal response to our own backgrounds and experiences — together these images reflect the rich and diverse character of England's countryside as a whole. Many different elements combine to create this character. Because of this there is tremendous variety in that character. To recognise the variation in countryside character is to understand how the many influences upon it combine to give a sense of place, to set a tract of countryside apart from adjacent areas. That is what this publication does.

Everywhere has character. As a society, we already place a higher value upon some areas of countryside than the rest. We do this with legislation by, for example, designating National Parks; by spending public money to help look after areas - through schemes such as Environmentally Sensitive Areas; and through our own behaviour, by going to certain places on holiday, for instance. Countryside character is present in all these areas and in the rest of the countryside. Recognising and understanding countryside character is equally important across the whole of England. How we choose to respond to that understanding is the next step, which is not undertaken in this publication.

Most of us have a strong sense of local pride. As we move rapidly towards a global society, we increasingly value the 'anchor' that our local identity gives us. We have pride in both our immediate surroundings, whether it be town or country, and also in feeling that we are part of something that is different, that has a unique sense of place. The character of the countryside is an important part of what many of us take pride in. It may be that we live in the countryside, or that it provides our workplace. It may be that we visit it often, or travel through it. It may even be that we have only experienced it through other media - literature, art, television. But for one or all of these reasons, we identify and take pride in the character of England's countryside.

⟶ p8

Two examples which show how the key characteristics of the South East & London combine to create character areas.

Thames Valley

The Thames Valley floodplain dominates the area as it spreads south from the Chilterns. Windsor Forest to the east and the steep river slopes in the north west of the valley are reminders of how the heavy clay soils were once thickly wooded. Elsewhere the trees have long been cleared for pasture or mineral extraction. Now gravel pits are a common feature.

The river winds across flat lands past well-populated towns such as Maidenhead and Slough and through the outer reaches of London. Here an extensive network of roads, railways and electricity pylons features prominently in the urban fringe landscape.

Historical and cultural associations characterise the valley, with Windsor Castle taking pride of place.

South Downs

With their rolling hills, steep slopes and sculpted dry valleys, the Downs form a typical chalk landscape. Viewed from the Weald, the dominant feature is the long ridge which runs from Winchester to culminate on Beachy Head's dramatic white sea cliffs. Areas of open short-turfed grassland, rich in orchids and other plants, are the result of intensive sheep grazing and give the Downs their characteristic smooth profile. River valleys cut through the hills to the coast, providing narrow belts of wet pasture, important for birds and invertebrates.

East of the meandering Cuckmere and its undeveloped estuary, one of the few on the south coast, tower the Seven Sisters cliffs. In marked contrast to the open grassland and arable areas of the east, the western end of the Downs is well-wooded.

1	North Northumberland Coastal Plain
2	Northumberland Sandstone Hills
3	Cheviot Fringe
4	Cheviots
5	Border Moors and Forests
6	Solway Basin
7	West Cumbria Coastal Plain
8	Cumbria High Fells
9	Eden Valley
10	North Pennines
11	Tyne Gap and Hadrian's Wall
12	Mid Northumberland
13	South East Northumberland Coastal Plain
14	Tyne and Wear Lowlands
15	Durham Magnesian Limestone Plateau
16	Durham Coalfield Pennine Fringe
17	Orton Fells
18	Howgill Fells
19	South Cumbria Low Fells
20	Morecambe Bay Limestones
21	Yorkshire Dales
22	Pennine Dales Fringe
23	Tees Lowlands
24	Vale of Mowbray
25	North Yorkshire Moors and Cleveland Hills
26	Vale of Pickering
27	Yorkshire Wolds
28	Vale of York
29	Howardian Hills
30	Southern Magnesian Limestone
31	Morecambe Coast and Lune Estuary
32	Lancashire and Amounderness Plain
33	Bowland Fringe and Pendle Hill
34	Bowland Fells
35	Lancashire Valleys
36	Southern Pennines
37	Yorkshire Southern Pennine Fringe
38	Nottinghamshire, Derbyshire and Yorkshire Coalfield
39	Humberhead Levels
40	Holderness
41	Humber Estuary
42	Lincolnshire Coast and Marshes
43	Lincolnshire Wolds
44	Central Lincolnshire Vale
45	Northern Lincolnshire Edge with Coversands
46	The Fens
47	Southern Lincolnshire Edge
48	Trent and Belvoir Vales
49	Sherwood
50	Derbyshire Peak Fringe and Lower Derwent
51	Dark Peak
52	White Peak
53	South West Peak
54	Manchester Pennine Fringe
55	Manchester Conurbation
56	Lancashire Coal Measures
57	Sefton Coast
58	Merseyside Conurbation
59	Wirral
60	Mersey Valley
61	Shropshire, Cheshire and Staffordshire Plain
62	Cheshire Sandstone Ridge
63	Oswestry Uplands
64	Potteries and Churnet Valley
65	Shropshire Hills
66	Mid Severn Sandstone Plateau
67	Cannock Chase and Cank Wood
68	Needwood and South Derbyshire Claylands
69	Trent Valley Washlands
70	Melbourne Parklands
71	Leicestershire and South Derbyshire Coalfield
72	Mease / Sence Lowlands
73	Charnwood
74	Leicestershire and Nottinghamshire Wolds
75	Kesteven Uplands
76	North West Norfolk
77	North Norfolk Coast
78	Central North Norfolk
79	North East Norfolk and Flegg
80	The Broads
81	Greater Thames Estuary
82	Suffolk Coast and Heaths
83	South Norfolk and High Suffolk Claylands
84	Mid Norfolk
85	Breckland
86	South Suffolk and North Essex Clayland
87	East Anglian Chalk
88	Bedfordshire and Cambridgeshire Claylands
89	Northamptonshire Vales
90	Bedfordshire Greensand Ridge
91	Yardley-Whittlewood Ridge
92	Rockingham Forest
93	High Leicestershire
94	Leicestershire Vales
95	Northamptonshire Uplands
96	Dunsmore and Feldon
97	Arden
98	Clun and North West Herefordshire Hills
99	Black Mountains and Golden Valley
100	Herefordshire Lowlands
101	Herefordshire Plateau
102	Teme Valley
103	Malvern Hills
104	South Herefordshire and Over Severn
105	Forest of Dean and Lower Wye
106	Severn and Avon Vales
107	Cotswolds
108	Upper Thames Clay Vales
109	Midvale Ridge
110	Chilterns
111	Northern Thames Basin
112	Inner London
113	North Kent Plain
114	Thames Basin Lowlands
115	Thames Valley
116	Berkshire and Marlborough Downs
117	Avon Vales
118	Bristol, Avon Valleys and Ridges
119	North Downs
120	Wealden Greensand
121	Low Weald
122	High Weald
123	Romney Marshes
124	Pevensey Levels
125	South Downs
126	South Coast Plain
127	Isle Of Wight
128	South Hampshire Lowlands
129	Thames Basin Heaths
130	Hampshire Downs
131	New Forest
132	Salisbury Plain and West Wiltshire Downs
133	Blackmoor Vale and Vale of Wardour
134	Dorset Downs and Cranborne Chase
135	Dorset Heaths
136	South Purbeck
137	Isle of Portland
138	Weymouth Lowlands
139	Marshwood and Powerstock Vales
140	Yeovil Scarplands
141	Mendip Hills
142	Somerset Levels and Moors
143	Mid Somerset Hills
144	Quantock Hills
145	Exmoor
146	Vale of Taunton and Quantock Fringes
147	Blackdowns
148	Devon Redlands
149	The Culm
150	Dartmoor
151	South Devon
152	Cornish Killas
153	Bodmin Moor
154	Hensbarrow
155	Carnmenellis
156	West Penwith
157	The Lizard
158	Isles of Scilly
159	Lundy

The Character of England:
landscape, wildlife & natural features

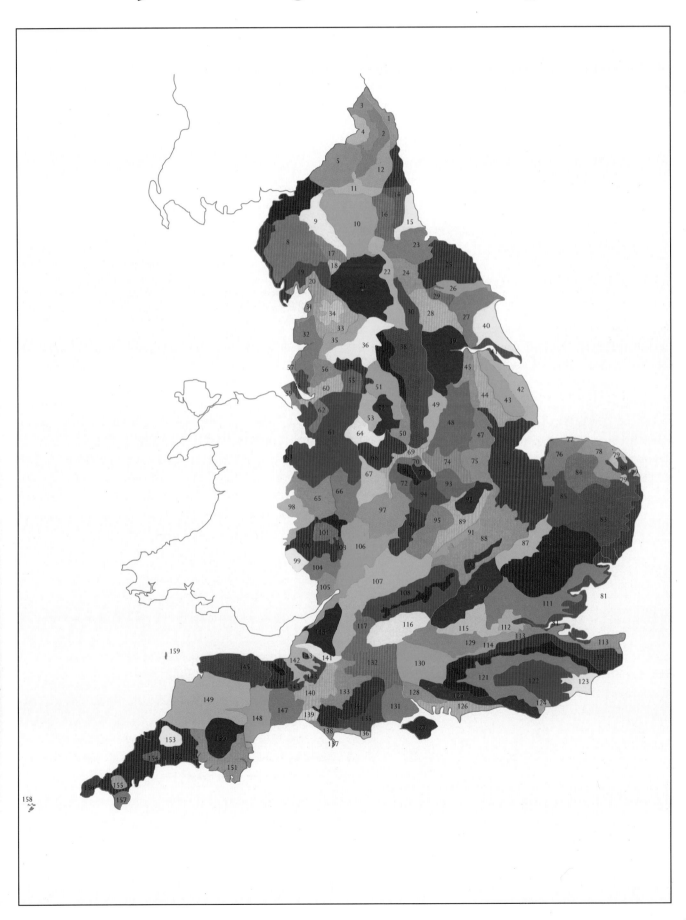

The irony is that as we increasingly begin to appreciate our local distinctiveness, we are also beginning to realise how vulnerable that distinctiveness can be. In an age of mass production, standardisation, economies of scale and international markets, those elements of our countryside that have traditionally been driven by local influences are being quickly eroded. The materials and style of new buildings, the breed of cattle in the field, the shape of the hedgerows, the village sign, the farm gates and buildings are just a few examples. In all of these there is a trend towards uniformity: it is becoming ever more difficult to identify from your surroundings which part of the countryside you are in. It is, therefore, more important than ever that we understand what contributes to the character of England's countryside. Then, we can recognise the impact on this character of the decisions we take, both as individuals and as a society.

The Countryside Agency and countryside character

The Countryside Agency is concerned with the whole of England's countryside.

The English countryside is a priceless national asset. It is fundamental to our national identity as well as a rich source for our local identity. This is reflected in popular public opinion (*Public Attitudes to the Countryside*, Countryside Commission, CCP 481, 1997, £4). The most remarkable aspect of England's countryside is its diversity. The Countryside Agency believes that it is in the national interest to protect and strengthen this diversity. Our work to identify and describe the character of England, which we are publishing here, is intended to:

- raise awareness of the diversity of countryside character we enjoy;

- increase understanding of what contributes to that character and what may influence it in the future; and

- encourage everyone to respect the character of the countryside and take account of it in everything that they do.

The Countryside Agency's predecessor, the Countryside Commission, had a long association with areas of the countryside that are designated as being of national importance (such as the National Parks and Areas of Outstanding Natural Beauty). It was active for many years in trying to encourage greater understanding and more active management of the wider countryside. Through this work, it became apparent that we lacked a consistent and comprehensive understanding of what gave the countryside of England its character. This is an essential starting point for guiding our own policies and decisions and for encouraging others to take account of the impact of their own decisions on the countryside.

The Countryside Commission worked with other bodies to develop the technique of landscape assessment (*Landscape assessment guidance, Countryside Commission, 1993, CCP 423*). This identifies those things that are having an influence on a tract of countryside and describes how the landscape reflects this. It has been applied at a wide range of scales, for a variety of purposes. Even so, much of England's countryside had never had such an assessment carried out which made it impossible to build up a national picture using landscape assessments.

The Countryside Commission identified the need for a new approach, which looked at the whole of England's countryside. This would use a consistent approach nationally. It would need to be at a broad enough scale to give national coverage, whilst ensuring that significant variation in the character of the countryside was picked up. It would provide a consistent national framework within which more detailed local landscape assessments would sit. This approach, which the Countryside Agency has fully adopted, is described in more detail below.

How we have defined the character of England's countryside

Our approach to mapping and describing the character of England's countryside can best be described as a combination of computer based statistical analysis and the consistent application of structured landscape assessment techniques. We initially piloted the approach in the south west of England (*The New Map of England: A Celebration of the South Western Landscape*, Countryside Commission, CCP 444, 1994, £20) from which a successful methodology was developed that was suitable for extending to the national scale. The south west pilot study produced a map of cohesive landscape character areas.

As part of the study, we asked a cross section of the public if they identified with the character areas produced - they did. On the strength of the pilot study, the Commission decided to develop the methodology for use nationally.

The National Mapping Project

The character of the countryside is the result of many different factors or variables. It is the way in which these combine that gives broad areas of the countryside a cohesive and distinctive character. The National Mapping project looked at how these variables combined across England as a basis for the mapping of distinctive character areas. The approach involved:

- identifying the variables that needed to be included;

- obtaining information on each variable for every 1 kilometre square of England; these are called the national data sets;

- combining all the national data sets through a computer based statistical analysis technique, known as TWINSPAN;

- using the results of the TWINSPAN analysis to inform the mapping of cohesive character areas.

The **variables** – these included physical influences (geological, topographical and soils based) and cultural and historical influences (human activity). They were selected by an inter-agency group which the Countryside Commission set up to oversee the countryside character work, following a lot of background research on availability of data and the feasibility of national coverage. In particular, the involvement of English Nature and English Heritage was essential in this process, ensuring that both the ecological and historical dimensions were properly reflected.

The **national data sets** – 12 national data sets were used. These are described in the box opposite. They were put together in a variety of different ways. Some simply had to be extracted from existing source material (eg altitude), others required interpretation of existing information (eg surface geology and ecological character). Some had to be specially created through empirical research (eg field pattern and density and industrial history).

Each data set has a number of attributes. The number of attributes varied between data sets. For example, the settlement pattern data set has only seven attributes, relating to the extent to which settlement is dispersed or clustered together. By contrast, the surface geology data set has 27 attributes reflecting the variety of solid and drift deposits occurring. For each data set, every kilometre square of England was assigned an attribute; hence, each kilometre square has 12 attributes. Full information on the attributes is contained in a Technical Report (*Countryside Character Initiative National Mapping Project, technical report of the computer phase, June 1997, Chris Blandford Associates - unpublished*). A map of each of the national data sets was produced, illustrating the distribution of all attributes across the country. Some examples of these as they relate to the South East & London region are shown in Figures 1 – 5 overleaf.

TWINSPAN analysis – the details of this process are set out in the Technical Report. The basic principle is that all the kilometre squares in the sample (the whole of England) can be divided up into a number of groups on the basis of the presence or absence of a particular attribute. This sub-division continues until an appropriate number of end groups are reached, each of which will contain kilometre squares with similar attributes. The map which resulted from this then informed the definition of character areas.

Map images were derived from the TWINSPAN analysis using all the national data sets and four selected physiographical data sets, respectively. They illustrate how physical factors, such as landform and geology, strongly influence character at the regional and national scale and how historical and cultural factors are significant in providing the more local variation on these broader patterns.

The National Datasets

Altitude: 10 altitudinal attributes, based on Ordnance Survey Digital Terrain Model

Landform: 10 landform classification attributes, based on original interpretation of existing altitude and slope data

Ecological characteristics: 12 ecological character attributes, using drainage and base status as determinants; provided by Soil Survey and Land Research Centre

Land capability: 7 inherent agricultural land capability attributes, based on soil type and drainage characteristics; provided by Soil Survey and Land Research Centre

Surface geology: 27 surface geology attributes, dervied from existing data on solid and drift geology; provided by British Geological Survey

Farm types: 17 categories of farm type, based on Standard Man Day data recorded through MAFF agricultural census; provided by Resource Planning Team, ADAS

Settlement patterns: 7 settlement pattern attributes, based on categorisation of Royal Mail Delivery Point Data; provided by Birkbeck College, University of London

Woodland cover: 8 attributes for woodland type and categories of percentage cover, derived from interpretation of Bartholomew's 1:100000 map series; based on Ordnance Survey

Field density & pattern: 16 categories of field pattern and field density, based on original interpretation of map data by Lancaster University Archaeological Unit, on behalf of Countryside Commission and English Heritage

Visible Archaeology: 12 attributes combining visibility and period, based on interpretation of original data on monuments and linear features provided by the National Monuments Record Centre of the Royal Commission for Historic Monuments in England

Industrial History: 16 categories of dominant industrial history, based on original interpretation of map and documentary sources by Lancaster University Archaeological Unit, on behalf of Countryside Commission and English Heritage

Designed parkland: 7 extant parkland density attributes, derived from comparison of 1918 Ordnance Survey series with current 1:50000 Ordnance Survey

Examples from the Countryside Character Programme National Mapping Project related to the South East & London region

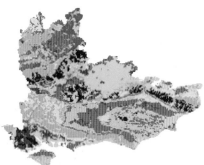

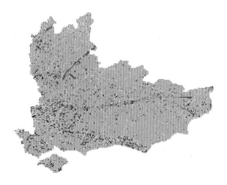

Figure 1
FARM TYPES

Reproduced and adapted from an original provided by FRCA.

Figure 2
ECOLOGICAL CHARACTER

This is copyright material and should not be copied without the express permission of the Cranfield University Soil and Land Research Centre.

Figure 3
VISIBLE ARCHAEOLOGY

Based on information supplied by kind permission of RCHME.

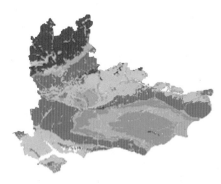

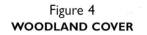

Figure 4
WOODLAND COVER

Based on the Ordnance Survey Map © Crown Copyright 1998
Licence No. GD272434

Figure 5
SURFACE GEOLOGY

Geological map © NERC. All rights reserved. Topographical map
© Crown Copyright reserved.

For all the above figures, colour visual representations derived from IDRISI image for information purposes only. Coastline is an approximation.

Informing the character mapping – the process outlined above was then used to help inform the definition of character areas, broad tracts of countryside exhibiting a cohesive character. This was also based upon a more conventional landscape assessment approach, which drew upon the knowledge and experience of a wide range of people involved in countryside planning and management, a considerable body of existing landscape assessment work and some limited additional fieldwork. The results of the TWINSPAN process were used to validate this more subjective view of countryside character and ensure that the character areas were defined in a consistent way across the whole of England.

The Character of England map: a joint approach

English Nature and English Heritage have both been closely associated with the development of the countryside character approach. English Heritage, as the government agency responsible for the historic dimension of the countryside, worked closely with the Countryside Commission in developing and sourcing the cultural and historical data sets, and advising on the broader process of characterisation. English Nature similarly worked with the Countryside Commission in respect of the soils derived data sets (ecological character and land capability) but their involvement in the mapping process has been more fundamental.

English Nature developed a similar approach to identifying and mapping the countryside according to the distribution of habitats and natural features, which they refer to as natural areas. This work was brought into the definition of character areas with a view to a single joint map of landscape, wildlife and natural features being produced. This was achieved, and the map is shown on page 7. Both English Nature and the Countryside Agency now work from the basis of this joint framework. Both recognise all the character areas identified on it. However, because physical influences are of primary importance in determining ecological variations, English Nature often aggregate the joint character areas into their larger natural areas.

Describing the character of England

Having identified and mapped the character of England, we have gone on to describe each of the character areas shown on the map. It is the descriptions for the character areas in the South East & London that are contained in this publication.

The descriptions have been developed through the wide ranging consultation process referred to above, which also informed the character mapping. Views from interested parties have been sought and material drawn from a great variety of sources. Nationally, over 800 people have contributed, through meetings, seminars and written comment.

For each area, the description seeks to evoke what sets it apart from any other. It aims to put our mental image of that area into words. Each description also provides an explanation of how that character has arisen and how it is changing, and gives some pointers to future management issues. The descriptions are not intended to prescribe any particular course of action as a response to that; only to inform the decision making process.

The character of England: shaping the future

The material contained in this publication describes the character of England's countryside at the end of the 20th century. This character has evolved over thousands of years, as a result of a complex interaction between nature and human activity. The pace of change over that time has ebbed and flowed and will continue to do so. The character of England is dynamic.

The identification and description of the character of England's countryside does not mean that we are seeking to 'freeze' that character at this moment in time. The purpose of the work is to ensure that we understand - from a widely accepted common reference point - the character of England's countryside. Only in this way can we all take proper account of that in all the decisions we make which will have a bearing on it. Greater awareness and understanding will engender greater respect and local pride. This will inform and shape change to make a positive contribution to strengthening countryside character.

We envisage this happening in a number of ways; for example by:

- **focusing national policies** – decisions and activities that have a major bearing on the character of the countryside are often driven by national and international policies, such as land use planning or the Common Agricultural Policy. There is increasing recognition that such policies need to be developed and applied more flexibly at a regional scale to improve their effectiveness and make them more responsive to local needs and priorities. The character of England provides a framework which can be used to provide a regional resolution for such policies, so that they take more account of the needs and opportunities within each region.

- **giving national meaning to local action** – encouraging local pride lies at the heart of ensuring that the character of England continues in all its diversity into the future. Local people have the greatest potential of all to recognise and strengthen local distinctiveness. The character of England provides a national context for local action, strengthening the link between local and national heritage, and providing a source of information and ideas to feed into local decision making.

Countryside Character is being published in 8 volumes, following the boundaries of the administrative areas of the Government Offices for the Regions:

North East
North West
Yorkshire & the Humber
East Midlands
West Midlands
East of England
South East & London
South West
(Merseyside is included in the North West volume.)

Greater Thames Estuary

Key Characteristics

- Extensive open spaces dominated by the sky within a predominantly flat, low-lying landscape. The pervasive presence of water and numerous coastal estuaries extend the maritime influence far inland.

- Strong feeling of remoteness and wilderness persists on the open beaches and salt marshes, on the reclaimed farmed marshland and also on the mudflats populated by a large and varied bird population.

- Traditional unimproved wet pasture grazed with sheep and cattle. Extensive drained and ploughed productive arable land protected from floods by sea walls, with some areas of more mixed agriculture on higher ground.

- Open grazing pastures patterned by a network of ancient and modern reed-fringed drainage ditches and dykes, numerous creeks and few vertical boundaries such as hedges or fences.

- Hedgerows are absent from the large, rectilinear fields with trees beginning where the marsh ceases and the ground starts to rise on land overlying the London Clay Lowlands. Generally, tree cover is limited to farmsteads and dwellings on the higher, drier pockets of ground.

- Distinctive military heritage on coastline such as Napoleonic military defences and 20th century pillboxes.

- Contrast and variety within the Estuary is provided by Sheppey, a long low island rising from a stretch of very flat marsh along the Swale estuary in Kent with low, steep, clay cliffs facing towards Essex across the Thames estuary.

- Numerous small villages and hamlets related to the coastal economy of fishing (at Mersea), boatbuilding and yachting. The historically important coastal cargo transport network of 'Thames Barges' developed as a result of settlement pattern.

- Modern day pattern of local parishes reflects the historical layout of settlements, surrounded by farmland on the higher ground inland, giving way to marsh down to the waterfront.

- Pressure on edges, particularly around major estuaries, from urban, industrial and recreational developments together with the associated infrastructure requirements often on highly visible sites against which the marshes are often viewed.

- The Thames edge marshes are themselves subject to the chaotic activity of various major developments including ports, waste disposal, marine dredging, urbanisation, mineral extraction and prominent power stations plus numerous other industry-related activities such as petrochemical complexes.

Landscape Character

The Greater Thames Estuary is the narrow strip of soft coastline between the Swale estuary on the Kent coast to

JOHN TYLER/COUNTRYSIDE AGENCY

The maritime influence is carried far inland by the pervasive presence of water in creeks and inlets, as here at Alresford, Essex.

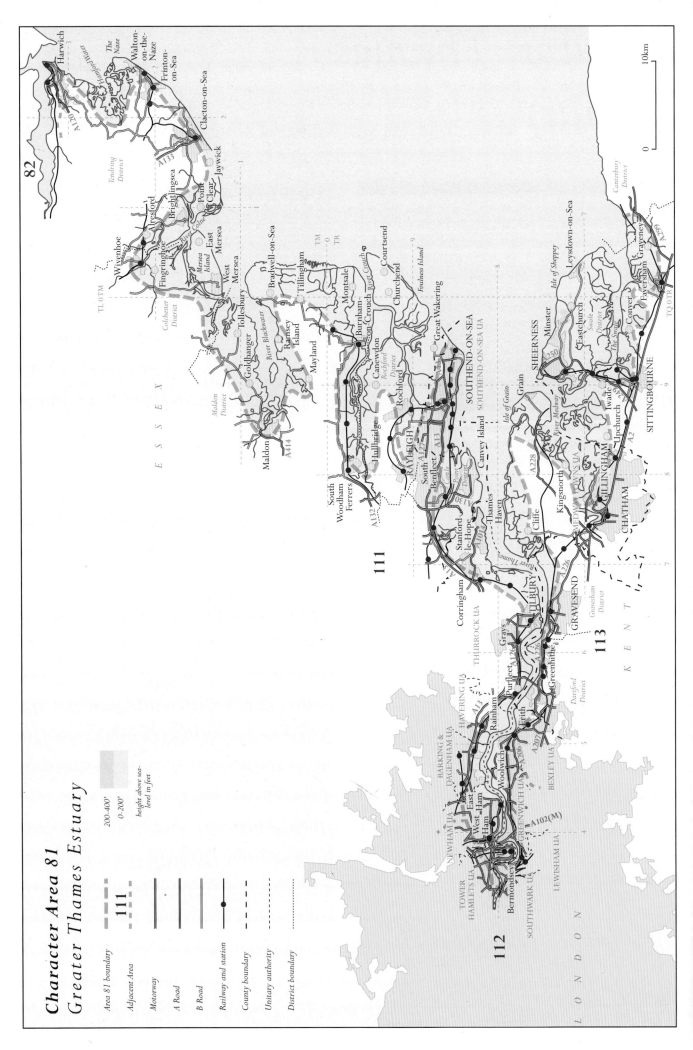

the south and the river Stour on the Essex/Suffolk border to the north. Although the term 'marsh' has been used since Anglo-Saxon times, to mean coastal wetland in general and salt-marsh in particular, the term is now also used to refer to former wetland and grazing marsh that has been drained for arable use, such as is found in this area.

The Estuary lies between the North Sea and the rising ground inland. In Kent the Estuary abuts the North Kent Plain while in Essex it borders the Essex Wooded Hills and Valleys to the north and the London Clay Lowlands further inland (both of which are subareas of the Northern Thames Basin character area). Further west, the Greater Thames Estuary extends fingerlike into Inner London.

The coastal scenery mainly consists of a maze of winding, shallow creeks, drowned estuaries, mudflats and broad tracts of tidal salt-marsh with sand and shingle beaches along the coast edge. The relatively permanent, branching, meandering creeks which dissect the salt-marshes fill and empty with the tide and provide an interesting temporal variation within the marsh landscape.

Within this essentially marshland character contrast is provided by the extensive areas, usually lying between coastal edge and rising ground, of former marshland where draining, levelling and improvement of the soil structure has allowed wheat and barley to be cultivated. This 'improvement' process has altered many of the characteristic features of the marsh landscape such as where the numerous meandering creeks of the grazing marsh have become straight dykes and ditches in arable areas.

Farms and larger settlements are located on the higher, drier pockets of land within the marshes, usually surrounded by stunted and windswept trees and hedges which are particularly prominent vertical features in the flat, open landscape. Decoy ponds with associated tree planting are also prominent landmarks. Dutch Elm disease has done much to alter the character of the marshes in recent years as the distinctive sentinel elm trees, once prominently scattered around the marshland, are now no longer a feature.

Low islands such as the Isle of Sheppey, Dengie and Mersea lie within the Estuary. Sheppey is a long low island rising from a stretch of very flat marsh along the Swale estuary in Kent with low, steep, clay cliffs facing towards Essex across the Thames estuary. The higher ground between Sheerness, Minster and Leysdown is a dense urban area with caravans, huts and bungalows at the eastern end. The marshes are largely inaccessible with few roads dissecting a landscape which is predominantly inhabited by sheep, cattle and wildfowl. There are also some areas of more mixed agriculture including a few orchards on the higher ground. The orchards enclosed by hedgerows, tree lines and windbreaks provide a contrast to the surrounding open

marsh landscape. Trees are rarities here and the small clumps that do exist help to mark the location of isolated churches and farmsteads on the pockets of higher land.

JOHN TYLER/COUNTRYSIDE AGENCY

The pillbox at Harwich, Essex is typical of many dotted along the coast, a reminder of the historical significance of the area in the defence of the land.

Physical Influences

The physical development of the Greater Thames Estuary has been dominated by the relative levels of land and sea. In the 9,000 years since the end of the last ice age, the sea has risen from 30 m below its present level and is currently rising at an estimated 2 mm per year.

The marshes themselves have been created and sustained from material carried by the sea from the north. This natural process of accretion has added some tens of thousands of acres to the marshes of Kent and Essex since Anglo-Saxon times. It is now reduced by man-made sea-defences.

Present day soils are derived largely from intertidal alluvial muds which give rise to stoneless, clayey, silty and loamy soils. This drift geology overlays the extensive London Clay. The present day soils have been extensively drained to give fertile arable land.

Historical and Cultural Influences

Evidence of first exploitation comes from Neolithic times when sea levels rose to around the present day level. Abundant Iron Age remains from the Essex Marshes are related to a local salt-making industry. The Red Hills are remains of salt-mounds marked by burnt earth, the location of such industry suggesting that marshland reed or sedge was a key source of fuel for the evaporation process. Later medieval evidence of salt-making sites, in the form of mounds, is to be found on the edge of the Kent marshes, in particular on the Isle of Sheppey.

At the end of the Iron Age, sea levels fell and the arrival of the Romans in Britain marked an intensive period of settlement made possible by their knowledge of wetland drainage. Farmsteads were developed on the higher ground and reclaimed marshland cultivated. Roman settlement, however, was short-lived. The sudden rise in sea level during the late Roman period, combined with poor drainage maintenance, caused them to abandon the Marshes but evidence of their fields are still visible today.

The later fall in sea level resulted in the creation of salt-marsh which was much prized by Saxons as pasture for sheep, the marshes often being owned by distant parishes. Canvey Island in the Essex marshes is still subdivided into numerous parts for various upland parishes located up to seven miles away. By the early Middle Ages, sea-banks had been built to protect farmland from the rising sea. Foulness Island on the Essex Coast was mainly enwalled during this period. The presence today of Saxon fishing traps and oyster pits in the Blackwater/Colne estuary are evidence of the importance of the sea and shoreline to early medieval economies.

Open grazing pastures are criss-crossed by a network of drainage ditches at Bowers Marsh, Essex. Typically for the Thames-edge these exist alongside major industrial development such as this petrochemical complex.

Following the later Middle Ages there are numerous records of surges and breaches with mention of special administrative bodies set up to oversee the upkeep of sea defences. A major use of Essex woodland at this time was as underwood for thatching sea walls. In order to combat coastal erosion, lines of posts and conifer branches were installed on the mudflats to trap silts at high tide allowing salt-marsh vegetation to colonise naturally. This is a method which is still in use today as the coastal protection scheme at Cudmore Country Park on Mersea Island demonstrates. At West Thurrock the sea walls were made of chalk transported from Purfleet at vast cost specifically for that purpose.

During the post-medieval period, further marshland was progressively reclaimed by the process of 'inning'. Coastal defences were constructed resulting in wet, sheep-grazed marsh within the sea walls and salt-marsh without. Between the late 17th century and today, further areas were enwalled as agricultural land at the expense of the salt-marshes. Many small innings were also lost as periodic surges breached both ancient and new sea banks.

Boats moored in the estuary at West Mersea, Essex, a focus for the local fishing and boat-building economy.

The recent and past conversion of the Estuary to arable use is today a declining trend. The risk of periodic flooding has led to the construction of hundreds of miles of sea wall defences. These are a vast, expensive and looming presence over the agricultural land behind but are now, once more, giving way in places where managed retreat and foreshore recharge are deemed an alternative to total sea exclusion.

Buildings and Settlement

The Greater Thames Estuary is characterised by a lack of major settlements and as such includes some of the least settled parts of the English coast. Farmsteads and villages are located on higher ground within and on the edge of the marshes. Industry, housing, caravan sites, transport routes and other structures now occupy what are often highly visible sites within the low-lying marshes due to post-war improvements in flood defence measures. Some settlements eg Clacton and Frinton, have developed as popular seaside resorts along the coast.

Many areas within the marshes remain very isolated, with only narrow dead-end tracks providing access from the wider road network linking settlements on the higher ground. Prominent embankments carry the more modern roads through the marshes, their raised profile discordant within the predominantly flat and open landscape.

Land Cover

Productive loams occurring on the marsh alluvium have encouraged the conversion of extensive areas of former unimproved wet grazing pasture to intensive arable cropping of wheat and barley within the sea walls.

Tracts of traditional, unimproved, wet grassland remain. These are extensive and particularly characteristic in Kent but less so in Essex. The grassland is mostly grazed by sheep and cattle although, around the fringes of some urban areas in particular, the grazing of horses is prevalent.

The mixture of saltings, mudflats, sand and shingle beaches beyond the sea walls is an important habitat for a wide range of waterfowl.

Virtually no trees or hedges grow on the exposed marsh except for a few isolated specimens on higher ground and some very localised scrub encroachment along road verges, railway embankments and some sea walls.

The Changing Countryside

- Since 1945, extensive drainage and fertilisation of the marshes for arable cropping and improved pasture, and to a lesser extent for industry, has led to widespread fragmentation and loss (64 per cent) of the traditional wetland character of the marsh.

- Tourism and formal recreation-related uses of the Estuary such as boating, water and jet skiing, new marinas and increasing visitor pressure have acted to influence the general feeling of remoteness and wilderness.

- Significant pressures on the landscape have resulted from new roads and the development of industrial complexes and their ancillary structures. The Thames Gateway and associated developments including transport are likely to further increase these pressures in the future. Such developments are particularly visible within the flat landscape of the Estuary.

- Increasing demand since 1945 for waste disposal sites and spoil heaps has further changed the character of the landscape. The landscape impacts of dredging are also a major issue within the context of the Estuary.

- Loss of elm from areas of higher ground is a notable change.

Shaping the Future

- The restoration of traditional cattle and sheep grazing pasture should be addressed. This might include the conversion of arable land to grazing marsh and pasture and the idea of managed retreat of the coastline.

- New planting to re-establish tree and shrub cover around farmsteads and other sites on areas of higher ground would help conserve the open character of the Estuary.

- The restoration of mineral and waste sites, including areas of disused industrial land, would offer opportunities to enhance the character of the landscape.

Selected References

Agricultural Development and Advisory Services (1995), *The Essex Coast Environmentally Sensitive Area: Landscape Assessment, (draft)*, Ministry of Agriculture, Fisheries and Food.

Agricultural Development and Advisory Services (1994), *North Kent Marshes Environmentally Sensitive Area: Landscape Assessment*, Ministry of Agriculture, Fisheries and Food.

Daniel Defoe's *Tour of the whole island of Britain* contains an amusing section on the Essex marshes.

Kent County Council, (1993), *Landscape and Nature Conservation Guidelines*, Kent County Council, Maidstone.

Milton, P (1991), *Essex Landscape Conservation Programme 1972-1989: A Review*, Essex County Council, Chelmsford.

Although this character area is one of the least settled parts of the English coast, a few settlements have developed into popular seaside resorts. These are the seafront gardens at Clacton.

MARK DYMOND/TENDRING DISTRICT COUNCIL

Bedfordshire and Cambridgeshire Claylands

Key Characteristics

- Gently undulating topography and plateau areas, divided by broad shallow valleys.

- Predominantly an open and intensive arable landscape. Fields bounded by either open ditches or sparse closely trimmed hedges both containing variable number and quality of hedgerow trees.

- River corridors of Great Ouse and Ivel compose cohesive sub-areas characterised by flood plain grassland, riverine willows and larger hedges.

- Woodland cover variable. Clusters of ancient deciduous woods on higher plateau area to north-west between Salcey and Grafham Water. Smaller plantations and secondary woodland within river valleys.

- Settlement pattern clusters around major road and rail corridors (A1 and M1) many with raw built edges. Smaller, dispersed settlements elsewhere. Village edge grasslands an important feature.

- Generally a diversity of building materials, including brick, thatch and stone. Limestone villages on the upper Great Ouse.

- Man-made reservoir at Grafham Water. Restored gravel working lakes adjacent to river Ouse, and water-bodies in Marston Vale resulting from clay extraction.

- Brickfields of Marston Vale and Peterborough form a major industrial landscape. Mixed extraction, dereliction and landfill.

- Medieval earthworks including deserted villages the major feature of visible archaeology.

Landscape Character

These claylands comprise most of central and northern Bedfordshire and western Cambridgeshire. There is a distinct boundary to the east, where they run down to the level fenlands, and to the south where they meet the chalklands which run between Dunstable and Cambridge. To the south west there is a more gradual transition towards the Upper Thames Clay Vales and Midvale Ridge. To the north lies the Yardley-Whittlewood Ridge, while the valley of the river Nene marks the junction with the adjacent Northamptonshire and Leicestershire Vales. Within, but distinct from, the Claylands character area the Bedfordshire Greensand Ridge to the south provides a contrasting narrow island of acidic soils with associated woodland and parkland.

JOHN TYLER/COUNTRYSIDE AGENCY

Predominantly an open and intensive arable landscape, with large fields often bounded by open ditches with few hedgerow trees, as seen here at Offord Hill, Cambridgeshire.

The area comprises a broad sweep of lowland plateau, dissected by a number of shallow valleys, including the rivers Great Ouse and Ivel. It is typically an empty gently undulating lowland landscape with expansive views of large-scale arable farmland, contained either by sparse trimmed hedgerows, open ditches or streamside vegetation. Further east, field size typically increases. There are scattered ancient woodlands which tend to be clustered most noticeably in a band to the north of the area; elsewhere the woods are more isolated, yet form important visual and wildlife features.

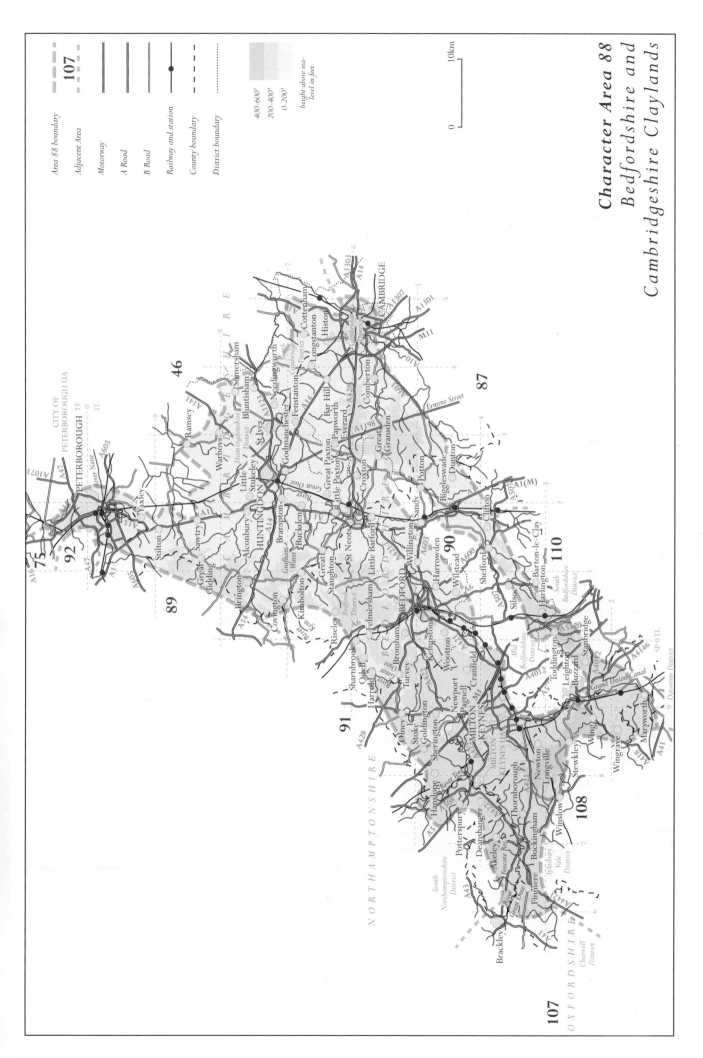

Character Area 88
Bedfordshire and
Cambridgeshire Claylands

Area 88 boundary
107 Adjacent Area
Motorway
A Road
B Road
Railway and station
County boundary
District boundary

400-600'
200-400'
0-200'
height above sea-level in feet

0 10km

River Great Ouse at Offord Cluny, Cambridgeshire. The shallow valleys of the Ouse and the Ivel provide distinctive local character within the claylands including flood plain grasslands, riverine willows and larger hedgerows, as well as an important recreational resource.

There are a number of distinctive sub-areas of varying scale. Firstly, between Bedford and the M1 is the Marston Vale, a broad valley dominated by the effect of clay extraction and the brick industry. Here, chimney stacks punctuate the skyline and the strong smell of burnt clay frequently permeates the atmosphere. Enormous pits exist throughout the Vale, a few of which are currently being worked. Other pits are either derelict, have been restored to water uses, or are utilized as major landfill sites. The latter create prominent domed landforms in the level Vale. The extent of these industrial areas is often concealed from the public roads but is more visible from the elevated railways and Greensand Ridge. Belts of mature poplars often emphasise the presence of these intrusive features.

Secondly, a similar landscape exists south of Peterborough.

Thirdly, the valleys of the rivers Great Ouse and Ivel pass through the centre of the plateau lands. West of Bedford the Great Ouse meanders down from Buckinghamshire, firstly around the northern edge of Milton Keynes and then through a picturesque and enclosed landscape of water meadows and attractive limestone villages towards Bedford. North of the confluence with the Ivel at Tempsford, the valley broadens to create long distance views and big skies. Here, the fertile alluvial soil and river gravels combine to create a mosaic of market gardening, mixed with past and present mineral extraction of sand and gravels particularly north of Sandy. River pollards and meadows line the flood plain and river, most notably between St Neots,

Huntingdon and St Ives, before meeting the fens at Earith.

Grafham Water, one of the largest man-made reservoirs in England, is an important base for water-based recreation and nature conservation. The lake is imposed on the local landscape, dominating the immediate locality but separated from the surrounding arable landscape by gentle hills and woods. A final sub-area is the corridor of the river Tove and Grand Union Canal to the west. Here mills, locks, weirs and riverine pollards create a distinctive environment. The canal then runs southwards through Milton Keynes alongside the river Ouzel passing through a series of linear parks and amenity lakes.

Physical Influences

The soils in the area are dominated by a variety of moderately permeable, calcareous, clayey soils. To the north these overlie a chalky boulder clay (glacial till), whereas to the south they overlie Jurassic and Cretaceous clays. The elevated clayland plateau to the west is dissected by the upper reaches of the Great Ouse which have better-drained soils due to the underlying local Jurassic limestone. To the east of Bedford and north of Shefford, the broader river valleys of the river Ivel and its tributaries have well-drained soils over alluvium and river terrace gravels.

The special properties for brick making of the Jurassic Oxford Clay have marked it out as a target for extensive extraction in the Peterborough and Marston Vale areas.

The heavy soils of the claylands and dense woodland deterred prehistoric farmers and Roman settlers who first congregated along the lighter soils in the valleys of the rivers Great Ouse and Ivel. Archaeological evidence is abundant in these valleys, including the use by Viking ships of the Great Ouse as far upstream as Willington east of Bedford, where there is evidence of a harbour and docks. The first Roman and medieval settlements were at the river crossings of the Ouse, including Huntingdon and Godmanchester, St Ives and St Neots.

With the improved ploughs of the Middle Ages, the population pressure grew on the higher heavier claylands and the pattern of agricultural landscapes developed. Many settlements from this time have subsequently either shrunk or been deserted which has led to a richness of archaeology in a more sparsely populated landscape. Remains include moated sites, deserted villages and ruined or isolated churches, for example Bushmead Priory.

John Bunyan wrote *Pilgrim's Progress* while imprisoned in Bedford jail. Fictitious locations in the novel drew inspiration from sites known to the itinerant preacher, for example the poorly drained Marston Vale is considered to be the 'Slough of Despond'. Oliver Cromwell, a contemporary of Bunyan, was born in Huntingdon in 1599. The small market town of Olney now famous for its Shrove Tuesday pancake race has an attractive broad High Street. It was home in the 18th century to the reformed slave trader Rev. John Newton and the poet William Cowper whose association led to the writing of the Olney Hymns.

The 20th century has brought a number of changes, noticeably in the brickfields of Peterborough and Marston Vale, which the London Brick Company significantly expanded from the 1930s. During the second world war airfields were built on the level plateaux. Many are now derelict but those at Alconbury, Cranfield and Thurleigh survive as important technological and military centres.

The Marston Vale, to the south and west of Bedford, has a distinctive local character resulting from a history of clay extraction and the development of the brick industry. Enormous pits exist throughout the Vale, many now being used for landfill before restoration to agricultural or recreational use.

Buildings and Settlement

The majority of the arable claylands are uniformly but sparsely populated. Small villages nestle in gentle valleys while isolated hamlets and farmsteads are widely dispersed, particularly north of Bedford. Linear settlements, like Riseley, are common in the area. Notable houses and grounds include Kimbolton Park and Croxton Park. The grandest example however is at Wrest Park, Silsoe, the estate of the de Grey family. The French Baroque/Rococo style house, built c.1835, is unique in England. The formal gardens (English Heritage) comprise canals, pavilions and radiating vistas within woodland.

High density housing development on the edge of urban areas, such as Cambridge, results in further development pressures on landscape features and the cumulative landscape impact can be very dramatic.

Traditional building materials in the villages comprise a mix of brick, thatch, render and stone but there is no over-riding cohesion to the area; rather more localised pockets of style or materials. Most notable are the warm limestone villages of the upper Great Ouse at Olney, Harrold, Odell, Turvey and Felmersham, many of which contain elegant Northamptonshire-style church spires and distinctive multi-arched stone bridges, for example at Harrold, Turvey and Bromham.

The towns along the lower Great Ouse contain a notable range of buildings including the High Street at Godmanchester which has many fine Georgian town houses. Along the river, causeways and medieval bridges – including the rare bridge chapel at St Ives – are distinctive features. Historic coaching towns along the Great North Road, for example at Stilton and Buckden, are now bypassed and provide the atmosphere of a bygone age. Kimbolton with its red tiled town houses is a small yet distinguished model settlement. The associated 'Castle' was the final home of Catherine of Aragon. It was later extended by Vanburgh and Adam. The Georgian Swan Hotel, on the Ouse at Bedford, is referred to by Pevsner as the most noble English hotel.

Settlement in the 20th century has continued from its historic pattern along the rivers and A1 corridor. There has been extensive yet undistinguished expansion of existing towns, eg Bedford, St Neots, Biggleswade and Huntingdon. These often present raw industrial and residential built edges to the open countryside, thereby degrading the river valley settings. Power lines and the gas fired power station at Little Barford provide further modern intrusions in this corridor.

To the west of the area adjacent to the M1, Milton Keynes has developed since the 1960s. The city, with its grid-iron road pattern, extensive open spaces, tree planting and sleek modern buildings, is both a showcase new town and major regional shopping centre.

Land Cover

This is a predominantly arable, intensively farmed landscape with large areas of winter cereals and oilseed rape on the higher clay plateau. There is a pattern of large rectilinear fields which are notably larger east of the Ivel/Great Ouse divide. To the east hedgerows are typically mixed but in poor repair and gappy. Further to the west, hedges are predominantly hawthorn but the quality and integrity improves together with a greater, though still limited, number of hedgerow trees, mainly oak and ash. Mature stag-headed trees are characteristic. Streamside willow and stands of poplars emphasize the river and stream corridors.

Clustered around many of the urban villages/settlements, are smaller yet significant areas of paddocks and pasture. Here a 'pony paddock culture' with mixed fencing, sheds and jumps creates a distinct local character, as evident at Wootton. Tree cover in gardens and village edge field corners is also greater than in the more open farmed landscape and provides a contrasting intimacy, as for example at Great Gransden. Pasture is common in the flood plain meadows along the river valleys.

The woodland cover is sparse, yet includes some important ancient woodlands, for example at Great Odell Wood, Marston Thrift, Wootton Wood, Brampton Wood and Monks Wood, which include oak/ash coppice woods, some of national importance. There is a greater concentration of woodlands in an elevated band between Salcey Forest and Grafham Water on the Northamptonshire/Bedfordshire border. Salcey Forest and Yardley Chase are the remnants of ancient deer parks and hunting forests which form distinctive historic landscapes that have remained largely intact compared with the surrounding intensive arable areas.

Along the river valleys of the Great Ouse and Ivel, significant areas of present gravel extraction and restored large water bodies are evident. In addition, within the Ivel valley on the flood plain soils, vegetables, horticultural cropping and glasshouses are a distinctive feature. To the north-east of the area, Grafham Water and its associated earth dams create a major man-made water body in the area.

The brickfields of the Marston Vale and south Peterborough create marked industrialised landscapes at the local scale. Active and worked clay pits, brickworks, landfill sites and large water-bodies, compose a mosaic of despoiled and restored land among the remaining agricultural uses.

The Changing Countryside

- Agricultural intensification and farm amalgamation, particularly to create larger arable fields. There are still isolated examples of this taking place today. Harsh management and neglect of hedgerows.

- Changing crop patterns, through subsidies and advances in farming practice, eg fewer spring crops.

- Loss and fragmentation of habitats, including grassland, ponds, ditches, spinneys and hedgerows. Dutch Elm disease in 1970s and 1980s had a major impact on woodland and hedgerow trees.

- Creation of open water-bodies, most notably Grafham Water.

- Extensive mineral extraction and landfill. Sand and gravel removal to river valleys. Clay extraction, brick manufacture and landfill to Marston Vale and south of Peterborough.

- Development along transport and infrastructure corridors, eg M1, A1. Sprawl and coalescence of towns and settlements often in river valleys. Development of Milton Keynes New Town.

- Growth of horticulture and associated glasshouses in Ivel valley. Subsequent decline of smaller holdings.

- Growth of 'pony paddock culture', stables and residual areas to edge of villages and towns, creating a piecemeal appearance.

Shaping the Future

- There is scope for the creation of new woodlands: smaller woods to river valleys and larger woods on higher plateau areas, with scope to enhance linkage within traditional woodland areas. The continued management of existing ancient woodlands is important.

- Landscape enhancement of the relatively industrialised Marston Vale and south Peterborough should include the assimilation of the stark landforms arising from landfill by extensive planting and sympathetic earthworks to respect the wider farmed landscape.

- The management of unimproved grasslands on settlement edges should include the retention of remaining ridge and furrow.

- The enhancement of wetland habitats including the corridors of the rivers Ivel, Tove and Great Ouse should include the re-creation and management of riverine grassland meadows and pollarding of willows. Less intensive farming adjacent to the rivers is important.

- Extensive planting schemes should be considered to reduce the impact of settlement edges, infrastructure corridors and isolated agricultural and industrial buildings. The re-establishment of hedgerows, hedgerow trees, species-rich verges and field margins would provide visual and wildlife corridors between woodland and water courses.

- The sensitive after-use of redundant airfield sites would benefit from integrated landscape strategies.

- A strategy should be considered for future mineral and clay extraction and the associated restoration of derelict and worked sites.

Transport corridors often contain both road and rail links which, together with numerous adjacent settlements, give a noisy and urban feel to these areas. Landscape features are isolated and fragmented and commonly undermanaged or innappropriately managed. Village edge grasslands are often ungrazed or overgrazed by horses with the attendant clutter of stabling and jumps.

Selected References

Automobile Association (1978), *Illustrated Guide to Britain*, Drive Publications Ltd.

Bedfordshire County Council (1995), *A Rural Strategy for Bedfordshire/Public Consultation Draft*, Beds C.C., Bedford.

Cambridgeshire County Council (1991), *Cambridgeshire Landscape Guidelines*, Cambs C.C., Cambridge.

Countryside Commission (1995), *Countryside Stewardship Targeting Statements for Bedfordshire*, Countryside Commission.

Countryside Commission (1995), *Countryside Stewardship Targeting Statements for Cambridgeshire*, Countryside Commission.

Forestry Authority (1995), *Reviews of Assessments of Landscape Character for the Counties of Norfolk, Suffolk, Essex & Cambridgeshire*, East Anglia Conservancy.

Pevsner, N (1968), *The Buildings of England - Bedfordshire, Huntingdonshire & Peterborough*, Penguin Books, Middlesex.

Pevsner, N (1973), *The Buildings of England - Buckinghamshire*, Penguin Books, Middlesex.

Scarfe, N (1983), *A Shell Guide to Cambridgeshire*, Faber & Faber, London.

Smith, J (1968), *Shell Guide to Northamptonshire & the Soke of Peterborough*, Faber & Faber, London.

Watkins, B (1981), *Shell Guide to Buckinghamshire*, Faber & Faber, London.

Bedfordshire Greensand Ridge

Key Characteristics

- Narrow escarpment formed of Lower Greensand, with distinct scarp slope to north-west and dip slope to south-east.

- Mixed land use on north-west facing scarp slope, including a high proportion of woods (both deciduous and coniferous), heath and pasture. Medium-sized arable and wooded landscape on dip slope.

- Panoramic views to north across claylands.

- Number of historic parklands and estates, including Woburn, Haynes, Shuttleworth, Sandy Lodge and Southill give the impression of a well-tended landscape.

- Settlement pattern includes estate villages and hamlets in folds of ridge. Local materials include ironstone, brick, thatch and render.

- Integrity of area breached by river Ivel valley.

- Existing and redundant sand quarries especially around Leighton Buzzard.

Landscape Character

The Bedfordshire Greensand Ridge is a narrow elongated area which lies south of Bedford, in a north-east/south-west orientation between Leighton Buzzard and Gamlingay. It is entirely surrounded by the Bedfordshire and Cambridgeshire Claylands.

It is the marked contrast of this island of 'Greensand' rising above the encircling clayland vales and low hills, which makes the area both attractive and distinctive within the wider regional setting. The lighter soils have typically created a marked pattern of land use with a relatively high proportion of woodland and parkland landscapes, mixed with smaller areas of pasture and heath. These distinctive elements are concentrated at selected locations along the ridge, while in other locations the character has been diluted rendering the contrast to the claylands less noticeable.

JOHN TYLER/COUNTRYSIDE AGENCY

The area has a mixed land-use pattern. On the dip slope, such as here at Haynes, it is a medium-scale arable and wooded landscape.

The area comprises two major components. Firstly, the north-western facing scarp slope which forms a strongly accentuated horizon from a distance with its mix of coniferous and deciduous woodland, pasture, arable and heathland. From the scarp slope there are panoramic views to the surrounding landscape, most notably to the north, over Marston Vale. At a closer standpoint, the scarp slope includes a series of sinuous secondary undulations enclosing a small-scale patchwork and more intimate landscape, for example at Great Brickhill and Millbrook. In contrast, the undulating dip slope provides the second component. This sub-area is a mix of arable and well-tended estate parklands, villages and woodlands. These give the impression of a carefully husbanded landscape where woodlands combine to create enclosure.

The continuity of the area is breached in a few selected locations, most noticeably and physically where the river Ivel breaks the ridge at Sandy but also where the A5, M1 and A6 transport corridors traverse the ridge. The southern boundary is marked by the river Flit which flows east along a well-treed watercourse through a small-scale intimate landscape of paddocks, pasture and arable fields.

Much of the typically characteristic Bedfordshire Greensand Ridge, including the parkland estates, is located on Cretaceous sands and sandstones. These deposits give rise to free-draining sandy acidic soils which have a strong influence on the vegetation. On the steeper scarp slopes there is risk of water erosion. A variety of sand-types occur including a pure 'silver sand' with a high silica content at Leighton Linslade, at the western end. Fuller's earth is present at Woburn Sands and Clophill where it has been worked from large quarries.

Locations with more diluted 'Greensand' character correspond to pockets of chalky boulder clay (glacial till) which overlie the sandstone. With the exception of the river Ivel valley and its fine loamy alluvial soils, which breaches the ridge west of Sandy, there are no major rivers. The scarp slope supports no watercourses. However, in contrast, the dip slope is drained by a series of streams which flow to the south to join the river Flit and river Ivel. Small lakes and ponds are associated with the parklands and estates.

Historical and Cultural Influences

In comparison with the adjacent claylands the poor fertility and lightness of the soils led to the attraction of the area for the creation of parkland estates, where hunting formed an important activity. The mosaic of medium- and large-scale woodlands, fields and pasture around the larger houses is still retained and gives the impression of stepping back

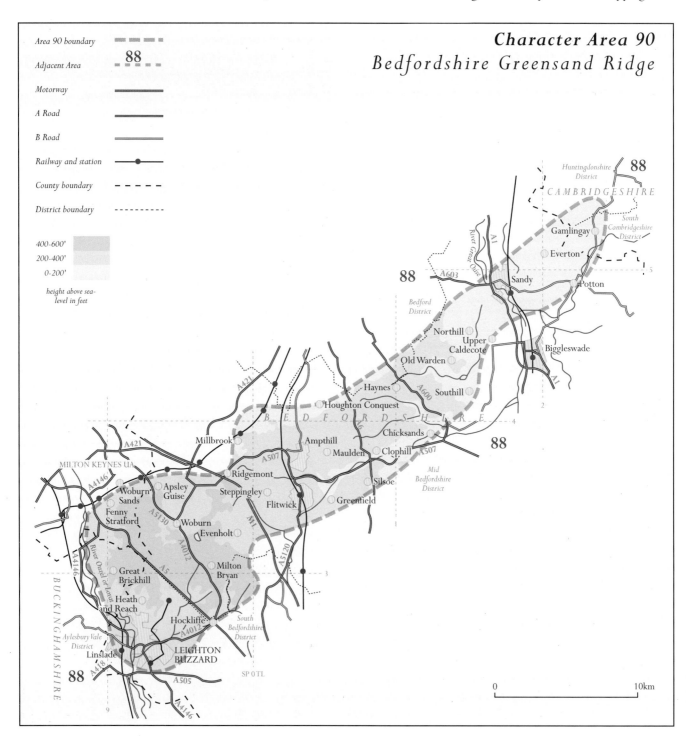

Character Area 90
Bedfordshire Greensand Ridge

Area 90 boundary	
Adjacent Area	**88**
Motorway	
A Road	
B Road	
Railway and station	
County boundary	
District boundary	

400–600'
200–400'
0–200'

height above sea-level in feet

into an earlier century, for example at Old Warden.

Some of the estates are retained in their traditional form, for example at Southill where the Whitbread family are the owners, while in others opportunities for tourism have been developed, such as at Woburn with the Wildlife Safari Park. Specialist users have also arisen, for example at Sandy Lodge, where the RSPB have their headquarters set in the grounds of acidic woods and heathland, and the internationally famous Woburn Golf Course – set amid the pine trees. Through the 20th century considerable afforestation using conifers has taken place at Millbrook and Woburn. Increased public access through the creation of country parks, Forestry Commission woodland and the Greensand Ridge Way, which follows the length of the ridge, have widened the public perception of this relatively private landscape.

JOHN TYLER/COUNTRYSIDE AGENCY

The Cretaceous sands and sandstones which underly the Greensand ridge exposed at Sandy Warren, Bedfordshire. These deposits give rise to free-draining acidic sandy soils which have a strong influence on the vegetation.

Buildings and Settlement

The Bedfordshire Greensand Ridge has a dispersed settlement pattern. The influence of the estate owners has kept the size of settlements restricted to small nucleated groups. This has controlled the amount of 20th century development, creating a pleasantly antiquated feel about parts of the area. Movement between settlements along the ridge involves a series of narrow winding roads and sunken lanes, often with rough verges of bracken. This complex pattern is only broken by the major north-south corridors of the M1, A1, A5 and A6.

The major towns in the area are generally located towards the edge of the escarpment, like Leighton Buzzard and Sandy, the most notable exception being the historic market town of Ampthill, which sits in the middle of the area behind the ridge and adjoining the Great Park.

A number of the villages comprise time capsules of a given style, often relating to the rebuilding of the great house in the vicinity. The Dukes of Bedford rebuilt Woburn Abbey in 1747-61 in the classical style. Part of the project was the relocation of the village of Woburn which today retains a distinctively complete and elegant Georgian High Street. At Old Warden the houses and village are of Victorian vintage. A model village was created by Lord Onslow with spacious thatched cottages in various architectural styles. The associated Shuttleworth House is of Italianate style. The estate also contains the Swiss Garden. A number of the remaining settlements contain attractive brick Georgian homes, for example those at Ampthill. Elsewhere, the traditional building materials are varied and include brick, sandstone, thatch and occasional ironstone – the latter being found in the churches around Ampthill. Tall and extensive estate walls in brick enclose some of the parklands such as Woburn while, within the woodland areas, timber picket fencing and clipped hedgerows are characteristic.

It may be surprising that, in view of the elevation of the area, few buildings dominate the skyline and the majority nestle in the valleys and woodland settings of the dip slope. Probably the most prominent landmark church is at Ridgmont where the spire punctuates the horizon above woodland close to where the M1 crosses the ridge. Houghton House provides another prominent landmark. This house, now a ruin, was built c.1615 and is reported to have been the inspiration for the 'House Beautiful' in John Bunyan's *Pilgrim's Progress*.

Land Cover

The area comprises a relatively organic and varied field pattern, interspersed with a high proportion of woodland cover compared with the adjacent areas. Cropping is concentrated in the chalky boulder clay areas of the dip slope and is predominantly cereals with some vegetable crops. Within the arable areas, the hedgerow cover is variable. In some locations, due to field amalgamation, it is comparable with the adjacent claylands. However, the well-husbanded landscape character of old is retained in pockets associated with the estates. Here the pattern of old mixed hedgerows with standard oaks survives.

The scarp and upper ridge contain the poorer acidic soils. Here, there are important heath habitats, some of significant wildlife value. On these poor soils the woodland cover is primarily coniferous, chiefly pine, for example near the Brickhills, Millbrook and Sandy. Alongside the woods, small areas of rough grazing and regenerating birch exist in the

The Greensand ridge has a number of impressive parklands and historic houses such as Woburn Abbey. Their surrounding estates are commonly well tended giving the impression of a carefully managed landscape where woodlands combine to create a feeling of enclosure. Shooting interests are important on these estates and strips of cover crops often have an impact on the local landscape.

undulations of the scarp slope. In contrast to these relatively modern woods, a number of ancient woodlands, supporting important acidic plant communities, are located on the ridge which help create the distinctive wooded skyline as seen from the north, for example Kings Wood, Wilstead Wood, Exeter Wood and Sheerhatch Wood. In other locations, the woods have a more mixed character, being actively managed for conservation, sport, and timber production. The parkland areas of pasture with mature trees and encircling shelter belts are a relatively small yet critical component to the landcover, due to their broader influence. Spring-fed wetlands and mires associated with outcrops of the Greensand aquifer are also found in a number of locations.

At the river Ivel, the presence of rich gravelly alluvial soils has led to the development of market gardening, with areas of glasshouses. There are also a series of past and current gravel pits, with old sites generally being restored as water bodies. The presence of the purer quality sands has also led to extensive quarrying at Heath and Reach, exposing significant geological sites. Other locations have subsequently been restored for use as Country Parks, for example at Stockgrove. The Woburn area contains deposits of the uncommon fuller's earth thereby creating pressure for continued extraction. To the south, the Flit valley contains a series of wetlands, old willows and pasture.

The Changing Countryside

- Localised agricultural intensification and farm amalgamation. Larger field sizes and hedgerow/field tree removal (now largely ceased) are reducing the area's distinctiveness from adjacent claylands.

- Pressures to reduce areas of traditional parkland for cultivation, forestry or tourism.

- Reduction of heath habitats by coniferisation and neglect leading to scrub invasion.

- Breaching of area by M1, A1 and A5 infrastructure corridors. Impact of extensive developments like Millbrook Proving Ground and the former Chicksands Military Base.

- Extraction of sand and fuller's earth reserves. Restoration for agricultural forestry and recreational after-uses.

- Growth and subsequent decline of small-scale market gardening units in the Ivel valley and at Potton.

- Encroachment of settlement to the edge of the Greensand Ridge, visible at Leighton Buzzard and Sandy.

Acid grassland and mixed woodland was once typical of the area but today is limited in its extent due to development pressures, mineral extraction and conversion to arable. Fragmentation of the heaths remains a problem. However, on a number of designated sites, such as the SSSI at Wavendon Heath Ponds, recent management has improved the wildlife and landscape value.

Shaping the Future

- The varied mix of deciduous and coniferous woodlands benefits amenity, recreation, wildlife and timber production.

- The maintenance of the strong architectural identity of small villages is important.

- There are opportunities to conserve and reinstate hedgerows, hedgerow trees and pasture.

- There is scope to manage existing heath habitats on the scarp slope and to create new areas of heath.

- The restoration of worked sand pits would create typical Greensand habitats.

- The contrast between the area – particularly the edge of dip slope – and the adjacent claylands can be emphasised by appropriate tree species. A varied scarp skyline with a mix of woodland, heath and pasture is important.

- There are opportunities to manage and re-create parkland through grazing and to care for and replant parkland trees.

- The conservation of river valley features, including wetlands and willow pollards, should be addressed.

Selected References

Automobile Association (1978), *Illustrated Guide to Britain*, Drive Publications Ltd.

Bedfordshire County Council (1995), *A Rural Strategy for Bedfordshire*/Public Consultation Draft, Beds C.C., Bedford.

Countryside Commission (1995), *Countryside Stewardship Targeting Statements for Bedfordshire*, Countryside Commission.

Pevsner, N (1968), *The Buildings of England - Bedfordshire, Huntingdonshire & Peterborough*, Penguin Books, Middlesex.

Watkins, B (1981), *Shell Guide to Buckinghamshire*, Faber & Faber, London.

TERENCE J. BURCHELL

Ironstone has been used for building along the Greensand ridge since Anglo-Saxon times. The ironstone churches, such as St John the Baptist at Flitton which is typical of the area, date from the 12th to the 19th century. Quarrying was small scale, localised and uncommercial with most villages having their own ironstone pit for regular building and repair needs. The Enclosure Acts of the early 1800s clearly marked the land set aside for these quarries.

Yardley-Whittlewood Ridge

Key Characteristics

- Broad plateau with shallow soils elevated above adjacent vales.

- A strong historic landscape character, largely due to the continued presence of extensive areas of ancient woodland.

- Mixed land uses of pasture, arable and woodland.

- Generally medium-sized fields with full hedges and hedgerow trees, mainly oak.

- Low density of settlement and consequently few local roads; cut through by major north-south canal, rail and road routes.

Landscape Character

The Ridge rises steadily up from the Bedfordshire and Cambridgeshire Claylands (which here extend in to north Buckinghamshire) to the south and east. In the north the land drops down to the Nene Valley, the southernmost of the Northamptonshire Vales. Thus, although only reaching elevations of some 150 m in the west and slowly dipping down to 80 m in the east, it is physically distinct from the adjacent low-lying vales and forms a noticeable broad plateau.

The area is predominantly agricultural in character, with a mix of arable, mixed and pastoral farming. Pastoral farming is predominant in the west, giving way to a more open, arable landscape as the land dips slightly to the east. However, the thin and variable soils have historically constrained agricultural development so that much of the area is wooded and has been so since at least the 13th century. The landscape elements form simple combinations, of stretches of arable alternating with pasture, with a backdrop of large, dark, woodland blocks. Woods such as Salcey Forest are extensive and have a network of rides and occasional open grasslands contained within the woodland – the 'lawns' which provided hay and pasture for commoners cattle.

The woodland blocks are largely oak or mixed with other broadleaves and, in some places, oaks planted in the early 19th century still remain. More recent planting of coniferous species has formed dense plantations and these can create particularly dark and impenetrable backdrops to the local farmland landscape. These dark blocks form striking contrasts with the fresh greens of spring foliage and the rich autumn colours of the deciduous woodland.

The Ridge is a broad plateau with shallow soils. The elevated position, predominance of arable usage and low hedges create extensive open views, with village churches often prominent on the local skyline.

From the gently undulating plateau top, the land can be seen to slope gently away in most directions with long views over the surrounding vales. This gives a feel of being elevated, of openness and expansiveness. Such views, however, are frequently cut off by the large blocks of woodland which are a constant feature of the plateau top.

Its elevation above surrounding land has made it suitable for telecommunications masts and airfields – one of the latter is now the Silverstone race track. The associated activities and facilities for occasional large numbers of visitors as well as other recreational facilities such as golf courses and parks, bring a suburban feel into local landscapes.

The few minor roads on the Ridge are bounded by hedges but have wide verges which are often herb-rich. Hedges are generally substantial and species rich and are often filled out with elm suckers. There are plenty of hedgerow trees, mostly oak with some ash. Many of these are mature and stag-headed, although some hedges show several young ash saplings growing up to form potential new hedgerow trees.

There are a number of parks in the area which, with their mature parkland trees, avenues and woodland rides, add to the historic feel of the landscape. The Grand Union Canal, running through the valley cut by the river Tove, creates a local landscape of waterways with locks, bridges and weirs.

The Ridge does have an historic feel to it, in particular in those parts which are contained by the extensive areas of woodland. These contrast with more open plateau areas which can be non-descript – indeed it has been described as a 'flattish, rather dull landscape'.

Physical Influences

The Ridge forms a low watershed between the catchments of the Nene to the north and the Great Ouse to the south. The Tove drains the vale in the north, turning at Towcester to cut through the Ridge at Grafton Regis and then flows south east and joins the Great Ouse.

There is a noticeable absence of other watercourses on the Ridge.

The area of the broad plateau is cut through by major north-south transport routes of canals, railways and roads such as the MI motorway.

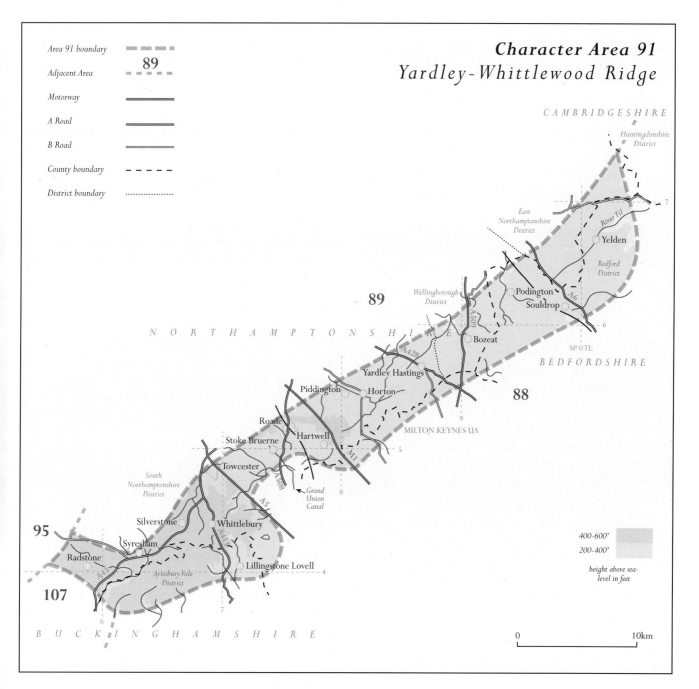

Area 91 boundary	
Adjacent Area	**89**
Motorway	
A Road	
B Road	
County boundary	
District boundary	

Character Area 91
Yardley-Whittlewood Ridge

CAMBRIDGESHIRE

Huntingdonshire District

East Northamptonshire District

River Til

Yelden

Bedford District

Wellingborough District

89

Podington
Souldrop

NORTHAMPTONSHIRE

Bozeat

SP 0TL

BEDFORDSHIRE

88

Yardley Hastings

Piddington   Horton

MILTON KEYNES UA

Roade

Stoke Bruerne   Hartwell

Towcester

Grand Union Canal

South Northamptonshire District

Silverstone   Whittlebury

Syresham

95   Radstone   Lillingstone Lovell

107   Aylesbury Vale District

BUCKINGHAMSHIRE

400-600'
200-400'

height above sea-level in feet

0   10km

Underlying the Ridge are Jurassic Oolitic limestones which run in a south-west to north-east alignment, parallel to the more substantial Middle Lias ironstones of Northamptonshire to the north west. Subsequent glacial activity has smoothed over this outcrop and left irregular drifts of boulder clay over the underlying Cornbrash. Accordingly soils are patchy and varied, ranging from a free-draining chalky till to less permeable clay. In places the underlying limestone comes close to the surface and has been quarried for local building stone.

Historical and Cultural Influences

There is some evidence of pre-Roman settlement, because the plateau was less boggy than the adjacent clay lowlands. Roman influence was limited to major routes crossing the Ridge which ran through two Roman settlements just to the north. Watling Street (now the A5) ran from London to Towcester and on to the north-west and another route passed through Irchester and on to the north.

During Anglo-Saxon times, clearance of woodland and the establishment of settlements continued. However, the main influence on the landscape, which is what largely creates its distinctive character today, was the appropriation of the extensive woodlands along the Ridge as Royal Forests from the 13th century. The woods of Whittlewood and Salcey were passed to the Dukes of Grafton. Whittlewood comprised 6,000 acres, of which 4,500 acres were woodland in 1608, while Salcey Forest (which includes Yardley Chase) covered 1,100 acres, and most of this was coppice. Such Forests provided a source of fuel and building material as well as hunting grounds for the nobility. Appropriated in this way, the area avoided the more intensive clearance of woodland, drainage and settlement that occurred on the adjacent clay lowlands.

This structure, of widespread forest, with 'lawns' for pasture, and small Forest villages (nucleated villages with open fields, whose residents had some rights over the Forest lands), continued until the early 17th century. Records show that, for instance around Knotting, clearance of some forest areas started at this time, to extend agricultural land, and continued through to the late 18th century. Clearance of woodland speeded up with the Parliamentary Enclosure Acts in the late 18th century and became more rapid in the early 19th century. Thus there are, until this time, historic references to extensive ancient forests around Melchbourne and to Odell Great Wood and Knotting West Wood where now there are large arable fields and few trees at all.

The poet William Cowper lived at Olney in 1767, moving to Weston Underwood in 1786, and spent much of his time walking in the woods.

This ride in the deer park at Yardley Chase is bounded by blocks of mature woodland creating a distinctive avenue view from the historic house.

Buildings and Settlement

The Ridge has a low population and the settlements, which are small and relatively few, tend to occur along the edges of the Ridge. Towcester, a busy small town, lies on the north-west edge of the area and Brackley, a rapidly expanding town, lies to the west.

Some of the few villages actually on the Ridge were Forest Villages, nucleated villages with open fields, (until the Enclosures) whose residents held rights over the Forest lands. Thus Ashton, Hartwell, Hackleton, Piddington, Quinton and Hanslope were all villages of the Forest of Salcey. During the medieval period, villages contracted as a result of the plague and later as part of the rural depopulation arising from the enclosures. The latter probably had less of an impact on the Ridge than on the surrounding lowlands.

Probably the most famous group of buildings and artefacts is to be found at Stowe Park. Now occupied by Stowe School, it was originally built in a formal layout, in the early 18th century, with two striking elm lined avenues running up to it. The remarkable series of buildings in the grounds were laid out between 1713 and 1763. In the 1730s, Kent introduced a more naturalistic style to the layout of the grounds.

Further parks and estates were established on the Ridge, as at Biddlesden, Melchbourne and Whittlebury. Formal landscapes, with massive avenues and woodland rides, are found at Castle Ashby and Chase Park. Rural depopulation again, in the early 19th century, left some villages more loosely structured and less compact, for instance Knotting. Adjacent towns such as Northampton and Wellingborough expanded rapidly with industrial activity in the 19th century, but with little apparent impact on the Ridge.

Building materials are varied with red brick and the soft local Oolitic limestone, ranging from warm greys to subdued ochres, both frequently used with either grey slate or red pantile roofing. Steep thatched roofs also occur, more frequently towards the east. This mixture of materials can be attractive in itself, as at Yielden, while other villages, like Whittlebury, have a more eclectic mix of building styles, including red brick houses with limestone frontages. But there are also some very attractive compact villages where the local limestone predominates as a building material, such as Shalstone and Ravenstone, and with a high proportion of thatched roofs, as at Alderton.

Land Cover

There is a relatively high woodland cover, of up to 15 per cent in Yardley Chase. These large woodlands, many of them now managed by the Forestry Authority, are of oak, or oak and ash standards, with coppiced oak, and an understorey of birch, hazel, alder and willow.

This woodland combines with permanent pasture, leys and winter cereals. Pasture is more dominant on the higher land to the west, giving way to arable cropping on the lower, less undulating land to the east. The recent influence of 'horsiculture', with its small paddocks and miscellaneous artefacts has an impact on land adjacent to settlements.

The elevated and wide plateau top makes it suitable for airfields, two of which – Silverstone and Santa Pod – are now used for race tracks. Silverstone is a Grand Prix circuit and, as such, attracts huge volumes of visitors on occasions while at Santa Pod there are a variety of other small industrial and miscellaneous activities, creating locally a very untidy and cluttered landscape.

Routes tend to cut across the Ridge rather than follow it. As already mentioned, two major Roman routes pass through on their way north. The river Tove cuts through the gap at Grafton Regis as does the Grand Union Canal and the main northern railway line from Euston. At Roade, in order to maintain gentle gradients, the railway is in a particularly impressive cutting, one and a half miles long, and 70 feet deep.

The Changing Countryside

- Agricultural intensification, in particular moving from pastoral/mixed to arable, has resulted in a consequent increase in field size, loss of hedgerows, fragmentation or loss of semi-natural habitats and damage to historic features. In the predominantly arable areas, hedges are over-trimmed and mismanaged.

- The replanting of woodlands with conifers, and the introduction of non-native broadleaf species into ancient woodlands, has had an impact both on the landscape and on the nature-conservation interest of the woodlands. The historic character of the landscape is particularly vulnerable to such changes in woodland cover and structure.

- Dutch Elm disease has had a dramatic effect over recent decades, resulting in the widespread loss of hedgerow trees, although oak and ash are more substantial components on these shallow soils than in the clay vales. The continuing occurrence of the disease prevents elm suckers from establishing as hedgerow trees.

A strong historic landscape character has been retained in areas such as Yardley Chase, with good survival of veteran oaks in the Deer Park.

DAVID WOODFALL/COUNTRYSIDE AGENCY

33

DAVID WOODFALL/COUNTRYSIDE AGENCY

The Ridge is mainly agricultural in character, and includes medium sized arable fields bounded by full hedges with mature trees, usually oak.

- Development pressures on the villages are evident but have been reasonably well contained. Pressures for leisure and recreational facilities, in particular golf courses, are increasing. Developments in the open countryside have had an impact on the simple but strong structure of the landscape and its historic character.

Shaping the Future

- The retention of the character and nature-conservation value of the woodlands could be achieved through management, to include replanting oak and replacing introduced species with native species. There is also scope for establishing new and maintaining existing broadleaved woodland on private land.

- The possibility of re-creating some aspects of the historic landscape, for instance by restoring 'lawns' which are now arable back to pasture should be considered. Similarly, opportunities exist for the improved management of hedgerows and protection for naturally regenerating hedgerow trees.

- Pressures for recreational facilities, such as golf courses and holiday villages, and for farm diversification need to be handled carefully and particular care taken to integrate such schemes into the landscape structure.

Selected References

Cobham Resource Consultants (1992), *A landscape assessment and strategy for Northamptonshire*, for Northamptonshire County Council and the Countryside Commission.

Steane, J M (1974), *The Northamptonshire Landscape*, Hodder and Stoughton.

Bigmore, Peter (1979), *The Bedfordshire and Huntingdonshire Landscape*, Hodder and Stoughton.

Northamptonshire Uplands

Key Characteristics

- Rounded, undulating hills with many long, low ridgelines.

- Abundant and prominent ridge and furrow with frequent deserted and shrunken settlements.

- Sparse settlement of nucleated villages on hilltops or valley heads.

- Mixed farming: open arable contrasts with pasture enclosed by good hedges with frequent hedgerow trees.

- Wide views from the edges and across the ridgetops.

- Straight, wide, enclosure roads, often following ridges.

- Little woodland, but prominent coverts on higher ground.

- Ironstone and limestone older buildings with a transition across the area. Brick buildings in some villages.

- Great variety of landform with distinctive local features like Hemplow Hills.

- Large and nationally-important historic parks.

Landscape Character

This long range of clay hills extends from the Cotswolds and the Cherwell valley in the south west to the low ground of the Leicestershire Vales around Market Harborough. In the west it abuts the lower ground of the Feldon and to the east subsides towards the Nene Valley within the Northamptonshire Vales. It is part of the Wolds landscapes that include the dip slope of the Cotswolds and extend to High Leicestershire and the Leicestershire and Nottinghamshire Wolds, but without the strong sense of identity of these areas, not least because it is very varied.

There are a number of historic parklands, often with avenues framing country house views, such as here at Watford, to the north east of Daventry.

In the central section, where it rises to the high points of Arbury Hill, Charwelton Hill and Naseby, it has a rolling, gently hilly landform, with long, level views criss-crossed by a regular pattern of hedgerows with frequent ash trees. These and the small, but very frequent, copses give many areas a well treed character which has been lost on some of the more level and fertile ground. Here arable cultivation has led to the reduction in size and number of hedges and the loss of hedgerow trees. Although there are some settlements prominently sited on hilltops, most lie within the small, sheltered valleys and this, together with the infrequency of the isolated farms and cottages, gives the area a remote and rather empty quality.

To the south of Daventry, the land is much more hilly and the undulations are sharper and more frequent. There is less of the glacial boulder clay which dominates so much of the central area, the fields are generally smaller and settlement is more frequent. Even within this two-fold division there is great variety, with distinctive hills as the land steepens in the north above the Grand Union Canal at Hemplow or around Catesby. Although woodland is generally scarce in the uplands, it is quite frequent in an arc in the south from Badby to Woodend which, with its undulating landform, creates yet another local difference.

However, there are undoubted unifying features across the Northamptonshire Uplands. The most obvious, and probably most important of these, are the extensive and well-studied areas of ridge and furrow and deserted settlements. They are most prominent and evocative in the evenings and winter when the low sun casts long shadows from them and they seem to dominate the landscape. The villages which have survived are generally small and nucleated. Ironstone is such a common feature of the older buildings, at least in the southern part, that the area is sometimes known as the 'Ironstone Wolds'.

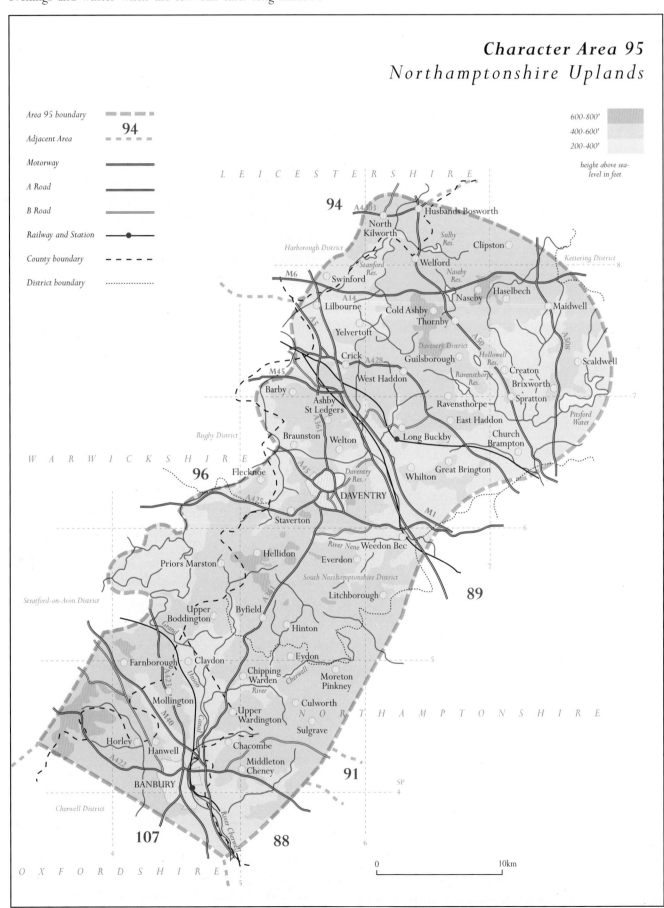

Character Area 95
Northamptonshire Uplands

Area 95 boundary

Adjacent Area

94

Motorway

A Road

B Road

Railway and Station

County boundary

District boundary

600-800'
400-600'
200-400'

height above sea-
level in feet

LEICESTERSHIRE

94

A4303

Husbands Bosworth

North Kilworth

Sulby Res.

Clipston

Kettering District

Harborough District

Stanford Res.

Welford

Naseby Res.

M6

Swinford

Haselbech

A14

Naseby

Lilbourne

Cold Ashby

Maidwell

A5

Thornby

Yelvertoft

Daventry District

A50

Crick

A428

Guilsborough

Hollowell Res.

Creaton

Scaldwell

M45

West Haddon

Ravensthorpe Res.

Brixworth

Barby

Spratton

Ashby St Ledgers

Ravensthorpe

A361

East Haddon

Pitsford Water

Braunston

Welton

Long Buckby

Church Brampton

Rugby District

WARWICKSHIRE

A45

96

Flecknoe

Whilton

Great Brington

Daventry Res.

A425

DAVENTRY

M1

Staverton

Hellidon

Weedon Bec

River Nene

Priors Marston

Everdon

South Northamptonshire District

89

Litchborough

Stratford-on-Avon District

Grand Union Canal

Upper Boddington

Byfield

Hinton

Farnborough

Claydon

Eydon

A423

Chipping Warden

Cherwell

Moreton Pinkney

River

Mollington

Upper Wardington

Culworth

NORTHAMPTONSHIRE

M40

Sulgrave

Horley

Hanwell

Chacombe

91

A422

Middleton Cheney

SP 4

BANBURY

107

88

Cherwell District

SP 4

River Cherwell

0   10km

OXFORDSHIRE

36

This sparsely settled area is of significant interest due to the survival of well preserved ridge and furrow as well as the frequent deserted and shrunken settlements that still remain.

The valley villages generally have an enclosed, well-treed and sheltered character in contrast to the open and exposed high ground. Perhaps even more characteristic are the few surviving cob buildings. The modest village houses are a strong contrast to the large mansions and manor houses which lie in the valleys on the slightly lower ground. Their surrounding parks are often very extensive and the estate character of the landscape is emphasised by the uniformity of the buildings in their adjacent villages. Elizabethan and Jacobean houses, such as Ashby St Ledger and Sulgrave Manors, are particularly well represented.

Although there were enclosures of the open fields which dominated the area from the 15th century onwards, the predominant field pattern and a strong unifying factor is that of parliamentary enclosure imposed on an 'up and down' landscape. Here the rectilinear pattern is frequently strongly visible. The straight, wide, enclosure roads which often follow ridges are also part of this planned character. From these ridges the essence of the uplands, described here by W G Hoskins, can be seen:

'In this hill country, partly isolated summits and partly high table land in places, the wind blows hard and cold … Up at Naseby next door to Cold Ashby … their voices are louder than anywhere else, they shout at each other to overcome the winter wind'.

Physical Influences

The area is underlain by the intractable clays of the Lias, capped locally by the ironstone-bearing Marlstone and Northampton Sands, and with a thick mantle of boulder clay (glacial till) in many areas: all of the sharper features have been smoothed away by a long process of denudation.

The uplands are 'the main watershed of Middle England'. At the southern end, the Cherwell arises near Charwelton and flows southwards, the valley narrowing downstream. The Warwickshire Avon rises on the eastern edge near Naseby to flow westwards and south-westwards, while the

north-eastwards flowing Welland rises near Sibbertoft, a few miles away. The tributaries of the Tove and Ouse originate in the south-eastern flanks to flow south-eastwards. Much of the eastern side of the area forms the upper catchment of the Nene, with the major tributary of the Ise arising in the far north east. Topographically, the upper Nene divides the Northamptonshire Heights to the north from the Cherwell/Ouse tablelands or 'Ironstone Wolds' to the south.

Historical and Cultural Influences

The history of the area is in many ways typical of a wolds landscape. It was originally covered in thick woodland over a soil not very attractive to early cultivation. Prehistoric activity and settlement encroached around the edges of the area within the river valleys and there were Iron Age hillforts, as at Borough Hill near Daventry. The area was an upland grazing and woodland resource for the surrounding settlements and was largely ignored by the Romans.

The early Anglo-Saxon settlements were also along the adjacent river valleys but the middle Saxon period saw the farmsteads (tons) spreading up onto higher ground and the outstanding late 7th century church at Brixworth on the edge of the area indicates that these were sites of major significance. The many woodland (leigh) names, however, illustrate that there were also substantial areas of woodland while the many place names ending in by demonstrate that Scandinavian settlement of the area was probably quite extensive. By the 11th century, there was quite frequent settlement although at a lower density than the surrounding more fertile areas.

Up to the mid-14th century colonisation proceeded rapidly. Most of the woodland went and nucleated villages, surrounded by open fields in ridge and furrow cultivation, dominated the landscape. The substantial churches reflect this main period of the area's expansion and colonisation, which went into decline following the disasters of the mid-14th century. Population shrank and settlements were deserted for a variety of complex reasons but all stemming from its limited quality for cereal growth. Ambitious landlords like the Spencers were able to accumulate large areas of land for grazing; in 1577 for instance their flocks at Wormleighton and Althorp numbered 14,000. Today the area is one of the classic sites for deserted settlements and ridge and furrow, overlaid by a mixture of Tudor and parliamentary enclosure hedges, with most of the woodland having long since disappeared.

As the population shrank and grazing dominated the landscape, so the great landscape parks and country houses like Althorp, Canons Ashby, Cottesbroke, Harlestone and Holdenby were laid out, some by major designers such as Repton and Brown. The strong landlordship that often

There are wide views from the ridgelines across the adjacent clay vales.

went with such parks is reflected in the estate villages. The Elizabethan and Jacobean houses, notably Althorp and Canons Ashby are particularly associated with the court life of that period, the poems of Spencer and the masques of Ben Jonson.

In the 18th and 19th centuries the remaining open land was enclosed, while in the 20th century the main changes to a substantially remote and rural area have been the major routeways of the M1 and A14 which cross it, the expansion of arable cultivation and modern farm buildings, and the construction of reservoirs around the edge of the area.

Buildings and Settlement

The main settlements of the area are small villages with red brick or ironstone buildings clustered around an ironstone church, allthough creamy-grey limestone is used in the north. There are scattered buildings in cob, which was largely replaced by brick in the 19th century. Pantile and tile roofs predominate throughout the area. Many of the villages are small, some with the earthworks of abandoned dwellings at their edges. Some, like Naseby and the aptly named Cold Ashton, are on prominent hilltop sites but others lie in sheltered situations at the heads of minor valleys. These latter villages are often attractively set within mature tree cover and have a unity resulting from common materials and design. Only around the edges of the area, along the Cherwell valley and to the north between Rugby and Daventry, have the villages become significantly enlarged by 20th century development. The remoteness of the central villages is emphasised by the minor roads that serve them, in contrast to the busy strategic east-west routes of the M1, A14 and A425 that cross the area.

Some of the country houses are buildings of great character. Cottesbroke, for instance is famed for its gracious proportions; Canons Ashby is built around the remains of the medieval monastery. Althorp House has the grand Georgian elegance of Henry Holland's design around an ancient core. But there are also fine buildings on a smaller scale, almost always in local stone, such as the manor houses at Ashby St Ledger and Sulgrave. In some cases the estate character of the landscape is emphasised by estate villages and lodges.

Land Cover

Most of the land is in agricultural use with a mixture of arable and pasture. The arable is quite extensive in the more level ground of the ridgetops. Here hedges can be quite low and hedgerow trees intermittent, while elsewhere the hedge cover is generally good. Within the pasture fields, ridge and furrow and the earthworks of deserted settlements are of particular significance. Woodland is generally sparse but there are some prominent woods in the south. The few blocks of ancient woodland like Badby take on a special value and interest in a locality where there are few areas of semi-natural vegetation and limited wildlife interest. Most of the tree and shrub cover, other than the hedgerows, is given by the spinneys dotted across the landscape, often on the higher ground. Around the edge of the area, reservoirs are a significant element within the land cover but the greatest variety, from the uniform pattern of pasture and arable within Tudor and parliamentary enclosure hedges, is given by the landscape parks.

The Changing Countryside

- Most of the area is remote and rural: change is mainly gradual and erosive.

- Intensification on the land most appropriate for arable has led to removal and reduction of hedges and loss of hedgerow trees.

- There is a general decline in hedgerow trees. Ash, the commonest tree, is particularly at risk from dieback.

- The woodlands are generally suffering from a lack of appropriate management.

- The area is of outstanding interest for its ridge and furrow and deserted settlements and these are vulnerable to ploughing up and unthinking damage.

- Features outside the area, notably the town of Rugby and the prominent radio masts, have an impact on the remote rural character of the landscape.

- There is pressure for sand and gravel extraction in the area of the M1 corridor, where it is allocated. Elsewhere it is restricted.

- Decline in quality of Parkland through management neglect, e.g. at Fawsley or conversion to more intensive agriculture.

Shaping the Future

- The conservation of parkland and ridge and furrow should be addressed. A co-ordinated approach between conservation organisations and farming interests to conserve the outstanding ridge and furrow and deserted settlements is important.

- Many villages would benefit from local design initiatives.

- There are opportunities to improve woodland management and to link new and existing woodlands.

Selected References

David Hall (1993), *The Open Fields of Northamptonshire* - the Case for Preservation and Ridge and Furrow.

Northamptonshire County Council (1985), *Nene Valley Management Plan Background & Strategy*.

Northamptonshire County Council (1989), *Nene Valley Management Plan Earls Barton to Wellingborough*.

Northamptonshire County Council (1994), *Landscapes Guidelines Handbook*.

Northamptonshire County Council (*Northamptonshire Heritage*)

Steane, J M (1974), *The Northamptonshire Landscape*, Hodder & Stoughton, London.

STEVEN WARNOCK

The intensification of arable cultivation on the area's rich red soils has led to a reduction in the size and number of hedgerows, creating an open landscape with a remote and empty quality.

Cotswolds

- Defined by its underlying geology: a dramatic scarp rising above adjacent lowlands with steep combes, scarp foot villages and beech woodlands.

- Rolling, open, high wold plateaux moulded by physical and human influences, with arable and large blocks of woodland, divided up by small, narrow valleys.

- Incised landscapes with deep wide valleys.

- Flat, open dip slope landscape with extensive arable farmland.

- Prominent outliers within the lowlands.

- Honey-coloured Cotswold stone in walls, houses and churches.

- Attractive stone villages with a unity of design and materials.

Landscape Character

The Cotswolds form perhaps the best-known of the stone-belt uplands that stretch right across England from Dorset to Lincolnshire. The dominant pattern is of a steep scarp and long, rolling dip slope cut into a series of plateaux by numerous rivers and streams. There is great variety of landform and vegetation and a number of distinct landscapes can be identified. However, in briefly describing these, the fundamental unity must not be underrated. This derives in part from the harmony of the ever-present honey-coloured oolitic limestone in walls, houses, mansions and churches. It dominates the villages which have a distinctive Cotswold-style derived from repeating simple elements. There are many other common elements such as beech woods, outstanding landscape parks, valley bottom meadows and a strong sense of a long period of settlement and human activity. The latter derives from the many outstanding features ranging from prehistoric monuments to the dry stone walls of 18th century enclosure.

At the western edge of the Cotswolds, the scarp face, fretted by deep combes, dominates the Severn Valley.

Dense beechwoods, tree clumps, scrub, semi-natural grassland and prehistoric earthworks, most notably the Iron Age hillforts, contribute to an attractive and imposing skyline. Although hedged fields divide up much of the scarp's pastures, there are surviving commons, including Cleeve Common. Settlements on the scarp are confined to a few sheltered sites, but there are frequent villages where springs emerge at its foot. Around Bath, Stroud and Winchcombe, the landform is characterised by deep, wide valleys, often accentuated by densely-wooded ridge crests. Tree-clad streams wind down the steep slopes where fields are often small with overgrown hedges but, on the ridge tops, the landscape is usually open arable divided up by dry stone walls.

JOHN TYLER/COUNTRYSIDE AGENCY

The use of Cotswold oolitic limestone for buildings is one of the most dominant and characteristic features of the area. It can be seen throughout the built landscape of the Cotswolds and is the basis of the great 'wool' churches.

Beyond the scarp to the north-west, there are outlying hills of which Bredon is the largest and best-known. They have an outward-facing radial form with field boundaries appearing to radiate from a central point. Several are crowned by ridges.

To the east of the scarp and its deeply-incised valleys, the landform becomes gentler and there are the broad rolling plateaux of the high Wolds. The large-scale, generally open landscape, is characterised by blocks of woodland and arable, but there are also lush, narrow, enclosed valleys forming a strong contrast, emphasised by the dry stone walls of the plateaux and the hedges of the valleys. Villages are near the spring lines, sometimes lying around a central common or green.

Finally, there is the dip slope which is yet more gentle than the high Wolds. The valleys, like those of the Windrush and Coln, are much broader and sometimes give the impression that they are simply undulations in the plateau. Arable predominates, but marshy valley bottoms with willows, alders and watermeadows still survive.

Physical Influences

The north-west-facing scarp reaches its highest point just north of Cheltenham, becoming less prominent to the north and south. The Jurassic oolitic limestone of the upper scarp

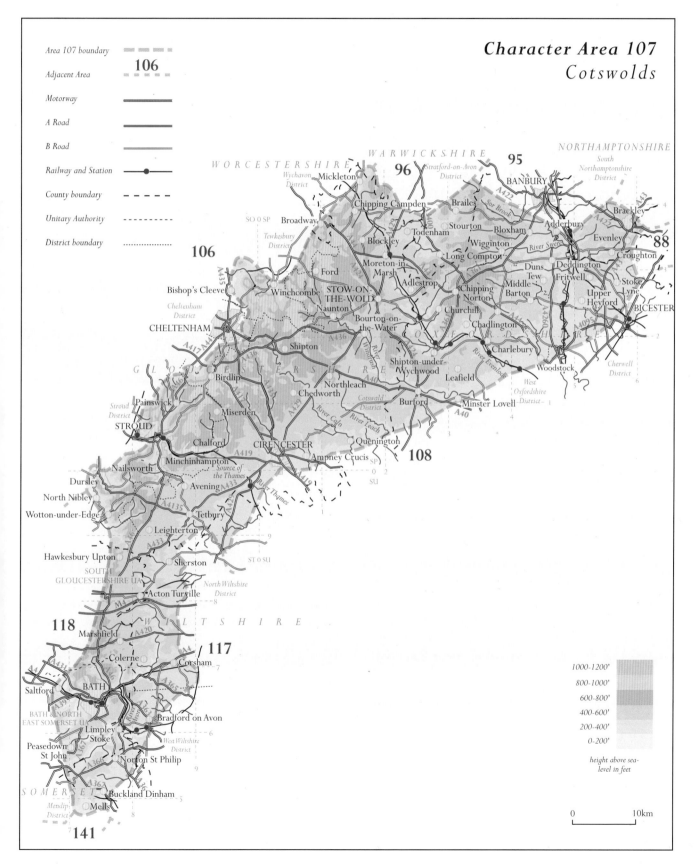

Character Area 107
Cotswolds

Area 107 boundary	— — —
Adjacent Area	**106**
Motorway	
A Road	
B Road	
Railway and Station	—•—
County boundary	— — —
Unitary Authority	- - - - -
District boundary	· · · · · ·

1000-1200'
800-1000'
600-800'
400-600'
200-400'
0-200'

height above sea-level in feet

0   10km

forms the freely-draining high land of the northern and western wolds, as well as the ridge tops between the steep valleys to the south and east. Steeply-incised stream and river valleys cut through the scarp, flowing westwards towards the Severn. To the south and east, the oolite dips beneath wetter clays which form broad valleys around the main rivers and streams which flow eastwards.

To the north east an undulating wolds landscape with wide views, large fields, dry stone walls, plantation and shelter belts is broken by a lush, enclosed and settled valley.

Jurassic rocks predominate, the strata dipping towards and becoming progessively younger to the south and east. Small areas of Oxford Clay and coarse, crumbly Cornbrash occur at the south-eastern extremity. The Great Oolite underlies most of the plateau area but the massive limestone escarpment to the north and west is formed by the underlying Inferior Oolite which, if anything, is even more sought after as a building stone. Lower down the scarp face, and surrounding the northern and western fringes, the Lias shales, sandstones and siltstones of the Lower Jurassic are exposed. These are soft and easily weathered and have slumped or eroded to form the hummocky ground, stream valleys and bays at the escarpment foot.

Many of the Cotswold soils are derived directly from the parent rock and tend to be alkaline and of low fertility. Thin, well-aerated, brashy soils derived from limestone are common on the steeper slopes, particularly to the west. More fertile, deeper, clayey soils of alluvial origin are present along the valley floors and on lower-lying land to the south and east.

Historical and Cultural Influences

The Cotswolds have some outstanding prehistoric monuments ranging from the Neolithic long barrow of Hetty Pegler's Tump near Uley to the many impressive Iron age hillforts like Bredon Hill and Meon Hill. They are evidence of substantial human activity which almost certainly saw the clearance of areas with light and easily

cultivable soils at an early date and it was probably these that formed the basis of the extensive Roman occupation of the area. Villas and lesser settlements were frequent and the road pattern of the Foss Way, Ermin Street, Akeman Street and Ryknild Street is still very apparent.

It is not entirely clear whether the Saxons took over a substantially cleared and settled landscape or whether the clearance of the heavier land took place during the Anglo-Saxon period. However, by the late 11th century, the area was extensively settled and there was little woodland. Common fields were in use soon after, if not before, the preparation of Domesday Book and, at that time and in the ensuing medieval centuries, much of the land was in large estates, both ecclesiastical and lay. There were vast open sheepwalks which formed the basis of medieval prosperity and sheep were moved seasonally from low to high ground.

A plateau of large-scale arable farmland with a sparse settlement pattern of isolated farmsteads and hamlets is a characteristic feature of this part of the Cotswolds.

After the disasters of the early and mid-14th century, large estates were consolidated and a prosperous cloth trade expanded from its early medieval beginnings with the many fast-flowing streams being used for fulling. Small market towns like Northleach and Chipping Camden expanded and many fine Perpendicular churches and merchants houses were built. The land market that followed the dissolution of the monasteries enabled the consolidation of the large estates, leading ultimately to the fine country houses and historic parks like Dyrham, Badminton and Compton Wynyates. Many of the villages owe their present uniform character to the strong influence of estates which, in many cases, has persisted down to the present day. Throughout the late medieval and post-medieval period, there was piecemeal enclosure of open fields, commons, waste and sheepwalks but many of the sheepwalks remained unenclosed until the late 18th and 19th centuries and the prominent rectilinear patterns characterise much of the higher ground today.

In the early modern period, the cloth industry concentrated in the valleys around Dursley, Stroud, Chalford and Painswick. Although it was originally a cottage industry, by

1800 large mills were built with cottages nearby. However, by the 1830s the industry was in decline and, apart from quarrying, agriculture has been the principal industry of the Cotswolds in the present century. There has been large-scale conversion from grassland to arable, removal of hedges and conversion of broadleaf woodland to conifers. The other major change has been the growth of tourism and the expansion of settlement.

Buildings and Settlement

Settlements throughout the area are united by the use of the Cotswold stone and a relatively small range of architectural styles. The great wool churches were built in Perpendicular style, mostly in the 15th century. They generally have profusely ornamented square towers although spires are sometimes found. It is, however, the high quality of the domestic architecture that is distinctive, typically comprising a steep roof of graded limestone 'slates', parapeted gables with finials, stone mullions, rectangular dripstones, dormer windows in subsidiary gables and four-centred arches over doorways. Ashlar is usually used on the front of buildings at least and the overall impression is one of diversity on a common theme of refinement and simple elegance, blending seamlessly into the surrounding landscape.

The principal towns – Bath, Stroud and Cirencester – lie on the very edges of the area and the fine qualities of the oolite-dominated townscape of Bath in particular is too well known to need description. The smaller towns and villages lie at the scarp foot, in the valley bottoms or on the valley sides with the gentlest gradients. Plans vary between compact and linear with some lying around a wide central green or common. Away from these sheltered town and village sites, usually never far from water, there are generally only small hamlets and isolated farmsteads, so that the higher ground often seems very sparsely populated. The settlements are linked by a complex network of roads. The oldest (the Roman roads) and the most recent (the enclosure road) sweep across the landscape in almost straight lines but the typical Cotswold road is a winding lane linking villages along the valleys and rising over the high ground.

Land Cover

Much of the high ground of the plateau is arable, broken by occasional woodland blocks and shelterbelts with dry stone walls but also with hedges. In the valleys, at least on the steeper slopes, pasture predominates and along the valley bottoms there are meadows and tree-lined watercourses. On the scarp slopes, scrub, beech woodland, hedges and tree clumps are present and some areas of species-rich grassland survive.

The beech woodlands are of national importance and have a characteristic, if limited, flora. Other woodlands, typically located on the upper slopes of valleys and on the flat plateaux tops, are more varied and contain a wide range of

The west facing Cotswold scarp supports high calcareous grassland and fine beech woods.

calcicole shrubs and ground flora. The unimproved grassland, too, contains typical calcicole species. The streams and marshes have varied marginal vegetation and unimproved wet meadows with alder and willow carr.

The Changing Countryside

- Agricultural improvement and conversion to arable have brought widespread loss of semi-natural habitats and landscape features in the period since the last war. Much of the unimproved, species-rich limestone grassland has been lost, marshes have been drained and hedges and dry stone walls removed. However, these changes have now more or less abated.

- Loss of unimproved grassland has probably been checked but scrub invasion through declining grazing is affecting what remains.

- There is pressure for expansion of villages and for the creation of new rural settlements, particularly those within easy reach of major towns and cities. Much new building has been infilling and unsympathetic in design and materials. Many farm buildings have been converted to residential use.

- Tourism and through-traffic have brought a requirement for upgraded roads, bypasses and through-routes with associated upgrading and an increased number of signs for minor routes.

- There is pressure for facilities at tourist honeypots, with associated congestion, erosion of footpaths, bridleways and viewing points.

- Dry stone walls are in long-term decline: the limestone walls become friable with age and require regular maintenance which is labour-intensive and expensive.

- Some small woodlands have been converted to conifers. Many existing small woodlands are unmanaged.

- There are continuing pressures for landfill, quarrying and extraction of gravel and minerals.

Shaping the Future

- Much of the scarp would benefit from an improved management of the limestone grassland and a reduction of scrub.

- There are opportunities for the sound managment of hedges, woodlands, copses and – particularly – the distinctive beechwoods.

- The sensitive management of wetland habitats of the valley bottoms including wet grassland, scrub, willows and the streams themselves should be addressed.

- There is much interest in the conservation of dry stone walls and hedge management. Priorities need to be set for the areas that are most important in the landscape.

- The quality of Cotswold villages is often jealously guarded. Local design initiatives offer a basis for turning this into precise guidelines and activity.

SIMON WARNER/COUNTRYSIDE AGENCY

Cotswold streams provide interest in the landscape and are generally of high quality supporting brown trout, dippers and, in a few areas, native crayfish.

Selected References

ADAS (1994), *Cotswold Hills ESA Landscape Assessment and Environmental Guidelines*.

Cotswold AONB JAC (1995), *Cotswold AONB Management Strategy*.

Countryside Commission (1990), *The Cotswold Landscape*, Countryside Commission, Cheltenham CCP 294.

Finberg, H P R (1973), *The Gloucestershire Landscape*, Hodder & Stoughton, London.

Hadfield, C and Hadfield, A M (1973), *The Cotswolds : A New Study*.

Glossary

calcicole: plant that grows best in calcareous soil

carr: a marshy copse

Upper Thames Clay Vales

This description consists of two sub-character areas: Wiltshire, Oxfordshire and Buckinghamshire Vales; and Vales of the White Horse and Aylesbury.

Wiltshire, Oxfordshire and Buckinghamshire Vales

Willow pollards along the Thames Valley and other river systems are distinctive features in the area.

Key Characteristics

- Broad belt of open, gently undulating lowland farmland on Upper Jurassic clays containing a variety of contrasting landscapes. Includes the enclosed pastures of the claylands and the wet valley bottoms and the more settled open arable lands of the gravel.

- The valley bottoms, with open floodplain landscapes displaying gravel workings and flooded pits, a regular and well-ordered field pattern, willow pollards and reedbeds along the water courses.

- The Vales in Oxfordshire are dominated by 18th century enclosure landscapes of small woods and hawthorn/blackthorn hedges. Former and current gravel workings along the Thames floodplain also include open water features. The distinctive character of Otmoor with its patchwork pattern of small fields defined by healthy hedgerows of elm add interest and variety to this area.

- In Buckinghamshire, the Vale is a predominantly pastoral landscape including regular fields within a well-defined network of trimmed hedgerows often with oak/ash hedgerow trees and some small blocks of woodland.

- Brick-built buildings within the Vales reflect the widespread use of the local clay as a building material.

Landscape Character

The Wiltshire, Oxfordshire and Buckinghamshire Vales form part of a larger belt of clay lowland that links the Cambridgeshire Claylands to the Avon Vales. This area consists of a broad loosely-defined clay belt of open, gently undulating lowland farmland and major river valley floodplains. The clay Vales are bounded by the limestone scenery of the Cotswolds to the north and the narrow limestone outcrop of the Midvale Ridge to the south.

Much of the Vales are of a mixed farmland character with a regular and well-ordered field pattern defined by thick hedgerows. More open floodplain landscapes are also a feature of the area, especially west of Oxford and into Wiltshire, where gravel workings and flooded pits are features in the landscape. Water courses contribute greatly to local landscape diversity with their numerous mature willow stands and pollards, and waterside reed beds.

The Oxfordshire and Wiltshire parts of the Vales are characterised by 18th century enclosure landscapes of small woods and hawthorn/blackthorn hedges. Hedgerow elms were a significant feature although these have inevitably disappeared but there are still many hedges where this species survives as a major shrub component. Former and current gravel workings along the Upper Thames

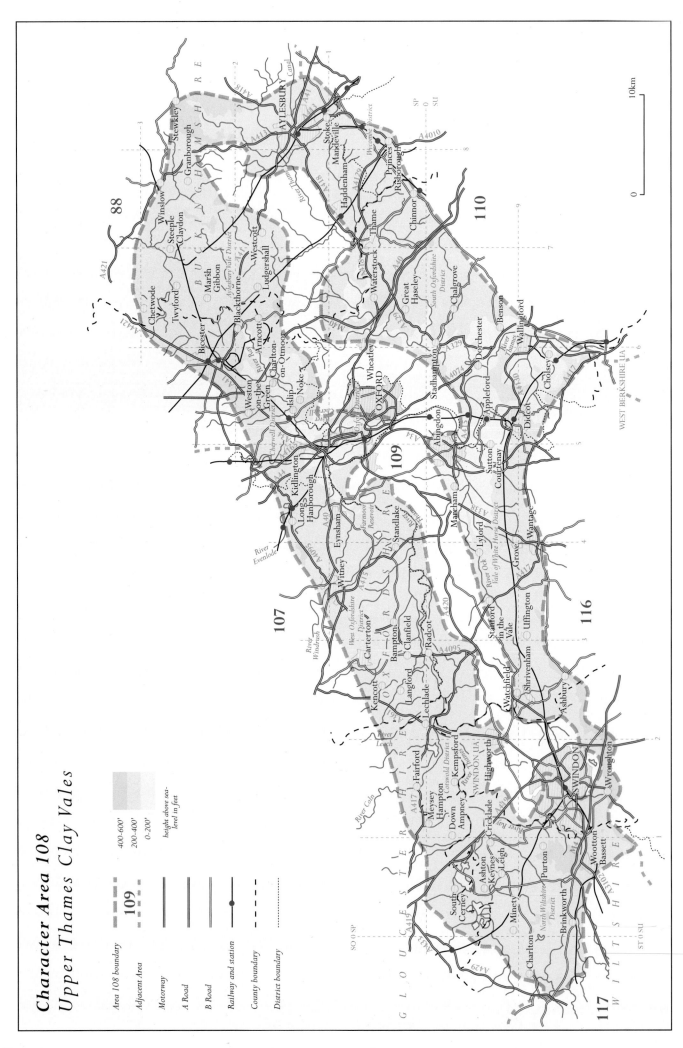

Character Area 108
Upper Thames Clay Vales

Area 108 boundary
109 Adjacent Area

Motorway
A Road
B Road
Railway and station
County boundary
District boundary

400-600'
200-400'
0-200'

height above sea-level in feet

10km

floodplain, many of which are now open water used for watersports and recreation, such as the Cotswold Water Park, are particularly characteristic of this area. Rivers and watercourses, particularly where tree-lined, are also important landscape features including the springlines which emerge from the base of the chalk escarpment. Further towards Buckinghamshire, the distinctive character of Otmoor adds interest and variety to the Vales. Noticeably devoid of settlement, Otmoor is a low patchwork pattern of small fields defined by healthy hedgerows of elm. Several distinctive villages fringe the area and are connected by a small road that skirts Otmoor itself.

Farther east into Buckinghamshire there is less arable land with pasture becoming predominant on the clay. The regular fields are bounded by a well-defined network of trimmed hedges with mature oak or ash hedgerow trees and interspersed by numerous small blocks of woodland.

Settlement within the Vales is characterised by brick-built buildings that reflect the widespread use of local clay as the principle building raw material. Nucleated villages are generally located on rising ground or confined to the raised gravel spreads above the valley bottoms. Scattered isolated 19th century farmhouses and historic parklands are a characteristic feature of the wider landscape.

Within the overall character of the Oxfordshire and Buckinghamshire Vales, much contrast and variety is provided by the pastures and hedgerows of the clay areas, the pollarded willows of the floodplains, the often hedgeless arable fields and the villages confined to the raised areas of gravel.

Physical Influences

Contained by limestone uplands to the north and by low hills and ridges to the south, the Wiltshire, Oxfordshire and Buckinghamshire Vales are underlain by a great expanse of heavy blue-grey Oxford and Kimmeridge clays. The topography of the Vales is flat although, to the east, the Buckinghamshire Vale is typically more gently undulating due to the thicker surface deposits. In many places, the clay is covered locally by gravel deposits centred along the major river valleys, and marked by extensive workings and flooded pits.

The Upper Thames drains the Vale to the west before cutting south at the confluence with the lower reaches of the Cherwell through the Midvale Ridge at Oxford. Wide expanses of terraced river gravels of limestone, derived from the Cotswolds, and wide alluvial flats dominate the Oxfordshire Vale. At the confluence of the Thames with the Windrush, Evenlode and Cherwell, distinctive tabular hillocks form low isolated features within the Vale where patches of more ancient pebbly drift rest on the underlying Oxford Clay. Soils are generally yellowish brown earth, gleyed in lower lying areas. The terrace and floodplain soils over gravel vary although west of Oxford the soils are dominantly calcareous with good drainage.

To the east, the river Ray joins the Cherwell at Islip and drains the wide basin of Otmoor where the soils are covered by a layer of peaty alluvium formed under marshy conditions before the land was drained for agriculture. The gently rising land along the northern rim to the east forms a watershed between the Ray and the river Ouse.

This area is underlaid by Oxford Clay with extensive deposits of gravel along the Thames Valley. Gravel pits have become a significant feature within the modern Vale landscape.

Historical and Cultural Influences

The straight-sided large fields enclosing the Vales are typical of a 'planned countryside'. Domesday Book records little woodland cover in the 11th century with scarcely any mention of place-names relating to woodland. However, by this time, Oxford's 'ford' across the Thames was in evidence, as were the grazed water meadows at Cricklade and at Oxford. Otmoor was being used for summer and autumn grazing.

A major contrast existed between the pattern of pastures and hedgerows associated with the clays, the pollarded willows on alluvium and the hedgeless arable fields and villages confined to gravel spreads within the river valleys. Modern day evidence of the reclamation of the wetter lands exists in the occurrence of 'moor' place names in the Cotswolds Water Park area and also Otmoor. Generally the older, smaller fields are limited to land next to the rivers while the larger arable/grassland fields dominate the higher, drier ground.

The sparse settlement pattern within the Vales was more or less established by the 11th century with the upper Thames area generally quite well-populated compared to the Vale further to the east. There were occasional hamlets, farmsteads or inns near river crossing points but the settlements tended to be on the higher ground around the edges of the gravels and loams along the river valleys due to the risk of flooding. Otmoor was, as now, largely devoid of any buildings or settlement.

Significant archaeological features are visible within the Vale. These include the Roman roads such as the Ermine Way, ancient field systems evident as crop marks along gravels and remnant embankments and ditches associated with royal hunting grounds. Numerous settlement sites on gravel spreads provide evidence of continuity of settlement from the Iron Age through the Saxon and Roman period and beyond although there are virtually no Palaeolithic or Mesolithic remains due to the difficulty of cultivating the heavy clay soils before the advent of crude tools.

Otmoor's distinctive patchwork pattern of small fields and hedgerows are thought to have inspired Lewis Carroll's chess board landscape in *Alice Through the Looking Glass*.

Buildings and Settlement

The overall pattern of settlement within the Vales follows the rim of the area with villages located on rising ground or confined to the raised gravel spreads within the flood-prone lowlands. Otmoor is devoid of settlement but is fringed by several distinctive villages comprising linear developments along the small road that skirts the moor itself. Some villages are more nucleated and isolated 19th century farmhouses are characteristic of many areas.

Brick-built buildings within the Vale reflect the widespread use of the local clay as a building material with plain-tiled roofs also common. However, there are some older stone-walled and stone-slated buildings particularly in the Oxford Vale, their character reflecting the influence of the Cotswolds to the north.

Land Cover

The Wiltshire, Oxfordshire and Buckinghamshire Vales is mainly a pastoral landscape dominated by stock rearing with areas of arable in some places. There are also some areas of old unimproved hay meadows north of Oxford with more diverse flora. Wetter areas are usually under grass ranging from ley grassland to unimproved pasture or meadows. The larger arable fields in contrast tend to be restricted to the elevated gravel terraces characterised by their better drained soils. The 'chequer board' landscape resulting from the juxtaposition of the arable and grassland fields in Otmoor is a notable feature within the wider, more uniform landscape.

Woodlands are generally scarce within the Vales and historically this has been the case for many centuries. Occasional coniferous trees appear within shelter belts around buildings on the areas of higher gravels within the Vale. These drier areas, which are less liable to flooding, also support a thick network of hedges with oak and ash hedgerow trees. In the past, many of these hedges would have included elm. Watercourses are often marked by lines of willows or black poplar. Lush waterside vegetation forms

irregular natural boundaries in some areas, while post and wire fencing and stone walls are found in others.

There are extensive areas of flooded gravel pits around the Cotswold Water Park where recreation is now the major land use. The very flat fields contain small ponds and are typically surrounded by ditches defined by the odd willow which thrives in the wet soil conditions. Cattle graze the fields where an often moderately pronounced pattern of ridge and furrow can indicate an older field system.

The Changing Countryside

- Deterioration of hedgerows due to a combination of undermanagement and neglect.

- Numerous and extensive gravel workings have altered the appearance and ecology of the open floodplain landscape in many places, resulting in benefits for wildlife.

- Intensification of agricultural activities resulting in the removal of hedgerows and enlarged fields, new farm buildings and structures in the landscape and neglect of landscape features such as farm ponds.

- River canalisation and land drainage.

- Planting of poplar plantations has changed the open character of many riverside landscapes.

Shaping the Future

- Hedgerows and field margins within arable fields would benefit from conservation management.

- The restoration of river corridors and wet meadows would benefit the area.

Selected References

Richards Moorehead and Laing Ltd (1989), *Buckinghamshire Trees and Forestry Strategy: Volumes 1, 2 and 3*, Richards Moorehead and Laing, Clwyd.

Reed, M (1979), *The Buckinghamshire Landscape*, Hodder and Stoughton, London.

Emery, F (1974), *The Oxfordshire Landscape*, Hodder and Stoughton, London.

Martin, A F and Steel, R W (eds), (1954), *The Oxford Region*, Oxford University Press, London.

Anderson, J R L (1970), *The Upper Thames*, Eyre and Spottiswoode, London.

Glossary

gleyed: waterlogged

Vales of the White Horse and Aylesbury

- A predominantly lowland agricultural landscape of open undulating vales.

- Mixed farming, dairy herds, hedges, hedge trees and field trees are all frequent and characteristic within the landscape. In many places, mature field oaks give a parkland feel to the landscape.

- The clays of the Vale of the White Horse support arable farming with some tracts of sheep pasture in medium sized and regular field pattern with few hedgerows or trees.

- Long views often dominated by Didcot power station and associated power lines.

- Aylesbury Vale is a continuation of the Vale of the White Horse, with a quiet, more enclosed agricultural character. Black poplar trees are distinctive features within the agricultural landscape of the Vale.

- The chalk scarp of the Chilterns and the Berkshire and Marlborough Downs form a backdrop for many views from the Vales to the south.

Landscape Character

The Vales of the White Horse and Aylesbury are low-lying undulating vales, open in character and largely dominated by agriculture, that lie below the Chalk scarps of the Chilterns and the Berkshire and Marlborough Downs to the south. To the north, the generally low ground is interrupted by the low profile of the Midvale Ridge.

Predominantly an agricultural landscape, arable fields, dairy herds, hedges, hedgerow trees and field trees are frequent and characteristic within the landscape. In many places, mature field oaks impart a parkland feel. The Chalk scarp of the Chilterns and the Berkshire and Marlborough Downs is prominent in many views from the Vales to the south.

The Vale of the White Horse supports mainly arable farming with some tracts of sheep grazed pasture. The field pattern of large regular fields is associated with few hedgerows or trees. Villages such as Baulking and Goosey built around distinctive greens are located on the gravels along the river Ock valley. Contrast is provided by the fruit orchards around Harwell which thrive on the light fertile sandy soils developed over the Greensand bench at the foot of the chalk escarpment. Long views are typical within the open landscape dominated, however, from many perspectives, by Didcot power station and its associated power lines.

Aylesbury Vale is a continuation of the Vale of the White Horse. The agricultural landscape continues over the low-lying and generally level topography of the heavy clay soils. Here, black poplar tree stands become distinctive features within the Vale. The farmed landscape is a geometric enclosure landscape of large farms set amongst large hedged fields with regular spaced hedgerow trees. In the vicinity of villages the fields are generally smaller and more irregular forming organic shapes within the wider landscape of large fields. Further contrast is provided by the river Thame which drains the Vale towards the Thames in the south west. Here, bankside willows fringe the river with flat open watermeadow landscapes adding to the interest and variety. A line of settlements from Bledlow to Wendover developed along the natural spring lines at the base of the Chilterns chalk scarp. Today, they include historic and distinctive market towns.

Low-lying agricultural land of arable and pasture is the dominant feature in the area. The field pattern here is open, modern and large-scale with agricultural intensification leading to hedgerow loss.

Physical Influences

This area is a broad lowland valley that widens between Goring and Abingdon before becoming narrower to the east where it has a more undulating topography, typically of low ridges and small mounds.

The Vale of the White Horse in the west is a broad belt of heavy blue grey Lower Cretaceous Gault Clay with some exposures of underlying Jurassic Kimmeridge Clay drained by the river Ock and the Thame. South of Swindon, the Vale slopes gradually down from the foot of the Berkshire and Marlborough Downs Chalk escarpment to form a gently undulating clay plain, here and there broken by minor hills of Greensand or Portland Limestone. Notable Chalk hill outliers rise from the middle of the Vale near Dorchester and Cholsey.

The Vale of White Horse passes eastwards into the Aylesbury Vale. Here, the wide unbroken valley is dissected by alluvial flats and low river gravel terraces around the confluence of the Ock and the Thame. Farther east into the narrower Aylesbury Vale, sandy brown earths – developed from the ledge of Greensand below the Chalk scarp of the Chilterns – provide some of the most productive soils in the area. Aylesbury Vale is drained by the river Thame and by numerous independent streams that flow south-west into the Thames. Where drainage is impeded along river courses, the underlying gleyed brown earths give rise to wet meadows.

Large hedgerow trees remain important elements in the Vale landscape.

Historical and Cultural Influences

In Neolithic times, numerous tribes colonised the river terraces downstream from Radley and ancient field systems are visible as cropmarks in the Thames gravels. Around Aylesbury the deserted villages, such as Quarrendon, Fleet Marston and Creslow, are also significant historic landscape features from medieval times.

Dorchester, on the Thames, was a Roman frontier post in defence against the Belgic tribes. The Romans laid down numerous roads to aid the conquest and later to act as trade routes connecting the settlement of Dorchester with wider areas. Although not visible today, groups of Roman farms were concentrated on the better draining loams of the gravel terraces along the river valleys, in particular the Thames. In contrast, the routes of Roman roads are still significant visual features in the modern-day road pattern.

The Domesday survey showed that the most densely populated part of the area was the dense narrow belt of spring-line villages on the Greensand at the foot of the Chilterns in Aylesbury Vale. Many of these settlements survive as historic market towns along the ancient route of the Lower Icknield Way. Much of this prehistoric trackway runs along the Greensand ledge.

Some of the earliest regional parliamentary enclosures were in the Vale, as descriptions of the Vale of the White Horse by Celia Fiennes indicate, 'it extends a vast way, a rich enclosed country'. The rate of parliamentary enclosure reached a peak in the second half of the 18th century as farmers responded readily to the new ideas of farm husbandry coming from neighbouring Berkshire and from Norfolk. Dairy farming developed rapidly within the Vale as new farming methods increased productivity from the rich clay soils. The predominant field pattern of large hedged fields, which is still present, dates from this time.

Villages that were slow to develop have remained small and retained their early settlement layout and old buildings. Aylesbury is the only town of any size, growing partly from its trade in Aylesbury ducks.

Buildings and Settlements

Springline towns and villages at the foot of the Chalk scarps are a characteristic feature of the Vales. Elsewhere, risk of flooding along the river valleys, such as the Thame, has resulted in a more sparse settlement pattern. Largely located on raised gravel patches, these numerous nucleated village settlements are often found centred around village greens with churches as focal points. The typical brick and plain-tiled buildings in the villages and hamlets have used the bricks originating from the numerous local clay quarries and brickworks.

Many buildings traditionally made use of 'wichert', a chalky marl mixed with straw, to plaster walls which were then often colour-washed. For example, the long curved walls and small windows of the buildings of Haddenham and Cuddington are of such construction. Villages located on the broad ledge of Greensand below the Chilterns were rarely built of the local sandstone. However, the use of chalk blocks or 'clunch' quarried from the Chalk hills to the south, together with thatch in some roofs, adds considerable interest and variety to the local scene. Notable buildings within the Vales include the Rothschild palaces at Mentmore, Aston Clinton and Halton.

Land Cover

The area has both pastoral and mixed farming regimes. The medium sized, regular shaped fields are largely improved grassland and arable with numerous wet meadows along the river terraces. The fields of the clay plains are cultivated up to the edge of each hill spur, until the paler earth of the Chalk is reached. Fields are enclosed by thick hedgerows with trees. Willows line the meandering course of the river channels such as the Thame. West of Aylesbury, the Vale is characterised by some small woods and tree clumps while, in contrast, to the east there are fewer woods and a notable concentration of orchards on the Greensand.

Industrial activities at Abingdon and Didcot, and in particular the power station, visually dominate much of the open agricultural character of the Vale landscape. Further variation in land cover is provided by the fruit orchards along the Greensand ledge below the Chalk downs which introduce local contrast and variety.

The Changing Countryside

- Loss of hedgerows to field enlargements.

- Large dominating developments and structures in the flat landscape such as Didcot Power Station and associated pylon lines.

- Pressures from new roads and road improvements.

- Localised recreation pressures.

Shaping the Future

- New woodland planting should be considered in many parts of the area. Trees – particularly the black poplar – are important landscape features.

- Many hedgerows are in need of restoration and replanting.

Selected References

Richards Moorehead and Laing Ltd, (1989), *Buckinghamshire Trees and Forestry Strategy: Volumes 1, 2 and 3*, Richards Moorehead and Laing, Clwyd.

Reed, M (1979), *The Buckinghamshire Landscape*, Hodder and Stoughton, London.

Emery, F (1974), *The Oxfordshire Landscape*, Hodder and Stoughton, London.

Martin, A F and Steel, R W (eds), (1954), *The Oxford Region*, Oxford University Press, London.

Anderson, J R L (1970), *The Upper Thames*, Eyre and Spottiswoode, London.

SIMON MELVILLE/ENGLISH NATURE

The open floodplain landscape of the Vale in Oxfordshire creates a flat 'chequer board' agricultural landscape with occasional small woods and hedgerows.

Midvale Ridge

Key Characteristics

- Low irregular wooded limestone ridge giving way to a series of isolated steep-sided tabular hills in the east which rise from the surrounding clay vales.

- Large geometrically spaced fields divided by regular pattern of hedgerows and trees supporting both arable and pastoral farming.

- Villages, typically built of local limestone, perched high up on spurs, hilltops and along ridges giving extensive views across the open, gently undulating, clay vales to the north and south.

- Visible archaeology dating from early Roman settlement of the area found on prominent areas of higher ground.

- Spring-line settlements associated with blocks of ancient woodland along the ridge.

- Contrast between the moderately elevated limestone hills and ridges and the surrounding low-lying clay vales.

Large geometrically spaced fields divided by a regular pattern of hedgerows and hedgerow trees supporting both arable and pastoral farming.

Landscape Character

The Midvale Ridge is a low, irregular outcrop of limestone that changes from a well-wooded ridge in Oxfordshire into a series of isolated steep-sided tabular hills in Buckinghamshire which rise above the surrounding clay vales. The Ridge separates the low-lying clay areas of the Oxfordshire and Buckinghamshire Vales to the north and the Vales of the White Horse and Aylesbury to the south.

The landscape is made up of woods and arable fields interspersed by numerous distinctive small villages. Woodland cover tends to be most extensive along the Corallian Limestone ridge in Oxfordshire while, in contrast, the Portland Limestone hills of Buckinghamshire have few large woods. Here, isolated trees and small woodlands are more typical. Fields are typically defined by a regular pattern of hedgerows and trees that enclose characteristically large and geometrically spaced fields.

Villages are found perched high up on spurs, hilltops and ridges giving extensive views across the open, gently undulating clay vales to the north and south. A local pattern of small fields often surrounds these villages in contrast to the more typical and widespread occurrence of large fields. Villages such as Brill have many stone buildings, typically of local limestone with red tiles or thatch common as roofing materials. The hilltop villages are very distinctive with village greens and thatched cottages typically set around the village church as a local landmark.

These villages are connected by a network of small sunken lanes with low trimmed hedges and hedgerow trees that wind up the slopes towards the hills and ridges. Below the limestone ridge in Oxfordshire where the clay vale meets the rising ground, spring-line settlements associated with blocks of ancient woodland are found.

Visible archaeological features dating from early Roman settlement of the area are a prominent feature on areas of higher ground. Parkland is a common feature within Oxfordshire, while windmills are distinctive landmarks throughout the area.

The moderately elevated limestone hills and ridges provide regional contrast and variety to the surrounding low-lying clay vales.

Physical Influences

The Midvale Ridge forms a low irregular ridge above the clay vales that gives way to a series of isolated steep-sided tabular hills in the east, rising above numerous intermediate valleys and basins.

The ridge comprises coarse and rubbly-textured Upper Jurassic Corallian limestones and sands, overlain in places by Kimmeridge Clay. These rocks form a distinct escarpment rising from the clay vales with a low and irregular north-facing scarp (100 m - 110 m AOD) and a very gentle dip slope that gradually falls, almost imperceptibly in places, to the Vale of the White Horse to the south. Lower Greensand caps many of the higher parts of the ridge such as Boars Hill near Oxford which stands proud of the Corallian Limestone at more than 150 m AOD. To the east, where the ridge becomes more broken up, a discontinuous outcrop of Portland sand and limestone overlies the clay and is in turn capped locally by Purbeck limestones and younger sand beds.

Soils are predominantly heavy rendzinas and sandy brown earths with areas of plateau sands giving rise to acidic soils. These soils are only suitable for arable use where well-dressed with lime and, in many places, are planted with conifers, in particular larch.

Apart from the upper Thames which cuts a steep valley between the limestone hills around Oxford, there is very little dissection by rivers along the ridge itself except for the springs at the base of the escarpment. Further east, streams and springs drain the lower slopes of the limestone hills south-west to the Thames via the river Thame.

Historical and Cultural Influences

The Midvale Ridge exhibits very little archaeological evidence of the Palaeolithic or Mesolithic period. The first significant settlement of the area occurred during the Bronze Age with further occupation during the Iron Age in places such as at Faringdon Folly and Boars Hill.

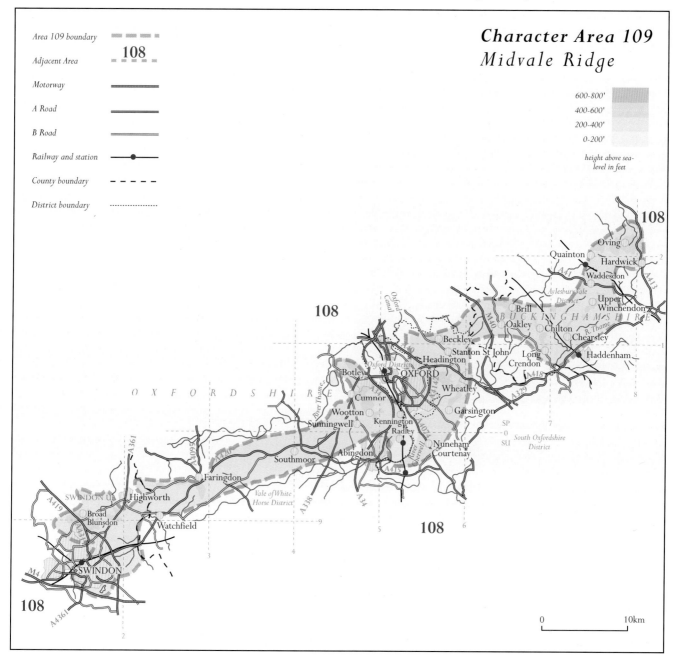

A local pattern of enclosed, smaller pasture fields often surrounds the villages in the Midvale Ridge.

From the 6th to the mid-9th centuries the area was fought over by the West Saxon/Wessex and Mercia kingdoms with the river Thames eventually forming the boundary between the two. During this period, Oxfordshire's oldest recorded community was built at St Frideswide in 735 and fortifications were built in Oxford to defend the kingdom against the invading Danes.

Small broadleaved woodlands of ash, field maple and small-leaved lime provide a splash of colour with dense bluebell 'carpets' in the spring. Woodland cover tends to be more extensive along the Corallian Limestone ridge in Oxfordshire.

Reference is made in Domesday Book to the good cover of 'Forests' in the area, such as Bernwood Forest, although it is unclear as to what proportion was woodland. Remnant ancient woodland from the Forests of Shotover and Bernwood dominate the ridge to the east and west of Oxford. Corallian Limestone was quarried at Wheatley during the 12th century and also from 1400 onwards at Headington. Oxford was noted for its tanning and woollen industries from the 16th to the mid-17th century. Historic

evidence shows that field sizes on the hills in the east were generally small-scale with larger open fields to the west. By the early 19th century, much of the area was considered good quality corn land although perhaps slightly too sandy in places.

Although difficult, navigation of the Thames was enhanced in 1624 by an Act of Parliament that opened up the river from Burcote to Oxford. In 1790 the Oxford Canal was completed allowing the carriage of coal and providing an important link to the rest of the canal network.

The area is closely associated with light engineering in general and agricultural machines in particular. The first steam rollers and ploughs were invented locally by a John Allen of Oxford in 1868. Swindon is renowned as the centre of the railway industry, with the development of the town closely associated with the growth of the Great Western Railway.

Buildings and Settlement

Away from the towns, the eastern part of this area is distinguished by the pattern of small villages perched on spurs above the lower-lying land with stone-built houses of local limestone, mostly roofed in plain tiles but also commonly thatched. In contrast, the villages along the western ridge are characterised by their stone walls derived either from the local rubbly Cornbrash or Corallian Limestone, with roofs generally of stone slates, The stone buildings are often of a simple and straightforward design in comparison to their limestone-built counterparts in the Cotswolds. The densely built-up city of Oxford lies on the Thames floodplain below a rural landscape of low limestone hills.

Notable buildings include the Oxford Colleges, which grew from the 14th century onwards, and Waddesdon which is owned by the Rothschilds and designed by the French architect Destailleur. Lying in the west of the area, Swindon is a dominant urban feature with considerable commercial, residential and light industrial development.

Land Cover

The mainly arable and grassland land use also includes a good woodland cover with, in particular, significant blocks of coniferous woodlands on the plateau gravel soils. Characteristic tree types include oak, ash, birch and larch many of which occur within ancient semi-natural woodlands such as the oak-dominated Bagley Wood. Coppice with standards occurs to the west together with forest woodlands such as Shotover. Some small patches of stony limestone grassland and isolated pockets of heath and acid grassland occur on the Greensand, such as at Cumnar Heath.

The Changing Countryside

- Agricultural intensification, in particular the expansion of arable cropping, leading to a deterioration and complete loss of hedgerows due to under-management and/or neglect.

Shaping the Future

- Restoration of field margins within arable fields and restoration and/or replanting of hedgerows, including establishment of new hedgerow trees.

- The management of extensive grassland.

- The less intensively farmed parts are an important characteristic of the area.

- The appropriate management of the riverine landscape should be addressed.

Calcareous grass-heaths are of particular nature-conservation interest, containing rare and distinctive plant communities.

SIMON MELVILLE/ENGLISH NATURE

MARTIN JONES/COUNTRYSIDE AGENCY

Large arable fields dominate much of the area. Agricultural intensification, in particular the expansion of arable cropping, has led to deterioration and, in some areas, complete loss of hedgerow pattern.

Selected References

Reed, M (1979), *The Buckinghamshire Landscape*, Hodder and Stoughton, London.

Emery, F (1974), *The Oxfordshire Landscape*, Hodder and Stoughton, London.

Richards Moorehead and Laing (1989), *Buckinghamshire Trees and Forestry Strategy: Volumes 1, 2 and 3*, Richards Moorehead and Laing, Clwyd.

Martin, A F and Steel, R W (eds), (1954), *The Oxford Region*, Oxford University Press, London.

Glossary

AOD: Above Ordnance Datum

Chilterns

- Chalk hills and plateau with a prominent escarpment in many places, and extensive dip slope with numerous dry valleys.

- Remnants of chalk downland on the escarpment and valley sides. Extensive areas of downland invaded by scrub.

- The most extensive areas of beech woodland in the country on the plateau, and 'hanging' woodlands in the valleys.

- Enclosed and intimate landscapes of the valleys contrasting with the more open plateau top and extensive views from the scarp to the clay vale below.

- Small fields and dense network of ancient hedges, often on steep ground. The agricultural landscape often dominated by hedges, trees and small woodlands.

- Many surviving areas of semi-open common land on the plateau.

- Scattered villages and farmsteads, some of medieval origin, displaying consistent use of traditional building materials including flint, brick, and clay tiles.

- Network of ancient green lanes and tracks including the Ridgeway which links numerous archaeological sites and settlements.

- Frequent grand country houses and designed landscapes occupying prominent positions on sloping valley sides.

Landscape Character

The Chilterns rise to just over 900 feet and stretch from the Thames in Oxfordshire across Buckinghamshire and Hertfordshire to Bedfordshire. The area includes the lower-lying substantial settlements of Luton, Dunstable, Hemel Hempstead, Berkhamstead, Chesham, Amersham and High Wycombe, as well as a section of the M40 and M1 motorway corridors. The Chilterns rise above Aylesbury Vale to the north, abut the East Anglian Chalk to the north-east and slope into the Hertfordshire Plateaux and River Valleys, and the Thames Valley to the south-east. The Berkshire and Marlborough Downs form the western boundary to the Chilterns.

Chalk streams with their associated waterside landscapes remain an important, if localised, landscape feature. Most of the chalk streams are affected, to some degree, by decreased flow.

The hills are formed by an outcrop of Chalk, overlain by clay with flints, up to a depth of four metres on the north-western side of the London basin. The Chalk strata have been tilted to create a dip slope that rises so gently towards the north-west that it generally has the character of a plateau. However, it ends abruptly in a steep scarp slope which forms the more dramatic north-western face of the Chilterns above Aylesbury Vale. The plateau is cut by a series of through-valleys that divide it into roughly rectangular blocks with many branching dry valleys further dividing these blocks and thereby creating a varied mix of landscapes. As well as the distinctive landform, the scarp is characterised by fragmented and occasionally substantial areas of unimproved chalk grassland with a uneven texture and colour. The influences of the underlying Chalk are apparent in the smooth, rounded sides of the numerous valleys that incise the dip slope. Most of the valleys were formed by glacial melt water but a small number of them support spring-fed streams. In recent years they have all been affected by drought and some by over abstraction. There are many coombes and dry valleys hidden away in the folds of the hills, sometimes giving rise to bournes (streams which flow intermittently).

The extensive areas of woodland dominated by beech on the plateau and the 'hanging' woodlands of the Chalk valleys are a characteristic feature of the area and make the Chilterns one of the most wooded lowland landscapes in England. Beech was selectively encouraged by management because of its value in the 18th and 19th century furniture industry. Today, the extent of the woodland and the grandeur of the 'cathedral-like' beech woods in particular, dominate the landscape and distinguish the Chilterns from other chalk landscapes such as the more open Berkshire and Marlborough Downs immediately to the south-west of the area.

The south-western boundary is formed by the river Thames as it flows past Wallingford, Henley and Marlow. Although part of the Chilterns, this belt of countryside is dominated by the river and its floodplain rather than by the Chiltern Hills.

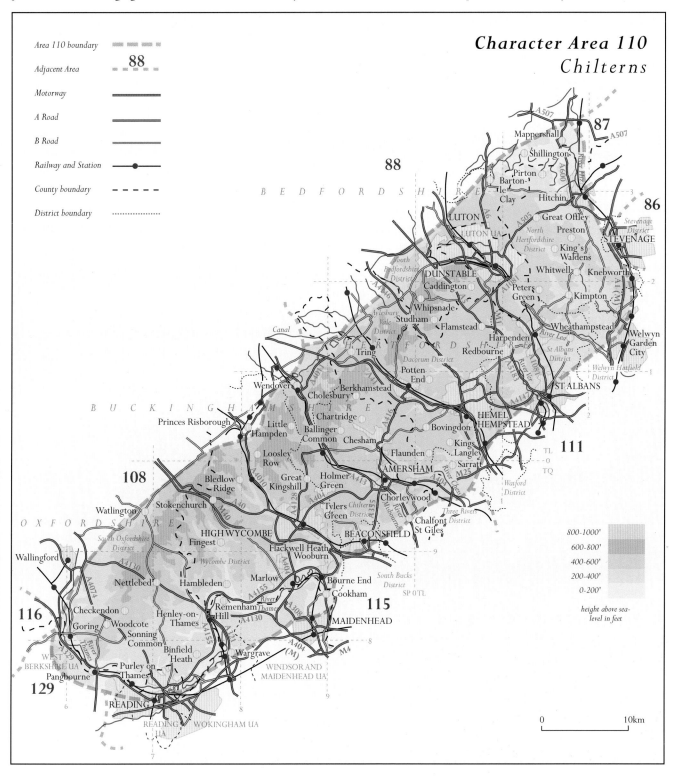

The escarpment, with its distinctive form, varies in character from the wooded scarp and gentler landform of the west, to the steep dramatic grassland scarp of the north east.

The escarpment varies in character with the more wooded scarp and gentler landform of Oxfordshire giving way to the more dramatic steep grassland scarp face of Buckinghamshire to the north-east. Sheep grazing is common on the improved chalk grasslands with remnants of species-rich pasture on the steeper valley slopes and scarp face. Scrub is invading chalk downland following cessation of large scale sheep grazing earlier this century and the effects of myxamatosis on rabbits more recently. Much of the largest area of surviving species-rich chalk grassland has been designated as an SSSI or National Nature Reserve. Many of these valuable sites are in public ownership.

Towns and villages of medieval origin are found throughout the Chilterns, the oldest are located in valleys with reliable water supplies. Most of these ancient villages boast Norman churches, village greens and ponds. From the mid-19th century, scattered linear villages have developed on the plateau, usually around commonland. During the 20th century there has been large-scale development along major road and rail corridors, typified by development along the Metropolitan line from the 1930s onwards. The result is that most Chiltern villages have grown rapidly during this century and house styles from the previous 300 years can be found in most of them.

Designed parklands and large gardens associated with grand historic houses make a dramatic contribution to the local landscape. The designed woodlands, tree clumps, parkland trees, lime avenues, houses and related buildings are distinctive in the Chilterns landscape and often occupy prominent positions on sloping valley sides. Designed landscapes such as Shardeloes, Tring Park, West Wycombe Park, Wycombe Abbey, Park Place, Remenham and Ashridge demonstrate the 18th century design of Bridgeman, Brown and Repton for which the Chilterns are particularly renowned.

Overall, the area has a predominantly quiet and prosperous farming character. The beech woods, the distinctive relationship between the Chalk scarp and the clay vale below, and the traditional villages are all significant characteristics of the landscape. When perceived from the extensive network of sunken lanes and tracks the landscape often feels hidden, enclosed and ancient. This give the Chilterns its special sense of place.

The Chilterns are formed by chalk, which creates the smooth rounded forms so typical of downland scenery. The chalk is exposed along the steep escarpment and along valley sides throughout the area. The dip slope is overlain

The Chilterns escarpment includes substantial areas of species-rich chalk grassland and scrub creating uneven texture and colour.

by clay with flints which supports extensive woodlands, medium-grade farmland and even remnant heath.

The valleys were primarily formed by glacial melt waters and are now dry. The main rivers are the Wye, Gade, Ver, Bulbourne, Chess and Misbourne. The Wye flows directly into the Thames whilst the others flow into the river Colne before joining the Thames. Small brooks known as 'bournes' flow in several valleys, fed by springs which periodically dry up.

A network of sunken lanes, known locally as hollow ways, are found on both the plateau and valley bottoms helping to link scattered settlements and woodlands.

Historical and Cultural Influences

The area has been continually influenced by human settlement since early Palaeolithic times. Neolithic clearance of woodland for agriculture and the development of an important Roman communications network established a settlement pattern still evident today and set the scene for the emergence of a distinctive wood-based industry and agricultural change in medieval times.

The earliest archaeological evidence of human activity in the area comes from Caddington where extensive flint working sites dating from the early Palaeolithic period (125,000 - 70,000 BC) have been discovered. Evidence of flint implements are common and widespread from the Mesolithic period (10,000 - 4,000 BC). The local importance of flint from the Chalk is still evident in today's landscape with the use of flint with brick in the walls of buildings and garden boundary walls.

The Neolithic period (4,000 - 2,000 BC) saw a dramatic period of landscape change when the introduction of agriculture to Britain led to the widespread clearance of woodland from much of the Chalk escarpment and river valleys. During this period and into the Bronze Age (2,000 - 750 BC) the Icknield Way was in use as a trackway along the scarp of the Chiltern hills and is associated with evidence of burial mounds on the adjacent higher ground. Evidence from the Iron Age (750 BC - 43 AD) confirms the developing importance of the Icknield Way as a major

line of communication and demonstrates the territorial nature of this period in the history of the Chilterns. Earthworks of former defensive hillforts and dykes to control trade are found along the scarp and also along the Thames Valley to the south. Their presence also probably defined tribal boundaries in the area.

The appearance of the landscape during the Roman period (43 AD - 410 AD) may not have been radically different to that of the Chilterns in the early 19th century. Small towns linked by a system of roads, a mosaic of small fields interspersed with large blocks of woodland, rough grazing on what was then the marginal plateau soils and a more intensively farmed arable landscape on the lighter soils of the valley bottoms. The pattern of settlement as we know it today evolved during this period with many late Iron Age farmsteads developing into Roman masonry villas distributed at regular intervals along the spring line and river valleys. These developed into small towns linked by a system of roads including the establishment of Watling Street and Akeman Street, two major lines of communication that became the A5 London to Dunstable and the A41 St Albans to Aylesbury roads. The presence of extensive areas of woodland provided the charcoal necessary for the emerging iron slag industry which was one of the earliest non-agricultural industries to exist in the Chilterns.

The period from the 5th century through to the Tudors saw a major change in the agricultural land use of the Chilterns. From the early 5th century onwards farmers in the Chilterns returned to subsistence agriculture as a result of the collapse of their markets and a reduced population due to the depredations of the Saxons. Marginal fields on the plateau were abandoned or maintained as rough grazing and, as a result, woodland cover saw an increase during this period. The landscape, as indicated in Domesday Book, appeared to be similar to that of today. The woodlands have never been cleared to the same extent as other areas and the current cover of approximately 20 per cent remains a high figure by UK standards. The Oxfordshire Chilterns has a woodland cover exceeding 30 per cent. The boundaries of woodlands are known to have changed significantly, reflecting constantly fluctuating agricultural and forestry economics.

Settlements were predominantly scattered in farmsteads and hamlets, a pattern still found in the Chilterns today, although much of the land on the plateau had still not been reclaimed for cropping. As the population increased, the pressure on the land led to an expansion in agriculture indicated by the creation of strip lynchets on steeper slopes. New farms and settlements were established on the plateau and new small fields were carved out of the extensive common woods that covered the ridges and allocated to a particular tenant.

Buildings and Settlement

The most notable feature of the vernacular buildings, both in villages and elsewhere, is the consistent use of materials especially the flints that occur in both the Chalk strata and the overlying clay-with-flints. In many places, flint is combined with brick both in the walls of older buildings and in the boundary walls around gardens. Most vernacular buildings also have tiled roofs, with the tiles often having been made from local iron-rich clay. Thatch has been used less, with notable concentrations in the Oxfordshire part of the Chilterns. The use of brick, flint and tiles is particularly characteristic of many of the historic farmsteads. The oldest farm buildings are commonly characterised by large timber-framed barns clad with black, horizontal weather boarding, brick and flint gable walls, which sometimes incorporate vertical ventilation slits and an owl hole. The consistent range of traditional building materials used in different combinations throughout the area contributes greatly to the distinctiveness of the landscape.

Settlements are linked by a network of ancient, commonly sunken lanes, some running straight along valley bottoms or ridge-tops while others wind up the scarp or valley sides. The sunken lanes pass through woodland, creating an enclosed landscape with an over-arching canopy of trees. On plateau areas and in some valleys the lanes can be lined with species-rich ancient hedges, the height and dense nature of which offer only limited views into the fields beyond. Much of the wider landscape is 'hidden' from the user of these lanes.

Along the loop of the river Thames, the towns of Marlow, Henley and Cookham expanded greatly in the 19th century. River frontages are characterised by ribbon development of summer homes.

Land Cover

Woodlands are a significant and characteristic feature in the landscape and occur throughout the area. Broadleaved trees dominate the Chilterns woodlands and include the grand beech woods and wooded commons of the plateau and the hanging woodlands of the scarp and valleys. It is the extent of woodland in general, and of the beech woods in particular, which distinguishes the Chilterns area from other chalk landscapes which are often more open in character. The unnaturally high incidence of beech owes its presence to the furniture making industry. There is a considerable amount of ancient woodland with a much greater variety of trees and shrubs, including oak, birch, holly, hazel on the more acid plateau and ash, wych elm, field maple and cherry on the escarpment. The favourable growing conditions for cherry helped to support widespread orchards, especially in the central part of the Chilterns. These orchards are no longer commercially managed and

are now disappearing rapidly. Juniper heath also survives in some places and very rare natural box woods can be found on the scarp. The woods also add significantly to the ancient feel of the landscape and to its intimate and hidden character.

The Chilterns are dominated by Grade 3 soils which are capable of growing cereals but with limited yields. The result is a mixture of dairying and sheep and arable farming. The mixture at any one time depends upon the economics of each type of farming. More recently, set-aside has become a notable landscape feature.

The type of crops grown are generally winter wheat and barley. Spring sown crops are now rare so there is little winter stubble which has consequences for many bird species formerly characteristic of the Chilterns.

The Chilterns landscape is dissected by transport corridors which run across rather than along the escarpment. Major roads, railway lines and canals are a significant feature within the area, the majority of which tend to follow the arterial valleys (the M40 is a clear exception). The Thames valley at the western end of the Chilterns is dominated by the river with its associated floodplains.

STEVE RODRICK/CHILTERNS AONB

The extensive areas of ancient woodland, secondary woodland and plantations make the Chilterns one of the most richly wooded lowland landscapes in England.

The Changing Countryside

- New commuter housing development and expansion of settlements by infilling leading to erosion of the traditional Chiltern's building style and adverse changes in the overall character of settlements. Recent developments on the edge of scarp-foot historic market towns are particularly intrusive. Suburbanisation through small scale but inappropriate development design.

- New road construction and road 'improvements' are a significant pressure on the small scale road network of the area.

- Intensification and changes in agricultural practice including the loss of characteristic chalk grassland on escarpment and valley sides because of scrub invasion and a cessation in traditional sheep grazing regimes. The loss of winter stubble means that fields are now green in the winter months. Increasing number of new crops appearing.

- Cumulative effect of localised removal of field hedgerows and an associated lack of appropriate hedgerow management. The reduction in the quality of hedgerows is considered to erode the character of many Chiltern valleys.

- Increase in horse-related land uses and development of new golf courses on former agricultural land.

- Elements of ancient countryside within the Chilterns, such as narrow winding lanes, organic field patterns and mature tree specimens, are particularly vulnerable to change.

- Remnants of parkland within the agricultural landscape are gradually disappearing.

- Increasing number of telecommunication masts on the skyline.

Shaping the Future

- The character of the transitional landscape between town and countryside needs attention.

- Management of popular recreational landscapes and sites would avoid environmental damage or deterioration.

- Schemes to re-establish characteristic chalk grassland at suitable locations, and to conserve those areas that remain, should be considered.

- Appropriate management would improve the quality of existing woodlands.

- Management and restoration of wooded commons would re-establish acid grassland.

- Landscape features which are remnants of ancient countryside including characteristic hedgerow patterns, old trees and lanes need positive management and conservation.

- The design of future development should reflect and help restore and reinforce a typical Chilterns character.

- Public transport, green lanes and quiet ways might be promoted to encourage people to visit the countryside without their cars.

- Many historic parklands are in need of conservation and management.

Selected References

Countryside Commission (1992), *The Chilterns Landscape CCP 392*, Countryside Commission, Cheltenham.

Hertfordshire Planning and Environment Department (1995), *Pre-Draft of Hertfordshire Landscape Strategy*, Hertfordshire County Council, Hertfordshire.

Richards Moorehead and Laing Ltd, (1989), *Buckinghamshire Trees and Forestry Strategy: Volumes 1, 2 and 3*, Richards Moorehead and Laing, Clwyd.

Reed, M (1979), *The Buckinghamshire Landscape*, Hodder and Stoughton, London.

Munby, L M (1977) *The Hertfordshire Landscape*, Hodder and Stoughton, London.

Northern Thames Basin

This description consists of four sub-character areas: Hertfordshire Plateaux and River Valleys; Essex Wooded Hills and Ridges; London Clay Lowlands and Essex Heathlands.

Hertfordshire Plateaux and River Valleys

Woodlands are an important feature of the Northern Thames Basin. Ancient parklands and wood pasture were once widespread. Those remaining, such as here in Broxbourne, harbour many veteran trees.

TREVOR J. JAMES

Key Characteristics

- A diverse landscape with a series of broad valleys containing the major rivers Ver, Colne and Lea and extensive areas of broadleaved woodlands being the principal features of the area. The landform is varied with a wide plateau divided by the valleys.

- Hertfordshire's large towns, the M25 and M1 motorways, railway line and prominent electricity pylons are also a major influence on character.

- Floodplain land is commonly arable sub-divided by hedgerow-deficient field boundaries. Open grazing land remains in certain areas.

- Many river valleys have been extensively modified by reservoirs, current and reclaimed gravel pits, landfill sites, artificial wetlands, river realignments and canals.

- Smaller, intimate tree-lined valleys supporting red brick villages provide a contrast to the more heavily developed major river valley floodplains. Within these river valleys, organic field shapes are common, defined by water courses and the legacy of woodland clearances rather than formal enclosure patterns.

- Broader plateau areas are mainly in agricultural use, with field patterns exhibiting the regular shape characteristic of 18th century enclosures.

Landscape Character

The Hertfordshire Plateau is a varied landscape characterised by a mix of settlements, woodland and mixed agriculture. It has a predominantly rural feel with few large developments but it is not notably picturesque: indeed it can have a confused, disorderly feel where the variation in land use and topography conflict. Landform is varied with a high broad arable plateau divided by more wooded and pastured valleys. Field patterns vary from the small organic shapes found in the north to regular rectangular fields found towards the Bishops Stortford area, the result of 18th century enclosures. Many of the enclosure fields have, however, had hedgerows removed and the landscape thus appears open and featureless in the east. The woodland cover comprises a number of small ancient beech and oak woods found mainly in the valleys to the west.

This area comprises much transitional countryside as rural Hertfordshire merges into the northern London suburbs. It is often despoiled by urban activity, particularly the motorways and associated services, power lines and so on. However, there is much local landscape diversity and

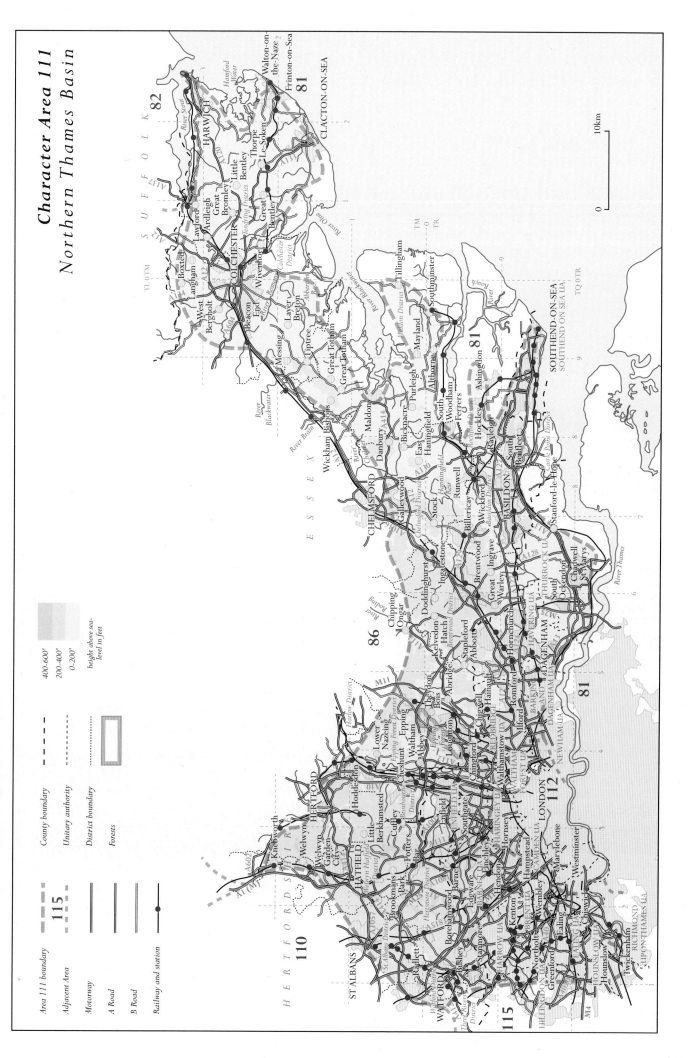

Character Area 111
Northern Thames Basin

Area 111 boundary

Adjacent Area 115

County boundary

Unitary authority

District boundary

Forests

Motorway

A Road

B Road

Railway and station

	height above sea-level in feet
400-600'	
200-400'	
0-200'	

10km

interest characterised by a patchwork pattern of fields and woodlands.

The higher ground of the plateau forms a distinctive backdrop to the river valleys. The more heavily wooded high ground of the plateau to the east gives 'tunnelled' views onto the relatively open farm land at the bottom of the valleys. The farmland has a well-wooded character due to the small organically-shaped fields having been carved from woodland and is still largely divided by well maintained hedgerows. This pleasant pastoral character becomes less apparent close to settlements where market gardening and grazing of horses has led to loss of hedges, hedgerow trees and a proliferation of wire fences and small sheds. The western plateaux are generally less well wooded and more developed than the plateau areas to the east.

Broxbourne Woods, an extensive area of woodland with almost continuous tree cover, comprises a significant feature within the plateau to the east. Views within the woods vary from the enclosed 'tunnel' effect of views from the woodland or from between hedges to sudden unexpected framed views over huge areas out and down to the Lee Valley and towards north London.

Historically, human development of this area has largely taken place within the river valleys, giving rise to structures and features of great heritage value. Electricity pylons and general industrial developments are often superimposed or adjacent to such features as the Roman Verulamium and historic houses and parklands. Motorways form significant developments within the area and often form discordant features through ridges.

Physical Influences

The area is quite complex topographically, having many valleys cut into the broad plateau landform which is often obscured by vegetation cover. Rivers drain the plateau into the Colne and Ver on its north-western side and into the Lea on its eastern side. In places, river erosion has created isolated landforms such as the Shenley Ridge.

The soils of much of this area are based on London Clay which produces heavy acidic soils often prone to waterlogging in winter months and to shrinking and cracking in summer. This has made them difficult to cultivate, which has resulted in a predominance of pasture fields.

The principal river valleys are occupied by the Ver, Colne and Lea. Many of these valleys are broad shallow landforms characterised by mainly well-drained and fertile friable brown earths likely to be alluvial deposits left by the river Thames. These brown earths in comparison to the acidic waterlogged soils of the London Clay plateaux are moisture retentive and relatively easy to work. The valleys, therefore, provide some of the most productive arable

farming in Hertfordshire while historically they formed the basis of the market garden industry within the Lee Valley. Gravel deposits beneath these fertile soils have for some considerable time been exploited for use in the building industry. This has given rise to the distinctive features of gravel workings and flooded pits in the area.

Historical and Cultural Influences

Four thousand years ago, neolithic farmers made the first impressions upon this landscape; their long barrows can still be seen today. It was not, however, until c.650 BC that human occupation made lasting marks when social changes, associated with the spread of knowledge and use of iron, led to the construction of defensive forts. It is unknown whether these early iron-using peoples or their predecessors penetrated much of the wooded clay plateaux of Hertfordshire.

Iron Age settlements and woodland clearings provided a basis on which the Romans built settlements and north-south roads which are still in evidence today. The full extent of Roman settlement is uncertain but it is thought that, when the Anglo-Saxons arrived at the beginning of the 5th century, extensive clearances had already begun. Hertfordshire's unique concentration of 'homestead moats' aligned with the grid pattern are thought to be influenced by Roman estate management techniques.

Names such as Blacklands and Black Acre seem to originate from the decay and burning of Roman sites, as many of the settlements in the centre and west of the county appear to have returned to forest.

The ends and greens of placenames are typical of the hamlets created through piecemeal clearing of the woodlands. Dispersed hamlets and single farmsteads dominated the map of Hertfordshire, with nucleated villages and triangular green villages resulting from settlements which developed around enclosures in dense forest.

The medieval expansion which occurred 250 years after the Norman Conquest was related to the increasing prosperity of the area and was the period in which towns took root. There was a movement of rural populations towards main roads, further clearance and new settlement. Much of the arable land in the 13th century was therefore of recent enclosure and cultivation, through piecemeal processes. There is a rich endowment of late medieval timber-framed buildings, moated sites, castles and homes of the wealthy from this period.

Late in the medieval period, following substantial population decline, the nature of field patterns changed as prosperity grew. Abandonment of small sites left an interlacing of tracks and paths between marginal settlements, many sunken winding lanes still being seen today.

The 16th and 17th centuries brought newcomers, rapid inflation and wealth to the area. The growth of London provided an increasing market and Hertfordshire became a source of homes and estates for new farmers and London merchants. Manors changed hands rapidly: a wealth of Elizabethan and Jacobean houses remain from this period and mark a number of major building phases. Examples include Hatfield House, built by Robert Cecil in 1607, and Balls Park and Tyttenhanger designed by the architect Peter Mills. Mid-17th century houses often adopted the Dutch gable style, as seen at Rohamstead, while in the late 17th and 18th centuries brick buildings were common.

Much medieval parkland in Hertfordshire was disemparked through the demand for profitable farming, eg Theobalds, one of William Cecil's parks. The site today is covered by Cedars Public Park. Cassiobury is an example of an impressive surviving park. Capability Brown and Humphry Repton both worked on many of Hertfordshire's parklands.

Follies and tombs remain as 18th century evidence of landlord influence, including the grotto at Amwell built by the poet John Scott and the tombs at St Alban's Abbey.

The narrow winding lanes, high hedges, *ends* and *greens*, hints of ancient furlongs, strip farming and individual clearings are a legacy of past agricultural practice. The reversed 'S' of the open furlongs can be seen to have dictated the piecemeal enclosure which continued into the 20th century. The least fertile areas were the earliest cultivated and the corn land of the heavy clay uplands was the first to be enclosed. Grazing continued on the wide greens along the roadsides, which can still be seen.

The pattern in the 18th century was of small irregular shaped fields resulting from enclosed furlongs, some unenclosed furlongs and unenclosed waste in the west. Associated settlement patterns were scattered; hamlets and isolated farmhouses on winding lanes remaining today.

Ley farming was common in the 16th century and the floating of water meadows to keep off frost in the 17th century. By the 18th century, however, new crops were seen and crop rotation practised. Clover, turnips, barley, peas, fallow, wheat and oats typified the mixture of crops seen. William Ellis was a popular agricultural writer of this time. Hedges were regularly layered - 'plashed' and the cuttings used for fuel.

Parliamentary enclosure was later (1845) and largely confined to the remaining unenclosed wastes and commons as piecemeal enclosure had already transformed the arable areas. Large rectangular fields, thorn hedges and straight roads from village nuclei to the parish boundary with wide grass verges are all a consequence.

Hertfordshire was considered the first and best corn county in England, largely due to its proximity to London.

Water has been used for the processing of produce and for local industries, particularly for the powering of paper and silk mills. Examples include Hatfield paper mill, which was converted from a fulling mill, and the silk throwing mill in Watford. Woodcrafts were important for furniture making and corn for straw hat and plait making.

Barley was grown for malt, making 'Maltings' an important part of the Hertfordshire landscape, the valleys of the Lee and Stort now being the cradles of the industry in Britain. Inns are consequently an important feature of the villages.

Modern communications, roads and waterways have made a lasting impact on this area, allowing the export of goods into London and the industrial revolution to reach west Hertfordshire. Canals provided cheap transport for paper and silk. Factories, strikes, commuters and intellectuals arrived in the county.

The railway landscape of the 18th century determined the routes which major communications have subsequently followed, the original routes in themselves being heavily influenced by local opposition, as in the case of Watford Tunnel. The Welwyn Viaduct (1848) designed by Lewis Cubitt is a lasting monument of the railways.

The area is now a zone of commuter homes, new towns and the Garden Cities of Ebenezer Howard, distorted by the trunk roads and M1 running from London northwards. It is a consequence of London's expansion, a new landscape superimposed upon the earlier, human landscape.

The plateaux contain several medium sized towns amongst the largest of which are Hertford, St Albans, Welwyn GC and Hatfield. All, such as Hertford here, are located within the river valleys reflecting the historical use of the valleys as a means of access.

Buildings and Settlement

The plateaux contain several medium-sized towns as well as several smaller towns and villages. The river valleys contain most of the largest settlements in the area including among others Watford, St Albans, Welwyn Garden City, Hatfield and Hertford. Their location within the valleys reflects the historical use of the valleys as a means of access into the heart of the area allowing for the clearance of the ancient 'wildwood'. Having been cleared, the valleys developed as the main routes through the area and provided good sites for early settlements. The valleys had easy access to water, were dry and sheltered, and also had good soils for agricultural development.

Land Cover

The eastern part of the plateaux are heavily wooded with some traditional coppice woodland, with oak as standards and coppiced hornbeam (the unusual prevalence of hornbeam related to its historical use as a quality firewood crop for London). Several areas have not been coppiced for many years, allowing the coppice stand to grow into quite dense 'high forest' with a limited understorey and reduced wildlife value. Where coppicing has been maintained or reintroduced, the woods have developed a multi-layered canopy creating an interesting appearance as well as being of greater ecological benefit. Birch and ash are also frequent in this area. The more western part of this region is less heavily wooded due to its proximity to a greater number of Roman roads such as Watling Street, now the A1(M), which would have allowed for easier clearance. This area has also been subject to greater pressure for development due to settlements along this road.

Field patterns vary, with those in the east being small and often organic in form. Some still look as though cut out from the 'Wildwood' and provide examples of wood/pasture agriculture. The western part of this region having been more extensively developed has a mix of ancient organic fields with the more rigid forms of the later Enclosure Act fields. Most fields are defined by hedges although fences are becoming more common, in particular in areas associated with horse grazing.

The river valleys contain some of the largest blocks of woodland in the county. The names of some of these woods give an indication of their species although many have been felled and replanted with non-indigenous species, such as former lime-woods which are now coniferous plantation. These woods often follow and accentuate the valley form, following the contours of the valley sides above flat and predominantly open valley floors. Large tracts of heathland were once widespread but are now only found as isolated remnants within commons such as Bricketwood Common or Colney Heath Common. In many places, the fields in the river valleys are large and open and the few hedges that do remain are often neglected remnants. Much of the valley land is under arable production. The Lee Valley contains a mix of gravel pits and heavy industrial development but is important as a recreational and wildlife resource, as are the Thames Water reservoirs which form significant landscape features.

The Changing Countryside

- Loss of trees through Dutch Elm disease.

- Loss of hedgerows due to field enlargement.

- Inappropriate management of set-aside land has led to an unkempt and muddled appearance to the landscape in some areas.

- Major roads such as the M1 and A1 have a major influence on the character of the landscape.

- Pressures for urban-related developments including electricity pylons and general industrial development which add clutter and appear discordant within the landscape. Associated problems such as fly-tipping and vandalism can also have a marked affect on landscape character.

- Agriculture has become a less dominant land use and recreation, both formal and informal, has become a significant land use.

- Green Belt designation has created development pressure on adjacent landscapes while at the same becoming neglected due to the 'hope value' of the land for future development.

- Gravel extraction has altered the character of the riverside landscapes.

Shaping the Future

- The conservation of woodlands and hedgerows partially through promotion of economically viable uses of these features would ensure their continuity.

- Agri-environmental schemes are needed to help enhance the landscape and nature-conservation value of farmland.

- The encouragement of appropriate land management in smaller farms would help retain the traditional, hedged, irregular field shapes.

- An overall strategy would help enhance the character of the landscape within the Green Belt.

- A coordinated programme of river valley restoration should be considered.

Selected References

Munby, L M (1977), *The Hertfordshire Landscape*, Hodder and Stoughton, London.

Hertfordshire Planning and Environmental Department (1995), *Pre-draft of Hertfordshire Landscape Strategy*, Hertfordshire County Council, Hertfordshire.

Glossary

plash: make or renew a hedge to enclose a wood

Essex Wooded Hills and Ridges

- Well wooded and prominent hills and ridges on a belt of sand often referred to as the 'Bagshot Hills' stretching through Essex from Epping Forest to Tiptree.

- Wooded commons with ancient and some secondary woodland defined in many places by peripheral medieval wood banks. Also notable medieval and later historic homes and their parks.

- Historically scattered and relatively sparse settlement pattern largely obliterated by modern developments including extensive residential developments and large towns.

- Landscape flattens out further north defined by straight and regular field patterns of late enclosure comprising of arable, horticulture and market gardening uses.

- Some significant areas of well-hedged landscape and ancient, semi-natural woodlands.

Landscape Character

The wooded hills and ridges form a transition zone between the South Suffolk and North Essex Clayland, which covers a large area of Essex to the north-west, and the lower lying London Clay Lowlands to the south-east.

There are several ridges including Epping Forest, Hainault, Thorndon, Galleywood and the Danbury to Tiptree ridge. These ridges are formed by the resistant beds of the underlying Bagshot Sands.

Most are crowned by characteristic woods, some of which are ancient with areas of secondary woodland on former common land.

Physical Influences

The hills and ridges rise above the London Clay lowlands to an altitude of approximately 100 m AOD and are capped in most instances by ancient drift gravels which overlie the fine sands of the Bagshot Beds. The highest point is Danbury Hill at 116 m AOD. The soils are easily cultivated but inherently very acid and stony and of low natural fertility. Numerous springs give rise to wet soils at the base of the Bagshot Beds and contribute to the generally limited potential of the hill slopes for agriculture. Paleosols occur in the Drift gravels, examples of which are preserved undisturbed in woodland at Epping Forest, Warley (south of Brentwood) and at High Wood.

JOHN TYLER/COUNTRYSIDE AGENCY

Wet grassland pastures in the many flood plains are a valuable habitat as well as a strong landscape feature. This example is on the northern edge of the Thames Basin at Hornestreet in Essex.

The ridges of Epping Forest, Brentwood to High Wood, Thorndon to Billericay and Danbury to Wickham Bishops are dissected by the valleys of the rivers Roding, Wid and Chelmer. The Ter, Brain and Blackwater also contribute to the drainage of much of the area while Hanningfield Reservoir provides a notable body of open water.

Historical and Cultural Influences

The higher land within the Essex Wooded Hills and Ridges was originally extensively commoned before gradually becoming enclosed into small farms and crofts. In contrast, the lower ground such as around Ingatestone and Hanningfield was essentially a tight patchwork of fields as shown on Tudor maps.

Wooded commons were widespread during the medieval period such as Tiptree Heath, a partly compartmented wood-pasture where a complex system of byelaws dictated woodcutting. Late enclosure had a major effect on these commons and few remnants remain today. Thorndon Country Park does contain remnants of Childerditch Common which have been preserved by the incorporation of the common into Thorndon Park during the 18th century.

Deer were introduced into substantial areas of wood-pasture during the 12th century to establish the Royal Forests of Epping, Hainault, Wintry and Writtle. Here, Forest Law protected the king's deer and governed woodcutting within the Forest. The Forest wood-pastures, where cattle, pigs, sheep and deer were grazed among pollarded trees, gradually gave way to extensive grazing plains. Enclosure and agricultural improvements of the 19th century destroyed much of the remaining Forest lands – only Epping bears a resemblance to its former existence. Epping Forest was purchased by the Corporation of London for Londoners by Act of Parliament – a significant cultural influence on this particular landscape feature.

Woodlands were typically extensively defined and embanked during the Middle Ages. Between 1250 and 1330 a large number of deer parks were created on private land. These parks were contained within a perimeter fence and usually contained some woodland which was often managed as compartmented coppices but also as uncompartmented pollards and grazing. Many of these parks have reverted to woodland with their parkland origins remaining in their names such as Park Wood.

The settlement pattern was largely one of scattered villages within a landscape that was relatively sparsely populated. An important Roman road ran north to south through the Essex Wooded Hills and Ridges connecting Colchester with London, the route of which is now followed by the modern A12.

Buildings and Settlement

The historical scattered and relatively sparse settlement pattern has been largely obliterated by modern developments including extensive residential developments and large towns. The present-day pattern of settlement follows the 19th century pattern of dispersion around an area where population was concentrated in numerous nucleated settlements which have since developed into substantial urban areas.

The A12, a former Roman road, comprises a major communications route through the character area connecting London with Colchester and the port of Harwich beyond.

Land Cover

This area includes the most wooded parts of Essex, with the hilltops and ridges crowned by woods. Many of these woods are quite ancient with large areas of secondary woodland on former common land.

Farmland in the lower lying areas is usually in the form of medium-size fields in regular or irregular layouts, with patches of small irregular fields often of greater antiquity.

The areas of Epping Forest and Hainault Forest have been largely unaffected by modern-day developments.

The Changing Countryside

- New roads and improvements, urban developments and unsympathetic location of overhead power lines are major changes that have affected the landscape.
- Loss of tree cover to Dutch Elm disease and to storm damage.
- Damage to archaeological features from development and agriculture.
- Pressures for new golf course developments.
- Pressures from increases in recreational use of the area.
- There have been major losses of ancient semi-natural woodland after the second world war, especially during the 1950s and 1960s, as a result of conifer planting and incremental clearance of the woodlands.

Shaping the Future

- Opportunities should be considered to support the existing woodland character.
- New planting would soften hard edges around settlements and individual buildings.
- Archaeological features are in need of protection and conservation.
- The area has a number of neglected and insensitively managed ancient woodlands and veteran trees.
- Many parklands are in need of conservation and protection.

Selected References

Scarfe N (nd), Essex: *A Shell Guide*, Shell.

Milton P (1991), *Essex Landscape Conservation Programme 1977-1989*: A Review, Essex County Council, Chelmsford.

Edwards, A C (1978), *A History of Essex (Fourth Edition)*, Phillimore, London.

Essex County Council (1992), *The Essex Environment: A Report on the State of the County's Environment*, Essex County Council, Chelmsford.

Glossary

AOD: Above Ordnance Datum

London Clay Lowlands

Key Characteristics

- Flat, extensive tract of traditionally unproductive farmland on heavy clay soils.

- Very sparse settlement pattern of hamlets and a few villages.

- Ancient planned landscape of long hedgerow boundaries and rectangular fields of mainly pasture – a contrast to the more evolved landscape of the adjacent boulder clays, wooded hills and ridges, and coast.

- Historical dominance of elm in the shrub and tree content of hedgerows.

- The overall landscape pattern reflects the simple rectilinear character of the fields and hedgerows.

- The open expanse of Abberton Reservoir provides contrast to predominantly enclosed nature of the landscape.

Landscape Character

The London Clay Lowlands lie south and east of the Essex Wooded Hills and Ridges, within the Northern Thames Basin, stretching from the outer suburbs of London at Grays and Thurrock, north-eastwards to the Dengie peninsula and the south side of Maldon. It embraces the town of Basildon, the village of Tolleshunt D'Arcy and the Abberton Reservoir and extends to include the Langdon and Hockley Hills. Much of the area is separated from the North Sea by the Greater Thames Estuary character area.

The field patterns and boundaries of this area display the characteristics of early planned landscapes, which contrast with the evolved landscape of the boulder clay plateaux and river valleys to the north and west. The field arrangements follow a simple roughly rectilinear pattern except where crossed by main water courses; some abut long hedgerow boundaries stretching for miles. These ancient patterns are considered to be Roman or possibly earlier.

Traditionally, arable farming has been difficult owing to the heavy and rather infertile nature of the clay. This has led to sparse settlement and an emphasis on pasture. The general arable use today is recent in historical terms.

A characteristic of the region is the historic dominance of elm which once provided both the tree and shrub content of hedgerows. The outbreak of Dutch Elm disease in the 1970s virtually destroyed the once considerable population of standing trees in the farmed landscape.

The south-east Essex Hills around Langdon, Hockley and Rayleigh comprise the only pronounced rise in topography within these lowlands. They are well-wooded, but much urbanised by the developments around Rayleigh and Southend.

Physical Influences

This landscape character area is underlain largely by London Clay, the dominant geological constituent of the London Basin. In the south the clay is overlain by river gravels and alluvium. The clay plain is broken only by the group of hills at Rayleigh, Langdon and Hockley, formed of the sandy Bagshot Beds capping the London Clay.

The generally flat and typically gently undulating lowlands are drained by numerous streams such as the Roach, Crouch and Blackwater which merge before widening out into the flat marshes to the east. To the north, the tiny Layer Brook has been dammed on its way to the Roman river to form Abberton Reservoir.

Most soils are heavy clays although lighter soils occur in some footslope positions. On level sites, winter waterlogging over impermeable subsoils is severe and drainage is needed to improve the soil for arable crops. Traditionally, the land was ploughed on the 'stetch', a form of ridge and furrow that promoted limited surface run-off. Most of the 'stetches' have been ploughed out and underdrainage systems using clay pipes installed.

The alluvial sands and gravel overlaying the London Clay are heavily extracted. This is a dominant land use in areas particularly close to the London fringe in the south of the character area.

MARK BOULTON/COUNTRYSIDE AGENCY

Historical and Cultural Influences

The London Clay Lowlands are characterised by their planned landscapes created on a very large scale during the Roman period. Over two large areas, a pattern of rectilinear landscape division exists based on axes which run straight for considerable distances, regardless of the local grain of the landscape. This pattern covers virtually the whole of the non-marshland part of the Dengie peninsula and the area from Thurrock in the south-west, north-eastwards to Wickford. It represents Roman field boundaries which are considered to be have been Imperial estates. The historical interest of these areas is often very subtle: indeed, the straightness of the hedges are easily interpreted as a sign of late enclosure. Moreover, the loss of hedgerow elm has left the landscape looking neglected and featureless.

There is evidence of early Saxon occupation of the Lowlands, especially in archaeological finds around Mucking in the south, and Rawreth and Wickford are possibly Saxon settlements. Over many centuries, the Saxons carved out ley settlements within the wooded ribbons and by 1086 much of the present day Essex landscape had already taken shape.

Seventeen groves dating from at least 1650 exist in the area of the Grays Thurrock pits surrounded by much development and mineral extraction.

Wooded commons, a form of wood-pasture often with elaborate byelaws governing woodcutting, were also a historical feature of this area. The largest and most highly organised example of a wooded common was the partly compartmented Tiptree Heath west of Abberton Reservoir. However, most wooded commons were uncompartmented, with grassland and pollard trees. Like all Essex Commons, these were greatly diminished by late enclosure.

London Clay soils are often difficult to cultivate and only sufficiently friable for cultivation over a very limited period. Farming in this area was traditionally mixed and permanent grassland would have been dominant here. The intensive wheat and barley production seen today is the result of ploughing and fertilising in response to agricultural policies of the 1950s and 1960s.

Buildings and Settlement

The town of Basildon began life as a post-second world war new town developed in response to the then current Government policy to reduce pressure on London housing. Southend is a 19th century seaside resort. Many of the villages and towns within the London Clay Lowlands are commuter settlements servicing the capital, the outer suburbs of which include such settlements as Grays and Thurrock.

Traditional buildings are of timber with brownish red plain-tiled roofs. Weatherboarding is usually more typical than colour-washed plaster as the principal walling material. The weatherboards are often painted white although traditionally they were painted black or tarred. The browns and reds of the tiled roofs form a contrast with the black or white painted weatherboards.

Land Cover

The 'plotland' woods of Laindon and Thundersley are a distinctive landscape feature found on former urbanised land where woods have sprung up on the sites adding interest and variety. Further interest and variety is provided by the hills around Langdon, Hockley and Rayleigh. These hills are quite well wooded relative to the surrounding land but have been heavily developed due to their location close to Rayleigh and Southend.

Abberton Reservoir forms a notable feature within the area with its convoluted shoreline and surface area of more than four square kilometres.

Large and regular fields of ley pastures dominate the poor heavy clay soils with intensive arable crops such as wheat and barley limited to a few improved areas where underdrainage systems have been installed. Hedgerows are generally species-poor with a high preponderance of blackthorn. The outbreak of Dutch Elm disease in the 1970s virtually destroyed the population of elm hedges, elm hedgerow trees and field trees within the farmed landscape but elm is now managing a comeback as a hedge species.

Various types of development and significant mineral extraction dominates the area around Grays and Thurrock, with substantial sand and gravel pits visible in the alluvial deposits that overlay the London Clay.

The Changing Countryside

- Past emphasis on arable production over the more traditional pasture use is contrary to the inherently infertile nature of the chalk-less heavy clay soils.

- Recent loss of former comprehensive tree and hedgerow elm cover, through Dutch Elm disease.

- Urban developments have extended out from London to influence much of the area, including the development of commuter settlements along major transport routes to the capital.

- Pressures for mineral extraction.

Shaping the Future

- Conservation of hedgerows should be considered through traditional coppicing techniques and, where appropriate, replanting of hedgerows – in particular with elm.

- The conservation of margins within arable fields is important to the area.

Selected References

Milton, P (1991), *Essex Landscape Conservation Programme 1972-1989*: A Review, Essex County Council, Chelmsford.

Jarvis, S M and Harrison, C T (undated), *In Search of Essex*, Essex Countryside, Letchworth.

Edwards, A C (1978), *A History of Essex (Fourth Edition)*, Phillimore, London.

Essex County Council (1992), *The Essex Environment: A Report on the State of the County's Environment*, Essex County Council, Chelmsford.

Buckley, D G (ed), (1980), *Archaeology in Essex to AD 1500: Research Report No 34*, The Council for British Archaeology, London.

Essex Heathlands

Key Characteristics

- Intensively farmed plateau encompassing an area of former heaths and commons on soils derived from ancient river deposits, much of which has an open, often relatively treeless character.

- Arable farming more common to the north, although horticulture and market gardening is also quite evident, particularly around the former heaths near Colchester.

- Straight and regular field patterns reflect the planned characteristics of late enclosure of this area and despite the presence of arable farming many hedgerows and woodlands have been retained.

- Abundance of archaeological features and remains identified by cropmarks and overlain by later physical features including hedgerows.

- Clusters of woodland, many of which are semi-natural and of ancient origin.

- Intricate pattern of hidden creeks and small valleys extending the influence of the coastal marshes inland.

Landscape Character

The Essex Heathlands, part of the Northern Thames Basin, are broadly bounded by the estuary of the river Stour and the Suffolk Coast and Heaths to the north, while the London Clay Lowlands and the Essex Wooded Hills and Ridges run into the area from the west. To the east lie the coastal marshes of the Greater Thames Estuary framed by the North Sea beyond.

The area essentially comprises a broad sandy plateau developed on soils derived from ancient river deposits. Historically it was dominated by extensive heaths and commons as shown by maps of the late 18th century where heaths embraced much of the land north of Colchester as far as Dedham. However, the area is now generally characterised by small isolated pockets of largely scrub-dominated heathland within a mixed agricultural landscape. In contrast to the more typical farming landscapes within Essex, much of the area is distinguished by a combination of improved grassland and arable fields, punctuated by a regimented pattern of horticultural and market gardening on the light sandy soils of the former heaths. Much of the former heathland has the straight lines and planned characteristics of late enclosure and is rich in buried archaeological remains.

A pattern of small but intricate creeks and small valleys break up the plateau edges where the land falls gently towards the Greater Thames Estuary along the coast. These distinctive features extend the coastal influence far inland creating contrast and variety.

River valleys form notable areas of often enclosed landscape within the broad plateau. These range from narrow steep-sided valleys with abundant woodland and small, well-hedged fields to more gentle valleys with wider floodplains and lush waterside vegetation.

Some clusters of woodland, many of which are ancient, are scattered throughout the area. However, much of the plateau has an open almost treeless character due to the loss of field boundaries in many areas.

Physical Influences

Broadly, the plateau landform is relatively flat with only minor undulations in relief. Notable variations include the locally steep-sided slopes of the Stour, Colne and Roman river valleys which, together with their tributaries, drain the plateau before discharge into the North Sea along the Essex coast.

The surface geology of the Essex Heathlands is dominated by sands and gravels deposited by a proto-Thames river, before it was diverted by ice sheets to its present course. Locally, around Tendring, deposits of wind-borne silty loam overlie the sands and gravels.

The soils are generally light and free-draining, supporting mainly pasture and areas of heathland. Less extensive but more fertile loams tend to support arable farming.

Historical and Cultural Influences

Although not as rich in visible archaeology as some other areas of Essex, numerous historic sites exist in the Heathlands especially around the Colchester area. These include old mills, crop marks, earthworks, hill forts, ancient settlement sites with associated barrows and prominent Roman castles. The light soils of the Heathlands, considered to have been relatively open and unwooded since prehistoric times, are particularly rich in buried archaeological remains that range from early Stone Age peoples to remains associated with the Roman occupation of the area.

Heathland was an important resource during medieval times in this area of Essex. Heaths were used extensively as pasture under commoners rights and heather and furze were cut for fuel. Many heaths were still in evidence in the late 18th century and formed a vast network, interspersed by wood-pasture where livestock was grazed amidst coppiced or pollarded woodland. Much of the Heathlands were subject to late enclosure as evidenced by the straight and regular field patterns, and the mostly enclosed settlements found within the Tendring plateau. Late enclosure destroyed most of the heathlands and those areas that were left untouched have reverted to woodland.

To the north and east of Colchester are extensive smallholdings dating to between the first and second world wars. These were established to re-settle the unemployed and homeless of the time and are a significant influence on the landscape in the Boxted and Ardleigh areas. A large number of these smallholdings are no longer farmed and current usage does not reflect the agricultural character of the area.

TREVOR J JAMES

The Essex Heathlands and Bagshot Hills lie towards the east of the area making a distinctive landscape. The broad sandy plateau now only survives as fragments within the wider arable landscape.

Buildings and Settlement

Scattered farms reflect the edge of former heathlands and the pattern of late enclosure, linked by a network of characteristically straight roads.

The principal building type characteristic of the Essex Heathlands are antique timber buildings with weatherboarding and white-washed plaster typical as walling materials. Brick is generally more common in the north of the Heathlands.

Colchester, the major settlement in the area, is a fine example of a walled Roman settlement and is claimed to be England's oldest recorded town, dating from 49 AD. The claim is based on the fine pre-Roman settlement of Cunobelin whose earthworks stand today to the south and west of the present day town. Colchester was a thriving Roman colony until, in 60 AD, its inhabitants were massacred in the Boudiccan Revolt. As a town, it was again thriving by Domesday and built its great wealth on cloth production and export.

Colchester retains part of its Roman city wall, the Roman/medieval street plan and the Dutch Quarter where immigrant Flemish weavers congregated. Of note, is a suberb example of Victorian civic architecture: the Grade 1 listed Town Hall.

Land Cover

The widespread occurrence of light free draining sandy soils supports mainly pasture and small areas of heathland while the less extensive but more fertile loams tend to support more arable farming.

The small isolated remnants of heathland are largely dominated by scrub and survive on the poorer soils amongst the mixed farming where agricultural improvements have not yet been applied. Late enclosure destroyed most of the heathlands and those areas that have been left untouched have now reverted to scrub and woodland.

Agricultural land use is generally mixed, with improved pastures, arable fields, horticulture and market gardening typical. The often large and regular fields are predominantly ley pastures with many fields under arable in the northern part of the area. Horticulture and market gardening is particularly evident around the former heaths near Colchester.

Woodland cover is typically confined to a few small clusters within the open character of the landscape. Some of these small clusters of woodland are semi-natural and of ancient origin. The typically straight hedges range in quality from the predominantly species-poor hedges with few hedgerow trees, to lengths of more healthy hedges within the arable farmed landscape.

The narrow steep-sided river valleys that dissect the broad plateau are relatively well-wooded compared to the wider landscape with small, well-hedged fields that characterise the floodplains associated with lush waterside vegetation.

The Changing Countryside

- Hedgerow loss, due to under-management or overcutting.
- Set-aside policies have not enhanced the open and intensively farmed character of the landscape.
- Loss of rural and agricultural character to suburban features.

Shaping the Future

- Woodland matters need to be considered, particularly the planting of trees around farmsteads and the creation of woodland groups.
- The restoration and replanting of hedgerows needs to be addressed.

Selected References

Edwards, A C (1978), *A History of Essex (fourth edition)*, Phillimore, London.

Milton, P (1991), *Essex Landscape Conservation Programme 1977-1989: A Review*, Essex County Council, Chelmsford.

Jarvis, S M and Hamson, C T (undated), *In Search of Essex*, Essex Countryside, Letchworth.

Buckley, D G (ed), (1980), *Archaeology in Essex to AD 1500: Research Report No 34*, The Council for British Archaeology, London.

Inner London

Inner London lies on the banks of the Thames where the river valley widens out into a broad floodplain. Alluvial gravels overlie the heavy London clay, and rise in gentle steps to form river terraces to the north and south. In places, sand and gravel glacial deposits form more noticeable low hills, as at Hampstead.

Berkeley Square, London. Plane trees are very typical of London's historic squares.

The gently terraced landform is almost completely obscured by the dense urban development. The central area of London comprises broad formal streets, lined by stone and brick buildings, with narrow streets in the commercial centre and planned layouts of streets and squares in the west end. Surrounding the centre are extensive housing areas, of lines of terrace houses, blocks of flats or estates of semi-detached dwellings, focussed around local shopping centres, offices and small manufacturing works.

Throughout, the dense urban structure is punctuated by a series of large parks and open spaces, in particular the royal parks – St James's Park, Hyde Park, Green Park and Regent's Park, near the centre. Elsewhere small local parks, cemeteries (some extensive, such as Highgate Cemetery, and others very small) and areas of common such as Hampstead Heath and Clapham Common break up the extensive urban area and provide a changing scene of vegetation and open space. Street trees play an important part, in particular the mature planes in the streets and squares of the West End, and the lines of flowering cherries in some suburbs. Many of the houses in the suburbs have well-stocked gardens, which contribute to a feel of greeness.

The waterfront along the banks of the river Thames is particularly striking, with new glass and steel office blocks juxtaposed against fine stone buildings from many periods, and the skyline is dramatically punctuated by features such as the dome of St Paul's Cathedral and office skyscapers in the city. Long views are also glimpsed of the new development at Canary Wharf. The Thames forms a connecting and unifying thread running through this historic capital city.

Much of the character of the urban area arises from the mosaic of layouts and buildings from many different historic periods. There is evidence of settlement alongside the river from several thousand years ago but the first permanent bridge was constructed by the Romans in 63 AD, at what was then the extremity of the tidal reach. This was the start of its long development as a major meeting point of road, river and sea borne traffic. It rapidly became an important commercial city, a network of narrow streets protected by walls and, today, names still reveal the locations of the gates – such as Newgate and Aldgate.

Unenclosed commons, such as Wimbledon Common, remain a very special environment acting as 'green lungs' for the city.

Largely built in timber, a large part of the city was destroyed by fire in 1666 which prompted a period of major rebuilding. Significant buildings were designed by notable architects such as Inigo Jones and Wren, famous for St Paul's Cathedral and a number of churches including St

Mary-le-Bow. The Palladian style of this period can still be seen for example at Burlington and Somerset Houses.

The city rapidly expanded, encroaching upon and absorbing adjacent settlements. The names of localities indicate the nature of the place in earlier times eg Hackney – a settlement in the marsh; Hampstead – a homestead or farm; and Paddington – the homestead of the Saxon Paeda family.

Many isolated pockets of open land occur, often associated with Royal Parks like St James's Park. They represent very important recreational and visual amenities.

To the north and west of the city, terraces and town squares were laid out in classical elegance, especially in Mayfair and Bloomsbury, where the characteristic mature plane trees now form a canopy over the gardens in the centre of the squares. The planned layout of much of the west end of the city continued through the 18th century, with the setting out of Regent's Park, Regent's Street and Oxford Street. Nash in particular left a legacy of elegant mansions and terraces in these areas while Robert Adam also had an influence, designing mansions such as Kenwood House.

To the east, massive docks were built to cope with the expanding trade of goods and terraces of workers' housing spread out north and eastwards. To the west, wealthy landowners whose names are now familiar through street names, such as Bedford, Grosvenor and Cavendish, began building extensive residential areas in the early 19th century. So London continued to expand and suburbs, focussed around local shopping centres, began to coalesce.

The confidence of the Victorian era was expressed through major public and municipal buildings, notably the Royal Albert Hall, the museums in south-west Kensington, the neo-gothic Houses of Parliament, Westminster Cathedral, Harrods, and several bridges over the river, including Tower Bridge. As the capital and the centre of commerce, London became the focus for the new railways and the main rail links with the rest of the country were installed.

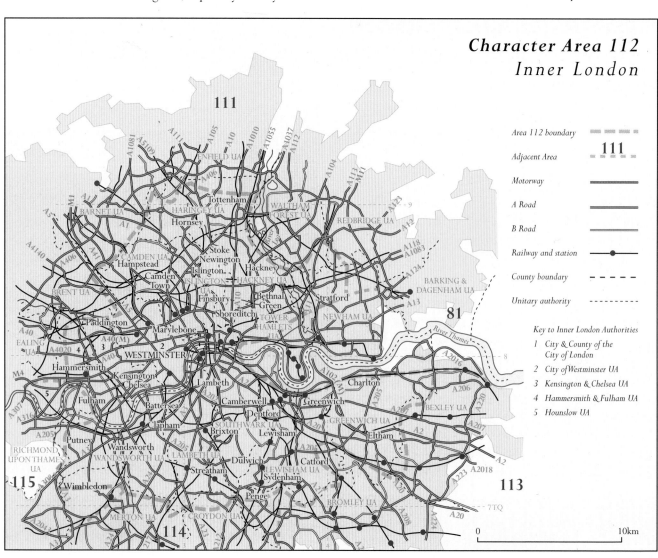

Magnificent station buildings were created, notably the huge hotel at St Pancras.

Building of extensive residential areas continued in the 20th century and inter-war semi-detached houses with generous gardens feature in many of the suburbs. Other features were added to the skyline, notably the Post Office Tower, the South Bank, Battersea Power Station, Centre Point, NatWest Tower and other office skyscrapers.

In each period, new building has combined with past structures with the result that there is a complex mosaic of urban styles and forms. Open spaces and street trees contribute to this varied structure, the whole reflecting the long and rich history of the capital.

Extensive areas of derelict land remain, particularly along the East Thames corridor, sometimes acting as valuable community greenspace. Redevelopment of the corridor is now underway in many places: for example the high profile Canary Wharf development.

The river Thames, flowing through the heart of London, is the key landscape feature. Inner London is also noted for its rich inventory of famous landmarks.

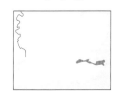

North Kent Plain

Key Characteristics

- An open, low and gently undulating landscape characterised by high-quality, fertile, loamy soils dominated by agricultural land uses.

- The exposed arable/horticultural fields have a sparse hedgerow pattern and only limited shelter belt planting around settlements and farmsteads. Gently undulating, the large intensively cropped fields to the west are mainly devoid of trees and hedges.

- Extensive areas of grazing marsh and reed beds.

- Lines of pylons dominate the open and often treeless landscape.

- Orchards and horticultural crops to the east predominate and are enclosed by poplar or alder shelter belts and scattered small woodlands.

- Discrete but significant areas of woodland and more enclosed farmland are distinctive and are confined to the higher ground around Blean and to the west, above the general level of the plain.

- Urbanisation and large settlements are often visually dominant in the landscape due to the lack of any screening woodlands or shelterbelts.

- Geologically, an outlier of the Chalk and, historically, an island separated from the mainland by a sea channel, Thanet forms a discrete and distinct area that is characterised by its unity of land use arising from the high quality fertile soils developed over chalk. Open and with few trees, the Thanet landscape is dominated by wide views over extensive fields of cereals, root crops and other horticultural crops.

Landscape Character

Lying upon the fine loam soils found between the London Clay underlying the Greater Thames Estuary to the north and the North Downs chalk to the south, the North Kent Plain is one of the most productive agricultural areas in Kent.

The landscape is open in character with a high proportion of arable land. It is characterised by a lack of hedgerows as field boundaries with only a few trees in the landscape. Limited shelter belt planting occurs mainly around small settlements and farmsteads on the few areas of higher ground. The landform is generally low but undulates and rolls giving local variations in topography. The intensity of agricultural production in general and conversion from pasture to arable and from one crop type to another, results in a diverse range of colours, textures and patterns in the landscape.

Within this overall picture it is possible to distinguish variations in landscape character resulting from the different combinations of land cover and local topography.

Lines of pylons marching across large, intensively cropped fields dominate the vistas in this open and often treeless landscape.

The western part is characterised by large and exposed intensively cropped fields, largely devoid of trees and hedges and dominated by the lines of pylons present in the landscape. The few trees and shrubs that do exist along roads and railways provide only limited contrast to the wider landscape. The built environment exerts a strong influence on the farmland character with urban areas around Dartford, Gillingham, Chatham, Margate and Broadstairs on Thanet, providing stark contrast to the predominantly open agricultural landscape.

Poplar-dominated shelter belts – or, north of Ash, alder – are particularly characteristic of the open and gently rolling eastern part of this area around the Great Stour Valley.

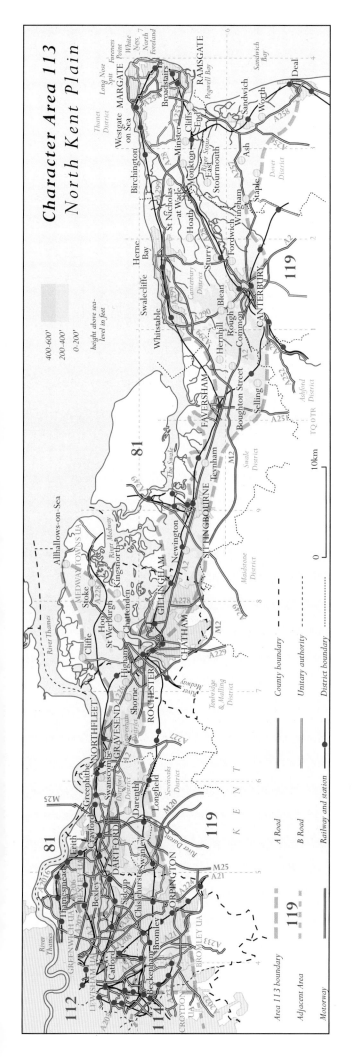

These familiar landscape features to the northwest and south east of Canterbury and around Faversham, relate to the locally distinctive land use of orchards, soft fruits and other horticultural crops. These thrive on the high quality brick earth soils, giving rise to the title 'Garden of England'. The regular patterns and rectangular shapes of the fields typical of this area are more usually defined by changes in crop type, rather than by hedgerows marking the field boundaries. Within this landscape, the few small woodland blocks and copses that do exist add a vertical element, and thus variety, to the horticultural scene. Further east still, the rolling landscape becomes more pronounced and feels much more open in contrast with the major fruit producing land to the west. The dominant landscape features are the orchards interspersed by a few, characteristically small and rectangular, arable fields related to market gardening.

To the east, shelter belts of poplars or alders enclose orchards, soft fruits and horticultural crops, reinforcing Kent's reputation as the 'Garden of England'.

The shelter belts aside, the overall feel is still one of an exposed and open plateau landscape with the only significant woodland confined to pockets of higher ground such as around Shorne, Chattenden and Blean. To the north of Canterbury, Blean supports the largest area of continuous woodland in Kent, with ancient trees found amongst the enclosed pasture and arable fields providing variety and contrast within the wider agricultural landscape. The unusual close proximity of these large woodlands to the sea creates a distinctive sense of place, unique within the context of the Kent landscape.

Thanet is a geological outlier of the Chalk and rises in altitude from the Chislet Marshes towards distinctive low sea cliffs above the English Channel. The Thanet plateau is characterised by its unity of land use arising from the high quality fertile loams. Open with few trees, the Thanet landscape is dominated by wide views over an extensive land cover of cereals, root crops and other horticultural crops. The magnitude of arable farmland on Thanet is only equalled in extent by the dominating presence of the characteristic massive skies with rapidly changing cloud formations.

MARTIN JONES/COUNTRYSIDE AGENCY

The heavily wooded higher ground around Blean contrasts with the rest of the Plain. These woodlands are unusual for their proximity to the sea and several are of high conservation value.

Physical Influences

Lying to the north of the Kent Chalk, the North Kent Plain is underlain by extensive Tertiary deposits, ranging from the light sands and pebbles of the Oldhaven, Woolwich and Thanet Beds to the heavy, difficult-to-work soils of the London Clay. Within the area, variations exist in the geographical extent and depth of the soils developed from these bedrock types. In general, however, they are deep, rich loams which support the distinctive Kent horticultural land uses, in particular the characteristic landscape elements of the orchards in the east.

The Tertiary beds give rise to the low gently undulating landform of the North Kent Plain through which the Darent, Medway and Great Stour rivers drain northwards to the Thames Estuary and the North Sea.

Thanet is an outlier of the same Chalk that forms the main body of the North Downs to the west. It was originally an island separated from mainland Kent by a sea channel, the remains of which are the entirely silted-up Chislet Marshes.

Underlying the area at great depth are Coal Measures. These have little surface expression, other than former colliery sites, spoil heaps and colliery villages which are a contrast to the usual Kent scene.

Historical and Cultural Influences

Prehistoric finds along the M2 corridor and on Thanet are indicative of long occupation of this area. Pieces of a skull (Swanscombe Man) from gravel pits close to the Ebbsfleet Valley are the earliest fossil human remains found in the British Isles.

The features of the present agricultural landscape probably began to be developed as the light soils were cleared during the Neolithic period and, by Roman times, the North Kent Plain was densely settled. Caesar's descriptions of Kent tell of largish arable fields interspersed with woodlands. Roman

influence on the landscape is evident in the Roman roads - particularly that linking Dover to Sandwich - and extensive remains at Faversham, Canterbury and the surrounding area. At this time, the Isle of Thanet was separated from the mainland by a channel along which it was posssible to sail from Richborough to Reculver. The impressive remains of Richborough Castle bear witness to the then attractive qualities of a large natural harbour; the channel is now silted and the castle sits forlornly in an agricultural setting. Richborough was one of many forts in a chain along the coast from Portsmouth to the Wash.

Historic parks, many of which are now lost, may be found on the junction between the plain and the chalk eg Goodnestone, Knowlton Court, Doddington Park and Cobham.

The rural population, largely scattered in small farmsteads across the area, had very few strongly nucleated settlements.

Buildings and Settlement

Dispersed settlement pattern with surrounding fields defined by a dense network of narrow lanes is typical of the area.

Settlement growth and urbanisation have been primary influences which have markedly changed the local landscape character. The development of Sandwich, Canterbury, Faversham and Sittingbourne, plus the sprawl around Dartford and the Medway Towns in particular, have all impinged on the character of the area.

Canterbury is a settlement of significant historical interest with notable buildings including the famous cathedral and cultural associations with Chaucer. Medieval prosperity is reflected in the buildings of small market towns such as Wingham and Fordwich.

The coastline of Thanet is heavily developed, particularly around Margate, Broadstairs and Ramsgate with tall buildings and structures such as tower blocks and power stations evident in the open farmed landscape.

Land Cover

The North Kent Plain is one of the most productive agricultural areas in Kent due to the fine loam soils and favourable climatic conditions. The agricultural character of the area is dominated by a high proportion of arable land with very little stock rearing. Large and exposed intensively cropped fields are common while hedgerows and individual trees are generally limited with few areas of unimproved pasture. The regular patterns and rectangular shapes of the fields are defined by the various crop types rather than by hedgerows.

Limited poplar and alder shelterbelts are associated with small settlements and farmsteads and are also found around orchards of soft fruits and other horticultural crops. A few small woodland blocks add variety to the horticultural landscape.

Significant woodland cover with outstanding nature-conservation interest is confined to pockets of higher ground to the west of the area and around Blean where heavy acidic London Clay soils support the largest continuous woodland in Kent. The more common species such as sweet chestnut, sessile oak, hornbeam and beech cover are found amongst the enclosed pasture and arable fields.

Thanet is high quality agricultural land and grows both cereals and horticultural crops, notably cabbages, in an open and treeless landscape.

Urban and industrial developments, such as Richborough power station, provide a stark backdrop to the predominantly open agricultural land and grazing marshes.

The Changing Countryside

- Widespread loss and damage to woodlands, hedges and hedgerow trees as a result of agricultural intensification.

- Loss of traditional orchards and hop gardens.

- Dutch Elm disease has affected remaining hedgerow elms.

- Pressures on the wider countryside arising from increasing urban sprawl, especially around the 'Thames Gateway' area.

- Industrial and commercial developments including associated pylons and masts.

- The North Kent Plain is a major communications corridor with future increases in traffic leading to pressure for new road schemes and improvement. Impacts on the landscape such as road lighting along the Thanet Way are particularly intrusive within the wider area. The A2 corridor connecting the major settlements is dominant and further urban expansion threatens significant archaeological remains of acknowledged interest in the area.

- The development of the Channel Tunnel High Speed Rail Link and widening of the M2 motorway will be major forces for change in the future.

- The impact of mineral working, including some chalk and widespread gravel extraction in the river valleys, remains an important issue within the area. Coal-mining has now ceased but its legacy remains as at Chislet where there are extensive tips.

- The restoration of proposed and existing large waste disposal landfill sites will continue to be a significant force for change upon the character of the North Kent Plain.

- Proposals for new reservoir developments will have a significant effect on the character of this area.

Shaping the Future

- New hedgerow, tree, woodland and shelter belt planting needs to be encouraged through appropriate agri-environmental land management mechanisms.

- The conservation of traditional orchards and hop gardens needs to be addressed.

- Landscape enhancement measures are an essential part of the future development of the 'Thames Gateway' initiative and as part of the development of the Channel Tunnel High Speed Rail Link.

- Sympathetic design and layout for road schemes are important in the open landscape of the North Kent Plain.

- Many disused mineral workings and landfill sites would benefit from restoration.

Selected References

Hull, F (1988), *Ordnance Survey Historical Guides: Kent*, George Philip, London.

Kent County Council (1993), *Landscape and Nature Conservation Guidelines*, Kent County Council, Maidstone.

McRae, S G, 'Agriculture and Horticulture' in S G McRae nd Burnham, C P (eds), (1973), *The Rural Landscape of Kent*, Wye College, Wye.

The distinctive chalk sea cliffs are a dominant feature of the Thanet coastline and provide a dramatic backdrop to the ecologically important marshes and reed beds.

Thames Basin Lowlands

- A small-scale lowland farmed landscape lying within a generally flat but gently undulating clay vale.

- Characterised by small mixed holdings with brick-built farms, a mosaic of small fields interspersed by oak/ash woods and shaws, field ponds, meadows, heathland and individual mature tree specimens.

- Gentle lowland character reinforced by river tributaries which meander through flat farmed valley landscapes with large areas of estate land.

- Some of the essential farmland character has been fragmented by the expansion of settlements and the associated major roads that dissect this area.

- Edges of settlements characterised by an unkempt appearance of wire fences, sheds, derelict hedgerows and weed-infested fields associated with pony paddocks.

Landscape Character

A small-scale farmed landscape sandwiched between the Thames Basin Heaths to the west and the North Downs to the south and east, broadening out towards the London suburbs immediately to the north. In many places the Thames Basin Lowlands retain a typical English farmed countryside, although the landscape itself has been largely lost or fragmented by the urban expansion of London across the northern parts.

The gently undulating farmland is interspersed with woods and shaws, villages and farmhouses. Fields are small or medium-sized and uneven, usually hedged and with some hedgerow oak. The flatter parts to the north and east tend to be more open and relatively featureless.

The interface between countryside and urban edge, including the edge of small villages, is typically characterised by an often unkempt appearance associated with horse keeping. Irregular fences and gappy hedges, run-down sheds and fields full of docks, nettles and ragwort give these landscapes a neglected feel. This untidiness is most apparent close to London where the rural landscape quickly merges with the expanded suburbs such as the Esher, Epsom and Ewell areas. The overall pattern of fields and woods is still evident but the landscape has been affected by the loss of traditional management and by a claustrophobic maze of housing typically interspersed with densely planted ornamental conifers in and around gardens.

Some areas are predominantly agricultural with a moderate woodland cover and a number of large villages. Shaws often spread fingers out from the woods to mesh with the field pattern, helping to make the landscape feel more wooded than it really is.

Gravel pits mature to form interesting lakes and provide good resources for informal recreation such as this one at Molesey Heath in Surrey.

Two rivers, the Mole in the east and the Wey in the west, meander northwards through this gentle lowland landscape towards the Thames. Their valleys are broad and flat and are marked by riparian wet woods and water meadows. The river scene around the Wey is complimented by the Wey Navigation Canal which continually enters and departs from the natural watercourse. North of the M25 the rivers become less rural and their landscapes more degraded, although quite unexpected rich fragments of countryside remain especially beside the Wey. The landscape of these rivers is mostly wide and open although often locally intimate in scale due to lush bankside vegetation. Between Leatherhead and Downside the Mole often rises in flood, forming great temporary lakes across the valley floor.

Views of the rising ground of the North Downs dip slope to the south are of a more open, larger-scale landscape. In the south-west, the sudden rise of the Hog's Back chalk ridge forms a dramatic boundary and, from the Hog's Back itself, extensive views are possible across the predominantly flat landscape of the Thames Basin Lowlands.

Physical Influences

This is an essentially lowland area lying within the London Basin. The land is a gently undulating plain for the most part, rising towards the dip slope of the North Downs to the south and east and to the Thames Basin Heaths in the west. Farther north, the land becomes flatter.

This area lies mainly on the London Clay with narrow sand outcrops comprising Reading Beds and Bagshot Beds, which run northwards from the North Downs. The soil developed over the London Clay is generally very heavy and clayey and therefore difficult to cultivate.

The Thames Basin Lowlands are drained by two principal rivers, the Wey and the Mole. Their valleys cut through the North Downs at Guildford and Dorking, and both rivers take a meandering course northwards to join the Thames at Chertsey Meads and Molesey in the Thames

Valley. The river terraces are composed of gravels with alluvial floodplains giving rise to extensive riverside grazing meadows. Peat is locally present in minor tributaries.

On the edge of the London suburbs, land use is characterised by horse paddocks, wire fences, sheds and derelict hedgerows.

Historical and Cultural Influences

The historical field pattern reflects variations in topography with areas of flat land typified by the straight and lean single-species hedges of the 18th and 19th century enclosures. In contrast, the more undulating areas support much older, wider and irregular hedges.

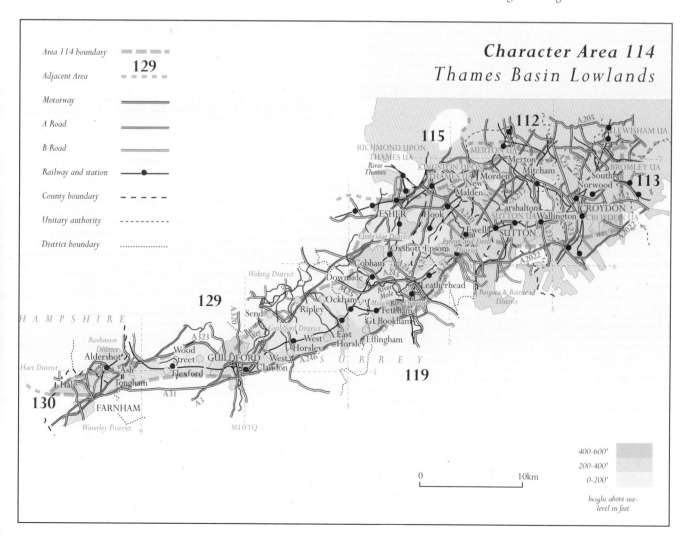

Many of the woodlands and shaws have banks around them showing signs of laid hedges, indicating historical boundaries.

A number of landscaped parks were prominent in the area; these include Claremont at Esher (now National Trust), renowned for Bridgeman's earthworks; Clandon by Capability Brown, and also Ockham and East Horsley. Most of these rural parklands are now intensively farmed but many of the parkland features still perceptibly influence the landscape with imposing oaks, limes and cedars scattered across their fields – in some places the decaying remnants of avenues, roundels and boundary walls can also be distinguished. The rivers have been significant influences in the development of these parklands such as Cobham Park situated on the river Mole.

On the Wey, north of the M25, there are traces of the former industrial use of the river and navigation in the form of old mills and factories.

Roads, such as the busy M25 motorway, and mineral extraction have fragmented much of the essential farmland character of the Thames Basin.

Buildings and Settlement

The density of settlement ranges from the relatively built-up landscape in the north-east, close to outer London, through to much sparser settlement in the west. Twentieth century development has expanded many villages until they appear to merge together, for example between Leatherhead and East Horsley on the A246, or again with Ripley and Send. Most settlements, however, retain a tangible village identity even when they have become engulfed in spreading suburbia; they hold a strong sense of locality and community.

Not surprisingly, the smaller villages relate much better to the surrounding landscape than those which are almost encapsulated by adjacent suburbs. Churches within these villages such as West Horsley and Ockham form important landmarks within the Lowlands.

In the west of this character area, the few settlements vary from scattered houses or farmsteads to small patches of more built-up estate developments. There are a number of distinctive brick and flint farmhouses with a similar building style built during the 19th century and also examples of fine half-timbered buildings.

Proximity to a large urban population means that the landscape is widely used for recreation. Most of the woodlands have well used footpaths through or alongside them and public spaces such as Esher and Epsom Commons are heavily used as recreational resources.

Dispersed settlements of mixed character are never far from each other, forming a network of villages. All are linked by sometimes congested country lanes and roads.

Land Cover

The Thames Basin Lowlands are predominantly a pastoral landscape dominated by hedged fields of permanent pasture over London Clay with some areas remaining as common or woodland. Field trees occur almost always in straight lines, indicating the position of vanished hedges. Oak is the most common hedgerow tree, though ash and field maple also occur. Most of the fields are bounded by hedges, although fences often replace hedges particularly when close to urban areas. There is some variety in the species richness of hedges: pure hawthorn hedges tend to be thinner and straighter, and to occur on flatter land, while the mixed-species hedges tend to be wider, irregular and to occupy more undulating land. Hedges often follow the course of streams and ditches, producing irregular field boundaries. Such hedges consist of irregular dense lines of great willow, hawthorn, ash and dog rose. In the north of the area, especially where the London Clay is overlain by gravels or alluvial soils, roadside hedges of pure elm are common.

The woodland is predominantly oak, with oak/ash on the more base-rich soils in the west, while oak/birch favours the less fertile, acidic land over the sands and gravels in the

82

east. Many woods comprise oak standards over hazel coppice with bluebells but oak high forest with sweet chestnut and ash is also found. Small areas of sweet chestnut coppice and conifer plantation also occur. Within woodlands, small pockets of wet willow wood can sometimes be found. The west of the area is generally more sparsely wooded but most of this is semi-natural ancient woodland. The base rich clay here gives rise to more species-rich woodland. The wild service tree, an ancient woodland indicator, is found in many woods and shaws. There are also former coppice woods of hazel and/or ash. Many woodlands have multiple uses such as pheasant rearing alongside timber production and well-used rights of way. In the north-east of the area, few of the woods are ancient as much of the woodland is the result of deliberate afforestation or natural woodland regeneration on heaths.

Former heaths such as Esher Common now comprise areas of dense secondary woodland interspersed with open scrub punctuated by groups of young trees, areas of gorse and bracken with some patches of heather. Ashtead Common is a distinct and unique landscape of gnarled old pollard oaks in pasture, once managed as wood-pasture but now invaded by bracken and birch. It also has some blocks of woodland including coppice with standards.

The rivers support riparian woodlands - with wet woods of alder, oak, lime, willow and poplar, plus hazel and holly. Scattered clumps of trees alongside the river course also occur including mainly alder, willow, poplar and oak.

Associated with the parklands, exotic ornamental trees make an occasional impact. Close to the suburban areas the character of indigenous vegetation is marred by ornamental conifers or garden escapes of rhododendron.

The Changing Countryside

- Urban fringe pressures such as land use conflicts between agriculture, housing, industry and recreational interests.

- Horse-grazed pasture with associated clutter is typical of landholdings.

- Recreational pressures, especially golf course developments, which seldom reflect the character of the landscape in particular adjacent to rivers.

- Lack of appropriate hedgerow management, especially damage by over-cutting.

- Loss of hedgerow and field trees.

- Fragmentation of field patterns into paddocks with loss of traditional boundary types.

- Loss of distinctive settlement character and inappropriate redevelopment of traditional barns and other characteristic built features.

- Low flows of rivers in summer exacerbated by water abstraction.

- Development of the M25 and A3 roads – amongst others – has had a major influence on landscape character.

Shaping the Future

- An over-grazing of the edges of woodland shaws needs addressing.

- There is scope for the conservation of existing hedges, hedgerow and field trees.

- The restoration and protection of water levels in rivers would help to conserve their landscapes.

- The removal of invasive species (including where necessary, trees) and a reintroduction of an appropriate grazing regime would help restore areas of open heath.

- Good building design in character with the area would enhance local distinctiveness within built-up areas.

Selected References

Brandon, P (1977), *A History of Surrey - The Darwen County History Series,* Phillimore and Co Ltd, London.

Surrey County Council (1994), *The Future of Surrey's Landscape and Woodlands – Part I: An Assessment (consultation draft)*, Surrey County Council.

Glossary

shaws: strip of trees or bushes forming the border of a field

Farming the London Clay soils is restricted to pasture and some arable crop production. It is a gently undulating landscape with fields divided by hawthorn hedges and mature hedgerow trees such as oak and ash. Commuter towns are frequent, such as Aldershot in the background here.

Thames Valley

- Hydrological floodplain of the river Thames as a landscape feature provides unity to the large areas of fragmented poor agricultural land.

- The western Thames valley is wide and flat with the river barely discernible, occupying only a small part of the wider geological floodplain.

- Woodlands characterise the north-western area, the wooded character extending up to the southern edge of the Chiltern Hills.

- To the south, the open Thames floodplain dominates with its associated flat grazing land, becoming characterised by a number of formal historic landscapes on higher ground such as Windsor Park.

- Towards London in the east, the natural character of the area is overtaken by urban influences; a dense network of roads including the M25 corridor, Heathrow Airport, railway lines, golf courses, pylon lines, reservoirs, extensive mineral extraction and numerous flooded gravel pits.

Landscape Character

The Thames Valley is a wedge-shaped area widening from Reading to include the Bracknell, Slough and Windsor areas, the Colne Valley and the south-west London fringes. As the river Thames enters the London suburbs of north Surrey, the floodplain is bounded in the distance to the south and west by low wooded hills which lie in the adjoining character area, the Thames Basin Heaths.

In the centre of the Thames Valley, the open Thames floodplain dominates. This is grazed pasture and includes a number of designed parklands on its higher ground. South of this are clay vales characterised by large regular field patterns and small woods. Further south the Thames Valley is edged by wooded ridges and rolling farmland. The central and northern parts of the area are dominated by medium-sized riverside towns such as Twyford and the

relatively high incidence of private rural houses and closeness to London give a slightly suburban air. However, the wealth of this district over a long period and its natural scenic attractions have left an overall atmosphere of sophistication, heightening along the river Thames and especially at Windsor with its Great Park characterised by rides, ancient woodland and ancient pollard trees.

Archaeologically and culturally significant, the river Thames has many special historic associations. Of these, Windsor Castle is one of the best known.

ROB FRASER/COUNTRYSIDE AGENCY

As the Thames flows towards London, its character is dominated by urban influences. Major roads, the M4, M40 and M25 motorways, pylon lines, Heathrow Airport, railways and golf courses dominate the local landscape. Around Slough, the Colne Valley and areas further east, the overwhelming influences are of lakes left from mineral workings and the vast raised reservoirs. Rapid development has often left new structures and buildings unrelated to the landscape around them. The overall impression is of a lack of cohesiveness, although older villages and woodlands survive in surprising seclusion.

At Walton-on-Thames, the Thames Valley becomes dominated by motorways and reservoirs. The area around Richmond reflects its royal patronage, the river Thames forming the focus within a series of formally designed landscapes.

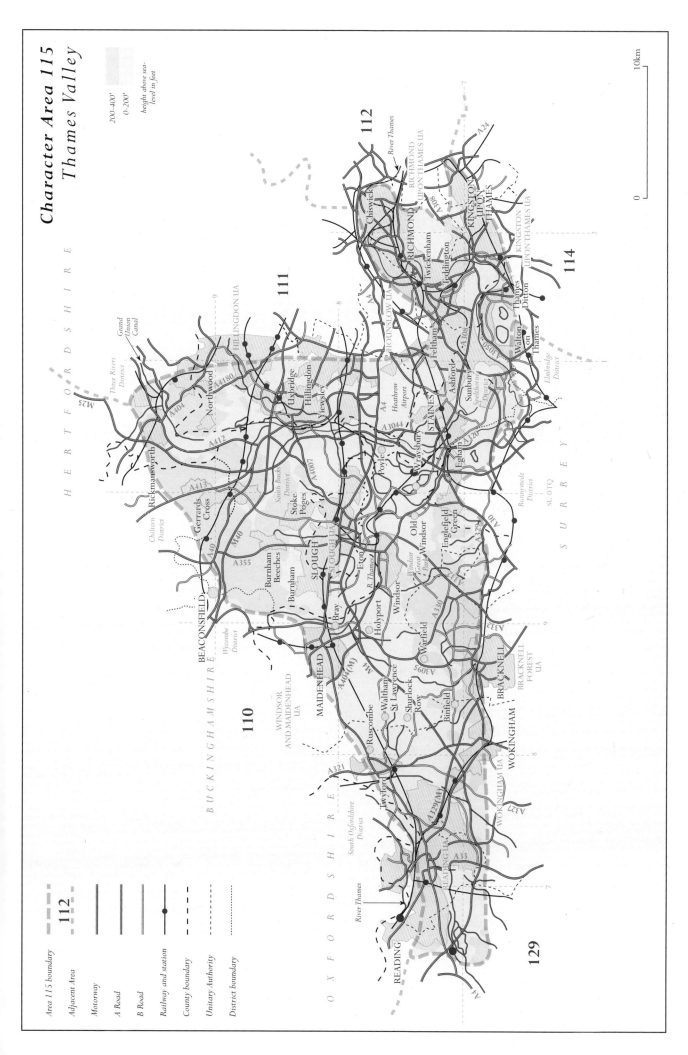

Character Area 115
Thames Valley

Area 115 boundary

112 **Adjacent Area**

Motorway

A Road

B Road

● **Railway and station**

County boundary

Unitary Authority

District boundary

200-400'
0-200'

height above sea-
level in feet

10km

0

ROB FRASER/COUNTRYSIDE AGENCY

The extensive river Thames floodplain is the dominant feature of the Thames Valley. The river meanders through fields of pasture and occasional arable, passing the riverside towns of Cookham, Maidenhead and Windsor.

Physical Influences

The underlying geology is London Clay, though much of it is overlain by alluvial sands and gravels.

In the south-west, the gently rolling valley sides give way to a fairly flat plain east of Reading. Much of this area is flat and close to flood level although in contrast Slough lies on slightly terraced land above the floodplain and Windsor Castle sits on a prominent local outcrop of the Chalk. Further north, the landform reflects the rolling hills characteristic of the nearby Chilterns landscape. Here, the Chalk is overlain by clay and gravel, giving rise to a plateau and a series of knolls at Knowl Hill, Ashley Hill and Bowsey Hill.

The Thames and its numerous tributaries wind across a landscape, formed by the action of the rivers, yet today the tributaries have dwindled through abstraction and drainage into insignificance relative to the dominating scale of modern development. Significant areas of land have been totally re-shaped by mineral extraction and by the presence of large reservoirs, many of them raised high above the natural ground level with steep, grassed embankments. These reservoirs supply London with clean water from the Thames and are internationally important for overwintering wildfowl.

The London Clay is typically dark bluish grey but brown at the surface when weathered and gives rise to heavy waterlogged soils occupied largely by permanent grassland and arable land throughout the Thames Valley. These clay plains were once thickly wooded but Windsor Forest is now the only significant surviving element of this once extensive woodland.

Historical and Cultural Influences

The apparent wealth and 'sophistication' of the Thames Valley are largely due to the area's proximity to London. The river is closely associated with numerous historical places and cultural events such as the signing of the Magna Carta at Runnymede.

This eastern part of the area has been drastically altered by the spread of outer London over the last century or so. The first edition Ordnance Survey maps of 1865 show that this area was an open, farmed landscape of regular fields suggestive of late enclosure and relatively treeless but with groups of trees and orchards around the small villages.

The identity of this flat landscape depended on the small scale features of trees and hedges which were easily removed. The scale, speed and range of development have left little sense of continuity. Yet despite this, there remain 'lost villages' such as Denham, Shepperton or Upper Halliford, where the small-scale architecture and the relationship between the village and its immediate landscape survive intact.

Buildings and Settlement

The wide clay floodplains of the Thames Valley are dominated by the towns of Reading, Bracknell and Slough, together with particular concentrations of development associated with the Airport and M25 and there are very few villages of more traditional character. Large houses set within 18th or early 19th century ornamental parkland, concentrated to the north of Bracknell, provide stark contrast with the sporadic modern development, including some commercial property and residential caravan sites, found further to the east.

Localised areas of species-rich hay meadows provide a splash of colour in the spring and summer as they flower alongside the river. Shown here are the ancient wet meadows at Cricklade, full of Fritillaries.

Many towns expanded greatly in the late 19th century together with several smaller villages and areas of dispersed development. Everywhere in these districts, housing is interspersed with open land, much of which includes golf courses. In the vicinity of Slough and Windsor, land ownership by Eton College and the Crown Estate has restricted the spread of development. Nearby to the east, at Ditton Park, there are research establishments in extensive grounds. In the Colne Valley, linear developments have extended out from the settlements along the roads. Substantial lengths of river frontage are characterised by the ribbon development of summer homes.

The M25, M40 and M4 corridors are a major feature of the Thames Valley with associated development often poorly contained and tending to dominate the floodplain. The fringe zone to Greater London has seen rapid and often haphazard development which gives the overall impression of a lack of co-ordination between the numerous activities and land uses. Heathrow Airport is a large dominating influence in the flat landscape around the M25. Areas of undeveloped land tend to be small and fragmented. This area is typified by the open expanses of development with few features to draw the eye apart from pylons which dominate the skyline. Fly-tipping, casual illegal use such as motorbike scrambling and incursion by travellers are common activities.

Land Cover

The clay floodplains comprise farmland interspersed with a matrix of small woods. There are some more substantial blocks of ancient woodland, such as in the Billingbear/Shurlock Row area, with some modern plantations of quite extensive woodland in other areas. The latter tend to be where the floodplains are fairly open, flat and relatively featureless, with regular field patterns suggesting late enclosure. The sloping banks of the Thames are occasionally dominated locally by quite extensive parklands.

The Thames Valley includes a mixture of farmland, small woods, golf courses and some small areas of orchards. Much of the lower Thames floodplain is fairly open, characterised by the limited tree cover. However, the parkland trees and extensive woodland of Windsor Great Park is a major exception. Some of the woodland is ancient and the park also contains ancient pollard trees which combine with the distinct tract of meadowland at Runnymede to create a unique landscape within the wider setting.

Farming is generally extremely limited due to demands made on the land for reservoirs and gravel pits, for numerous school playing fields or for the extensive grounds of research establishments and the like. Reclamation of disused mineral extraction sites has resulted in large expanses of lake and wetland which provide important habitats for wildlife and are also valuable recreational resources. Willows, belts of poplar, hawthorn, elder, and alder are particularly characteristic of these areas.

Green Belt land within the urban fringe is characterised by some remnant areas of agriculture or market gardening although these landscapes are often impoverished, with few trees or hedges. Keeping of horses is also fairly widespread within these areas typified by the sometimes tall straggly lines of bushes and trees and generally unkempt appearance of the landscape with frequent patches of scrub.

Burnham Beeches comprises a wooded plateau of unfenced common land with small areas of heath dissected by narrow, winding lanes. As such, Burnham Beeches provides variety and contrast within the generally developed character of the wider Valley.

The Changing Countryside

- Golf course development pressures.

- Designed parkland features within farmed landscapes at risk from changing agricultural activities and lack of management for individual trees.

- General development pressures owing to proximity to London in particular both existing and proposed major road corridors including lighting and signage, expansion of urban areas, and airport development/associated activities. Much of this development is unrelated to the character of the surrounding area and has significantly contributed to the overall fragmentation of the landscape.

- Incipient pressure from non-farming use of small-sized holdings, notably horse grazing and land held for 'hope value'. Also pressure from recreational uses and associated facilities within the Green belt and urban fringe in general.

- River Thames itself is a focus of increasing recreation both on and off the water, as are the historic riverside towns, woodlands, commons and restored gravel workings.

- Pressures for the sub-division of land holdings and associated pressures of new buildings, fencing and other developments more usually related to urban fringe land uses.

Shaping the Future

- The conservation of woodlands and locally important individual trees is important to the character of the area.

- The conservation of wooded commons and, where applicable, restoration to heath should be addressed.

- New planting would help to assimilate new and existing development into the landscape, to replace lost features such as hedges and hedgerow trees and to reinforce existing woodland.

- A number of traditional haymeadows are in need of restoration.

- The restoration and management of many mineral extraction sites – particularly by the creation of wetlands – should be addressed.

- There are opportunities for the conservation of historic landscapes and historic features within farmland – particularly adjacent to the river – such as pollarded willows and parkland.

Selected References

Babtie Public Services Division (undated), *A Landscape Strategy for Berkshire: Consultation Proposals*, Berkshire County Council.

Surrey County Council (1994), *The Future of Surrey's Landscape and Woodlands – Part I: An Assessment (consultation draft)*, Surrey County Council.

Richards Moorehead and Laing Ltd (1989), *Buckinghamshire Trees and Forestry Strategy: Volumes 1, 2 and 3*, Richards Moorehead and Laing, Clwyd.

JOHN TYLER/COUNTRYSIDE AGENCY

South of the Chilterns, the flat open landscape spreads out. Large open fields are interspersed with occasional woodland and scrubby hedgerows.

Berkshire and Marlborough Downs

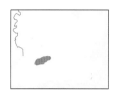

- High, large-scale rolling chalk downland characterised by intensive arable farming, sparse woodland cover and few hedges or hedgerow trees becoming more enclosed towards the east.

- Dramatic scarp on northern edge.

- Well-wooded dip-slope characterised by mixed farming with tree-lined arable fields.

- Tree belts and clumps punctuate the skyline in many places.

- Dry valleys forming deep combes with steep slopes and some remnants of grazed chalk grassland.

- Scattered small hamlets clustered along valleys with fast chalk streams, wet and grazed pastures, hedgerows and small woodland blocks.

- Includes the Vale of Pewsey's meadows and orchards and the beech avenues and ancient oak glades of Savernake Forest.

- Many sites of archaeological significance including numerous scattered barrows, Neolithic stone circles, earthworks, Roman roads and ancient tracks, and also the distinctive chalk white horse carvings characteristic of this area.

- Historically linked to the Chilterns landscape by the Ridgeway which runs along the top of the chalk scarp.

- Horse gallops are a common feature linked to the numerous racing stables on the Downs.

Landscape Character

The Berkshire and Marlborough Downs is an area of distinctive landscape character encompassing broad expanses of essentially open downland dissected by numerous dry valleys, richly-farmed vale and valley landscapes with many extensive areas of woodland.

Part of the extensive Chalk deposits in south and east England, the Downs meet the river Thames and the Chilterns along the wooded Goring Gap to the east while, south of the Vale of Pewsey and woodlands of Savernake Forest, lie the Hampshire Downs and Salisbury Plain. To the north and west, the low-lying clays of the Upper Thames Clay Vales and the Avon Vales provide the setting to the Downs, the vale villages sharing many characteristic features with those on the Downs. The Vale of Kennet forms the southern boundary to the Berkshire Downs.

The Neolithic stone circle at Avebury, part of a World Heritage Site, is evidence of the early occupation of the Berkshire and Marlborough Downs.

The escarpment of the Berkshire and Marlborough Downs is a prominent relief feature reaching over 250 m AOD, sweeping round in a huge arc from near the Buckinghamshire/Oxfordshire border to the north of Devizes in Wiltshire. Much of the downland is an elevated dip-slope plateau, dissected by a network of dry valleys, much like other downland areas such as the Chilterns. Although numerous, the dip slope dry valleys or 'combes' become shallow and gentle features towards the scarp resulting in smooth rounded hills, giving a typically rolling or undulating landform.

With the move towards intensive arable farming, the chalk grassland has been replaced by vast, rectilinear fields of

Character Area 116

Berkshire and Marlborough Downs

Legend:
- 109 Area 116 boundary
- Adjacent Area
- Motorway
- A Road
- B Road
- Railway and station
- County boundary
- District boundary
- Forest

height above sea-level in feet
- 800-1000'
- 600-800'
- 400-600'
- 200-400'
- 0-200'

0 _____ 10km

cereals. These large arable fields, coupled with a lack of hedgerows or tree cover, save for the few clumps of planted beeches, make for an open homogenous character with a simple but strong structural form. The dry valleys provide a pleasing contrast to the chalk plateau; the valley landforms hidden from view by the undulating topography. It is on the scarp itself and on the steeper sides of the dry valleys that the remaining tracts of traditional chalk grassland can be found. These remnants of former sheep pasture provide visual interest in contrast to the monotony of arable fields and are of considerable wildlife conservation value with their distinctive wild flowers amid the springy turf, maintained by the grazing of numerous rabbits.

To the south and east, the open downland character gives way to increasing numbers of tree belts and woodlands, including the heavily wooded rolling hills of Savernake Forest on the isolated area of clay south-east of Marlborough. Beech in particular thrives here, a species often occurring as planted avenues among the ancient oaks and the more recent conifer timber crops. The settlements here are small and scattered in contrast to those in the valleys of the open downland, where a broad scatter of clustered settlements are linked by the more major roads and lanes that tend to follow the dry valley bottoms.

On the exposed higher downland, numerous tracks, byways and footpaths cross the intensively farmed but sparsely settled landscape. Many of these are quite ancient in origin, such as the Ridgeway. Within this vast expanse, isolated farm buildings, post-and-wire fences and the odd clump of trees or shelterbelts form the only significant elements.

Physical Influences

The Berkshire and Marlborough Downs are underlain by Cretaceous Chalk, the surface of which is often covered by a stony layer of clay-with-flints. Sarsen stones, isolated remnant blocks of weathered Tertiary sandstones with a hard silica cement, are a particular feature. Solifluction processes have transported these blocks down slopes resulting in distinctive dry valleys dotted with sarsens. The black or brown tinted soils of this area are predominantly light, free-draining and generally thin except wherever clay-with-flints caps the chalklands. This creates areas of damp heavy soils which support major areas of woodlands such as Savernake Forest.

The open rounded chalk downs form an elevated plateau of typically rolling or undulating topography, incised with dry valleys or combes. These characteristic chalk landscape features were formed by surface streams during the Ice Age when permafrost impeded sub-surface drainage. The Vale of Pewsey to the south of the Downs is not a true river valley but an undulating lowland vale of subdued terrain. This anticlinal structure has had its crest denuded to expose

the Upper Greensand, while Chalk forms inward facing escarpments to the north and south. The Vale is entirely drained by the river Avon, which flows south through Salisbury Plain, while the upper reaches of the river Kennet have cut a significant valley running west to east through the Marlborough Downs towards Hungerford and into the Vale of Kennet. The majority of the high open downland is now water-less due to the porous nature of the chalk bedrock.

JOHN TYLER/COUNTRYSIDE AGENCY

This area is characterised by a large scale, open, rolling downland landscape with intensive arable farming on the dip slopes and a dramatic scarp slope along its northern edge.

Historical and Cultural Influences

The Berkshire and Marlborough Downs have been settled since Neolithic or early prehistoric times as the numerous barrows, and other prehistoric earthwork features that are scattered around the chalk downs, testify. The Neolithic stone circle at Avebury, the ceremonial mound known as Silbury Hill plus the adjacent West Kennet longbarrow on the Marlborough Downs are collectively designated as a World Heritage Site. Further significant archaeological features are found on the north scarp of the Berkshire Downs around White Horse Hill. These include the Bronze Age hillfort of Uffington Castle, the Neolithic chambered longbarrow of Wayland's Smithy built from massive sarsens and the striking figure of the White Horse itself, dating from the first century, cut into the chalk scarp face.

Linking these sites was the Ridgeway — a broad track created by early peoples and their livestock, considered one of Britain's oldest 'green' roads. The Ridgeway follows the highest part of the chalk scarp linking Avebury with Ivinghoe in the Hertfordshire part of the Chilterns. The landscape through which the Ridgeway passes remained much the same up until about two centuries ago when new

Enclosure Acts came into force. The Ridgeway was enclosed by hedges and banks to prevent livestock straying onto newly cultivated fields.

Much of the open sheepruns, that gave rise to the distinctive close-cropped chalk grassland turf, turned to scrub or ploughed fields as the price of wool fell and cereals became more productive. Many of the open panoramic views became interspersed by planted clumps and belts of trees as a result of farmers' attempts to shelter their crops sown on the windswept plateaux.

The chalk hills and plateaux were abandoned hundreds of years earlier as prehistoric peoples began to clear the lower river valleys and vales of the thick scrub and forest, allowing the first settlements to be established close to water supplies. Subsequent invaders, such as the West Saxons, also favoured the valleys and carved out their farmsteads on the valley floors, leaving the high grassy downlands for their sheep. This settlement pattern has changed little up to the present day.

Woodland is a distinctive feature in the Downs landscape both as prominent beech 'hangers' and shelterbelts on the clay caps.

Buildings and Settlement

The Berkshire and Marlborough Downs are generally thinly settled, with most settlements largely clustered along valleys. On the chalk uplands a broad scatter of modern farm buildings and large horse racing establishments are prominent in the thinly populated open landscapes, while the distinctive valleys that intercut the Chalk plateau contain generally compact villages and hamlets. These nucleated villages have Saxon origins and are often evenly spaced along the valleys, with thatch, red brick and weather-board characteristic of the cottages and barns. These villages often contain attractive historic buildings many of which have knapped flint and weathered chalk in their walls and locally-occurring sarsen stone for their foundations.

Marlborough and Pewsey are the main settlements in the area, both historic agricultural market towns inextricably linked to their respective wider landscape settings.

Dry valleys and their steep coombe sides still support important areas of chalk grassland.

Land Cover

Few areas of traditional chalk grassland have survived on the Downs except for limited tracts on the scarp itself and on the steep sides of dry valleys. These few areas support colourful lime-dependant wild flowers among the short rabbit-grazed springy turfs. On some steeper slopes, juniper and hawthorn scrub is frequent and beech is the dominant tree type occurring as characteristic clumps on numerous hill crests in the area.

Much of the open chalk downland, although traditionally pasture for sheep grazing, has now been ploughed up and replaced by neatly cultivated fields for arable crops or, in many areas, by race horse gallops.

The fields are mainly large within the richly farmed valley landscapes which includes the particularly fertile Vale of Pewsey's meadows and orchards. On the open chalk uplands, the predominantly large rectilinear fields are largely defined by post-and-wire fencing, with very few hedges. In contrast, the fields on the lower slopes tend to be more irregular with managed hawthorn hedges that frequently contain oak hedgerow trees, within numerous blocks of woodland and shelterbelts.

On these lower slopes, woodland is a significant land cover. Areas such as Savernake Forest are characterised by the ancient semi-natural oak glades, juxtaposed with planted beech avenues and more recent commercial forestry plantings of conifers. The conifers thrive on the heavy soils generated by the thick mantle of clay on the south fringes of the Downs.

This wooded landscape is criss-crossed by a winding network of lanes, often with high grassy banks which link the small farm settlements and clustered hamlets to the wider road network, including the M4 motorway which crosses between the Marlborough and Lambourn Downs.

The Changing Countryside

- Field amalgamation, leading to loss of hedgerow features on the Downs, and widespread arable farming and commercial forestry has changed the character of some areas.

- Clearance and lack of management of historic woodlands, including several former Royal hunting forests, has altered the woodland character.

- Scrub invasion of chalk grassland due to removal of traditional management regime.

- Replacement of former sheep pastures with arable fields or race horse gallops resulting in the loss of characteristic chalk grassland.

- Spread of new land uses such as golf courses and pig-farming have changed the appearance of significant areas of the Downs.

- Changes to the appearance of the downland landscape have occurred as a result of inappropriate management of set-aside land.

- Pressure for new roads and improvements to existing roads.

- Pressure for new motorway services, petrol stations and other associated developments along major routes.

- Recreational pressures from conflicting interest between walkers, motor-cyclists and off-road vehicles on downland tracks.

Shaping the Future

- Many archaeological features have suffered damage in recent times and deserve further conservation and protection.

- The open nature of the higher areas of downland, including important views, is an important aspect of the local character.

- The management and restoration of chalk downland and associated woodland (including hill-top shelter-belts) should be considered.

Selected References

Yarrow, I (1974), *Berkshire*, Robert Hale and Co, London.

Babtie Public Services Division (undated), *A Landscape Strategy for Berkshire: Consultation Proposals*, Berkshire County Council.

Landscape Design Associates (1993), *Newbury District-Wide Landscape Appraisal*, LDA, Peterborough.

Stedman, A R (1960), *Marlborough and The Upper Kennet Country*, Butler and Turner, Marlborough.

Glossary

AOD: Above Ordnance Datum

VALE OF THE WHITE HORSE DISTRICT COUNCIL

The numerous ancient field systems, barrows and other prehistoric earthworks along with the 'white horse' provide dramatic visual evidence of a long history of settlement.

North Downs

Key Characteristics

- Dramatic and distinctive Chalk downland with a continuous and steep scarp giving extensive views across Kent and Surrey towards the South Downs.

- The broad dip slope gradually drops towards the Thames and the English Channel. The dip slope is incised by a number of valleys or 'coombes' of the rivers Stour, Medway, Darent and Mole.

- Chalk soils on the scarp, at the base and in the dry valleys, support areas of high-quality unimproved chalk grassland. Clay-with-flints soils on the upper parts of the dip-slope supports oak/ash woodland and scrub with beech/ash/maple is common on the valley sides, such as on Box Hill.

- Land use includes a few pockets of traditional downland grazing but (especially in Kent) it is largely dominated by arable fields. These fields at the base of the scarp have extended their regular pattern up the sides of the Downs.

- The North Downs are a rural landscape with scattered flint-walled farmhouses and large houses. Towards London, while some valleys of species-rich grassland are still retained, the character changes to urban, with the topography masked by the built-up areas.

- The south-eastern end of the Downs becomes increasingly open and more intensively farmed as it widens before ending abruptly at the distinctive chalk cliffs of Dover. In places, it is undulating with dry grassed valleys and ridgetop woodlands.

- In some areas, major motorway and railway corridors introduce a discordant feature into an otherwise quiet and peaceful rural landscape.

- In the east, the lower dip-slope is characterised by high quality, fertile, loamy soils that support extensive tracts of cereals, root and other horticultural crops.

- Woodland and shaws cover much of the dry valleys and, in places, they are a characteristic of the ridgetop.

- Lanes follow the lines of old drove roads in many places.

Landscape Character

The North Downs escarpment is a striking and dramatic feature in the surrounding landscape. The Downs run from the narrow ridge of the Hog's Back in west Surrey, into south London and across Kent, widening eastwards to end abruptly at the distinctive landmark of the White Cliffs between Deal and Folkestone.

On the wide northern dip slope in east and mid-Kent, the North Downs merge into the plateau of the North Kent Plain and become urbanised in many places, such as south of Croydon or at Chatham. Farther to the west in Surrey, the Hog's Back marks the narrow divide between the Thames Basin Lowlands to the north and the Wealden Greensand to the south. The steep south-facing scarp of the North Downs rises to over 180 metres above the Greensand and is still more than 150 metres above sea level at Folkestone on the south Kent coast.

Arable farming is common on the more fertile soils of the gently undulating dip slope.

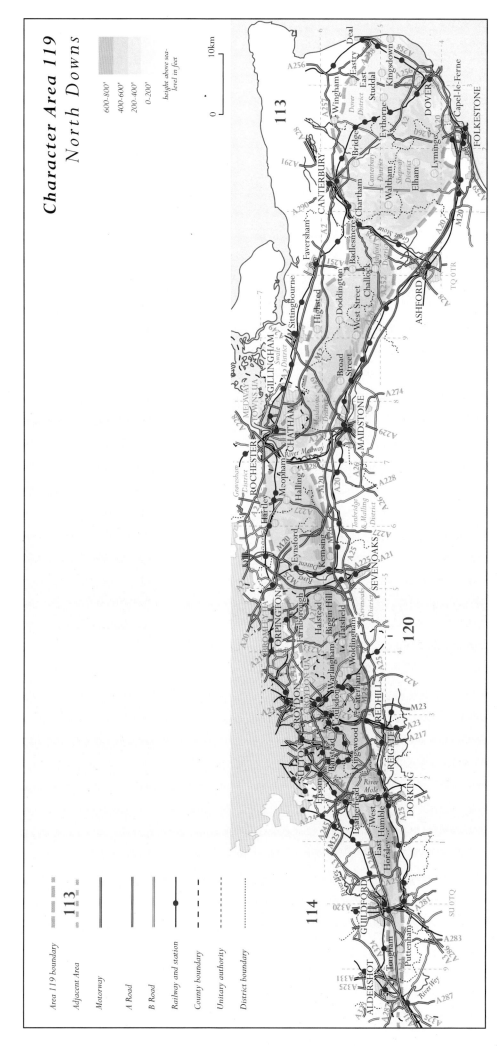

Character Area 119
North Downs

Area 119 boundary

Adjacent Area 113

Motorway

A Road

B Road

Railway and station

County boundary

Unitary authority

District boundary

height above sea-
level in feet

0-200'
200-400'
400-600'
600-800'

0   10km

The feature that gives unity to the character of the North Downs landscape is the strong Chalk topography and the open expanses of rolling downland. This strong landform is emphasised further by the pattern of woods and shaws which cover the numerous dry valleys.

Much of the North Downs has remained isolated and undeveloped as a result of the steep topography. The area contains a few large towns such as Chatham or Guildford but the majority of the major roads skirt the hills, leaving most of the area secluded and unspoilt. Bisecting the Downs at Rochester, the river Medway is associated with busy transport routes, industry and mineral extraction which detract from the rural and unspoilt character. The rivers Mole and Wey also cut narrow passages through the Downs at Leatherhead and Guildford.

Physical Influences

The Chalk forms the backbone of the North Downs which constitute the northern rim of the Tertiary London Basin. To the south lies the Wealden anticline exposing older Cretaceous strata.

The steep south-facing scarp face of the Downs is incised by a number of dry valleys which form wide gentle coombes dominated by the chalk soils. In contrast, the upper part of the dip slope is capped with extensive drift deposits of clay-with-flints. The rivers Stour, Medway, Darent, Wey and Mole also cut through the scarp to form deep valleys, showing evidence of river capture in many places.

Historical and Cultural Influences

In prehistoric times much of the region, including the Downs, was likely to have been covered in dense, deciduous woodland. Evidence of early human activity or settlement within the area is provided by the prehistoric megaliths on the scarp in western Kent. The main areas of significant settlement are thought to have developed primarily along the river valleys as traces of Roman, and possibly earlier, habitations show. A slow colonisation of the poorer lands on the exposed upper Downs occurred up to the Middle Ages and it is this historic settlement pattern of parishes – with boundaries that take in an area of downland, scarpfoot and chartland – that form the basic framework for the present network of settlements found in the area.

The open nature of the Downs owes its appearance to the once widespread regime of grazing by stock and the development of drove roads to move animals to summer pastures or market. Other well-used tracks exist: the North Downs Way which follows the ancient path across the ridge and the Pilgrim's Way taking the righteous to Canterbury.

To the east the Downs still show evidence of their importance as defensive sites; hill forts (such as Bigbury) and second world war remains are relatively common features.

The North Downs landscape has inspired numerous well-known writers and artists who collectively found the area to be a rich source of ideas for their work. For instance, Godmersham Park in the Great Stour Valley between Ashford and Canterbury is believed to have been the setting for Jane Austen's *Mansfield Park*. The dramatic and distinctive White Cliffs of Dover feature not only in Shakespeare's play *King Lear* but also came to symbolise the whole country during the second world war through the famous Vera Lynn wartime song.

MIKE WILLIAMS/COUNTRYSIDE AGENCY

The Devil's Kneading Trough near Wye is one of a number of dry valleys that incise the steep scarp slope. Where traditional grazing practices are no longer maintained, scrub is invading the important chalk grasslands along the scarp face.

Buildings and Settlement

The North Downs is a rural landscape punctuated by a few large settlements such as Guildford, Chatham and Dover. The Kent part is marked by a scattering of small villages. However, where the Downs underlie London towards Croydon and Sutton, they are increasingly dominated by urban development interspersed with a number of species-rich grassland valleys.

Tree-lined tracks and lanes run diagonally down the scarp linking the Downs with the Wealden Greensand to the south. The enclosed lanes are narrow, twisting and steep-sided. Overhung with yew, wayfaring tree and whitebeam, they offer only restricted views in contrast to the extensive views possible from the top of the scarp.

Toward the east, the land becomes more open and intensively farmed, before ending with the renowned white chalk cliffs between Deal and Folkestone.

Buildings of local materials are a significant feature in the landscape of the North Downs, with the use of flint, from the Chalk, as a building material providing a link between the physical and cultural landscapes. The rich orange-reds of Wealden bricks have been commonly used for the corners and door and window surrounds, framing the cool greys and whites of the flints being used in walls.

The Channel Tunnel terminal development dominates the views from the escarpment at the eastern-most end of the Downs where it widens before ending abruptly at the White Cliffs of Dover. The M25 and M20 transport corridors cut through the North Downs (and run parallel in Kent) introducing a discordant feature – plainly visible from the scarp – into an otherwise quiet and peaceful rural landscape.

Land Cover

The land cover of the North Downs is relatively homogenous being largely influenced by soil derived from the extensive occurrence of chalk and clay-with-flint.

The North Downs are more wooded than many other southern Chalk areas, particularly in west Kent and the eastern parts of Surrey between Guildford and Leatherhead. Oak and ash are typical of the upper part of the dip-slope while a mix of beech, ash and maple are commonly found on the chalk soils of the dry valley sides. Much of the upper scarp is wooded with woodland or hawthorn scrub extending onto the dip-slope. In Surrey, extensive areas of

On parts of the dip slope, such as here in Kingswood, Challock, sweet chestnut coppice dominates, with often spectacular carpets of bluebells.

yew with box woodland exist giving a distinctive dark green appearance to parts of the scarp.

Many parts of the Downs retain tracts of species-rich unimproved chalk grassland and, towards the eastern end, traditional grazing is still practised. In contrast, there are also large areas of the chalk grassland on the scarp and valley sides that have been ploughed for arable use.

The Changing Countryside

- Increasing pressures on farmland due to the expansion of urban areas, fragmentation of holdings and pressure from intense recreation use near urban areas; vandalism, fly-tipping and erosion of footpaths are typical issues.

- Scrub invasion of unimproved chalk grassland due to a reduction in grazing levels on the scarp face.

- Removal and lack of active management of trees and woodlands.

- Increased traffic congestion, pressure on car parking facilities and litter are significant problems associated with increasing recreation.

- Noise and visual intrusion from development of new roads and railway lines with extensions to existing routes particularly affecting the scarp; planting associated with highway improvements has resulted in loss of characteristic views from roads along the Downs – for example, along the Hogs Back.

- Storm damage to escarpment woodlands.

- Chalk pits and quarries have dramatically altered the appearance of the landscape. Scars on the scarp face have arisen from past chalk extraction forming highly visible features within the surrounding landscape. Potential adverse impact on the landscape from working of chalk pits for agricultutusal lime.

Flint from the chalk soils is a characteristic building material of the scattered farmhouses and large houses of the north Kent Downs.

RICHARD BARTLEY/WYE VILLAGE DESIGN GROUP

Shaping the Future

- The restoration of suitable arable areas to chalk grassland and traditional management regimes should be considered, together with the conservation of existing unimproved chalk and remnant grassland.

- The wooded character of the scarp face and elsewhere depends on continued management and regeneration.

- Retaining and re-creating views from the scarp crest and from highways would emphasise the open character of the Downs.

- Restoration of habitats previously lost to past chalk extraction and the enhancement of disused sites and spoil heaps would assimilate them more fully into the character of the Downs landscape.

- Many historic parklands are in need of restoration.

- Positive planning and design guidelines are needed to assimilate major transport corridors into the landscape.

- The character of the Downs landscape and its settlements would be enhanced by working with communities and promoting good design.

Selected References

Countryside Commission (1995), *The Kent Downs Landscape CCP 479*, Countryside Commission, Cheltenham.

Kent County Council (1993), *Landscape and Nature Conservation Guidelines*, Kent County Council, Maidstone.

Surrey County Council (1994), *The Future of Surrey's Landscape and Woodlands – Part I: An Assessment (Consultation Draft)*, Surrey County Council.

White, J T (1977), *The South-East Down and Weald: Kent, Surrey and Sussex*, Eyre Methuen, London.

Hull, F (1988), *Ordnance Survey Historical Guides: Kent*, George Philip, London.

Glossary

shaws: strip of trees or bushes forming the border of a field

Wealden Greensand

- Large belt of Greensand typified by its scarp/dip-slope topography and by extensive belts of ancient mixed woodland of hazel, oak and birch together with more recent coniferous colonisation and plantations.

- Large sections of the winding Upper Greensand escarpment are noted for their steep 'hanger' woodlands with areas of remnant heath and wet heath.

- Settlements are generally scattered villages and hamlets linked by deep, overhanging, winding lanes with some small, irregular fields remnant of Saxon clearances.

- The Wealden Greensand in Hampshire and West Sussex comprises areas of high ground supporting a mosaic of open heath, beech/ash or oak/hazel/ash wooded hangers – or pine forest in Sussex – and rough grazing. There are broad river valley plains which support arable farming on light soils with large geometric fields.

- In the western Surrey area, the Wealden Greensand is flat with much heathland and former heathland. Towards the east, the slopes become steeper and are generally densely wooded with an extensive oak/birch/pine cover, numerous small woodlands and also 18th century conifer plantations. Farming is predominantly mixed with dairy pastures in small irregular fields with well-maintained hedgerows and shaws. The latter give a wooded feel to the area.

- In east Surrey and western Kent, there are many wooded commons ('charts') with oak/birch woodland.

- Tree-lined winding sunken lanes connecting small settlements built of sandstone or malmstone and the overall undulating and organic land form combine to give a sense of intimacy to the landscape.

- In the east of Kent, the Wealden Greensand has a gentler and more open aspect than the wooded west. This part of the area is also more marked by development with the presence of major towns and communication corridors such as the M26/M25/M20 and railway lines.

- Fruit growing is still a characteristic feature of the Kent Greensand.

- Older deer parks and more recent 18th century parklands are a distinctive feature of the Wealden Greensand with extensive views out over the Low Weald.

Landscape Character

This long, curved belt runs across Kent parallel to the North Downs and through Surrey, moving south to adjoin the Hampshire Downs before curving back eastwards to run parallel with the South Downs in West Sussex. Its local character varies as a result of changes in local topography, soils and landuse but it is unified throughout the area as a result of underlying geology, scarp/dip-slope topography and the distinctive spring-line settlements below the Downs.

JOHN TYLER/SUSSEX DOWNS CONSERVATION BOARD

Rural cottages display the estate colours.

Extensive belts of woodland, both ancient mixed woods of hazel, oak and birch and more recent coniferous plantations, give the area a well-wooded feel in many

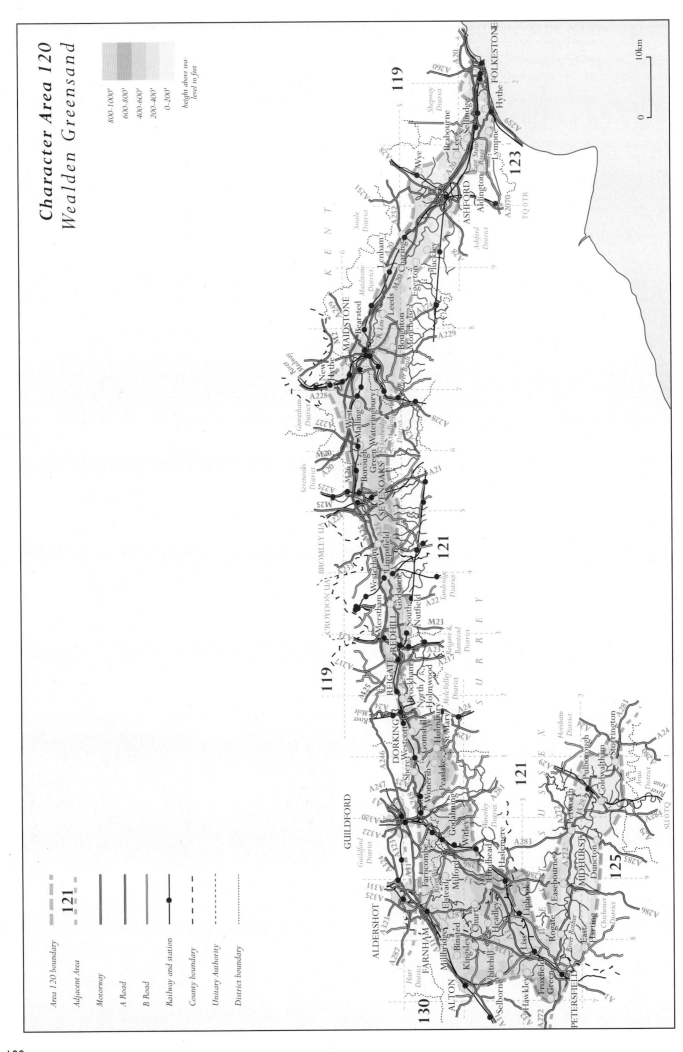

Character Area 120
Wealden Greensand

800-1000'
600-800'
400-600'
200-400'
0-200'

height above sea-level in feet

Area 120 boundary

121 Adjacent Area

Motorway

A Road

B Road

Railway and station

County boundary

Unitary Authority

District boundary

0   10km

places. The dramatic 'hangers' of East Hampshire are a dominating local influence within the Wealden Greensand. Contrast is provided by more open areas of sandy heath and wet heath found on the acidic soils, by the rivers and also by the mixed farming found throughout the belt.

Wooded slopes form the backdrop for pasture valley bottoms with tree-lined rivers.

To the west in Hampshire, Sussex (and west Surrey), the Greensand forms an intimate landscape with a diverse character. Landforms of the western Wealden Greensand vary from the more-or-less parallel sandstone ridges to the dramatic and steep scarp slopes and the rounded clay vales containing river valleys with broad plains. This variety is evident for example, in the Upper Greensand bench at the foot of the Downs in Hampshire. The small pasture fields and linear woodlands of the ridges give way to larger and more regular field patterns where the Greensand merges into the Gault clay. This arable landscape of large geometric fields is encouraged by the light fertile soils of the river Rother plain which cut through the sandstone. It provides a local contrast with the more intimate nature of the sandy soils dominated by small pasture fields. These sandy soils on the higher ground support some extensive heathland. The area is a mosaic of open heath (with some pine encroachment), beech/oak woodland and rough grazing. A few areas of high quality heather heath remain, such as at Iping Common. Other areas of former heath have reverted to rough grazing or have been planted with conifers. Sand and sandstone are quarried and exposed on the Lower Greensand ridges below which springs, fed by the sandstone aquifer, occur at fairly frequent intervals.

A notable feature of the southern arm of the Wealden Greensand is the extensive wetlands of West Sussex, in particular those associated with the river Arun and Amberley Wildbrooks where the water levels are controlled by sluices and the flat, treeless landscape is given vertical interest by the numerous reed-filled ditches.

Further north and east from Hampshire into Surrey, the slopes become steeper and are typically densely wooded; the steep 'hanger' ash or beech woodlands of East Hampshire being a locally dominating feature. Some of the woodlands are of oak/birch/pine but there are also conifer plantations which introduce harsh lines into an otherwise undulating and unstructured landscape. There are many small woodlands scattered through the area. Farming is mixed, with a high proportion of dairying. Hedgerows are in good condition and mark the boundaries of the small irregular fields.

The intimate, almost secretive, feel of much of the west of the Wealden Greensand (that is Hampshire, Sussex and west Surrey) is reinforced by the deep stream-cut gulleys and tree-lined winding sunken lanes leading to small settlements built of sandstone, or more locally, malmstone. Even the larger settlements retain a link with the landscape, not least through the use of local building materials.

This mixed intimate character continues across Surrey with woodland cover increasing. This is the most wooded part of the area with a high proportion of ancient mixed wood. Much of the woodland is, however, the result of conifer plantations on former heathland. Open heath is left only on commons such as Reigate Heath or at Frensham. Wooded commons known as 'charts' are a characteristic feature of this part of the Greensand as it moves into western Kent where the wooded topography intensifies and is particularly dramatic. Besides the woodland, the Surrey Greensand is characterised by open rolling farmland. In the south a traditional farmscape of small fields and thick hedgerows is retained. On flatter land, however, arable use is more common resulting in a loss of typical character. Some of the farmland in this heavily populated area is given over to small holdings and pony paddocks which can appear scruffy and unkempt, particularly where hedgerows are damaged and replaced with wire fences. The main river valley is the river Wey which cuts a broad watery plain with open meadows and typical waterside vegetation, including willow and alder. The Surrey Greensand is particularly important for recreation, as it is easily accessible from London and many of Surrey's major towns. The overall landscape, although mixed, is unified by the wooded character engendered by the many woodlands and shaws. In many areas the settlements and gardens bring a suburban feel and some smallholdings can often appear out of place. This can sometimes diminish the more natural character but provides contrast and variety within the landscape.

Further east, into Kent, and beyond the dramatic wooded topography, the Greensand becomes less distinctive. Although sunken lanes and hidden valleys are a feature of the area around Sevenoaks and Maidstone, the landscape here, being less wooded, does not give such an impression of intimacy unless contained by remaining hedgerows and shelterbelts. The area is also more marked by modern human influence with major towns such as Maidstone, Sevenoaks and Ashford and numerous communication routes. Notable among the latter are the M25 and M26 near Sevenoaks and the M20 and rail lines around Ashford which follow the vale below the North Downs scarp. Generally the Kent Wealden Greensand in the east has a sandy and heathy feel and the landscape is relatively more open with mixed farming. The central area of the belt near the Medway, where lighter loams occur, is a major fruit growing area with orchards and associated windbreaks, plus chestnut coppice for hop poles. These introduce a more regular pattern of straight lines into the landscape. Hop growing is particularly common around Maidstone. Further east, however, both orchards and hops are being replaced by arable fields which are often irregular in shape reflecting the changes in landform. At its south eastern extreme the Greensand forms a notable scarp, formerly a sea cliff, giving extensive views over Romney Marshes. Panoramic views across the Low Weald are frequent and extensive from the Greensand ridge above the scarp face.

Designed parkland is a common feature within the greensand. Much of it is threatened by fragmentation through lack of appropriate management.

Physical Influences

This region includes the outcrops of Upper Greensand, Gault and Lower Greensand. In general terms the Upper Greensand and Lower Greensand form escarpments, separated by a clay vale formed on the Gault Clay.

The wide range of lithologies, from clay to sandstone in close proximity, give rise to many localised variations of land use and woodland cover. The soil ranges from poorly-drained alkaline over the Gault to free-draining acidic over the Folkestone Beds.

In the west, below the chalk escarpment of the North Downs, a low bench of Upper Greensand at the foot of the chalk escarpment is deeply incised in places by springline streams. Further away from the chalk escarpments, Gault Clay lowlands give way to the Lower Greensand rocks which include Folkestone Beds, Sandgate Beds and Hythe Beds. The coarse-grained, acidic and free-draining Folkestone Beds form a broad escarpment often associated with tracts of heaths and commons. The Sandgate Beds which give rise to heavier and wetter soils are often dominated by pasture. Major rivers such as the Rother flow in narrow alluvial floodplains across the easily eroded Sandgate Beds. The most elevated and steeply undulating relief is formed by the resistant calcareous sandstone (known as ragstone) of the Hythe Beds which form the main part of the escarpment. They support lime-tolerant plant communities in the otherwise generally acidic soil conditions of the Greensand region.

Areas of soft sandstone are easily eroded producing distinctive sunken lanes in the Greensand, cut deeply into the rock below the surrounding land surface. These lanes are historical and characteristic features of the landscape and are also used as part of the modern road system.

In contrast to the North Downs, surface water is an important feature on the Greensand. Streams and rivers drain off the dip-slope and there are many flooded quarry workings which are commonly hidden by trees from distant views.

Historical and Cultural Influences

The Wealden Greensand has been occupied since earliest times. Evidence of early occupation at Oldbury Hill in Kent is provided by the presence of palaeolithic flint tools and, at Abinger, traces of a neolithic hearth from c5000 BC suggest that this could be the oldest village in England!

Bronze Age tumuli are evident near Petersfield and are common on the higher ground of heathlands in Sussex. Iron Age forts exist, for example at Holmbury, Anstiebury and at Oldbury Hill. The Pilgrim's Way prehistoric track of the North Downs runs parallel to the Greensand and is closely associated with these features.

In contrast to the winding, eroded, sandstone lanes of the wooded west, Roman roads radiate from Canterbury to Ashford and Lympne and thence to Maidstone.

The Wealden Greensand area has significant woodland and estate parkland. The former has always been diverse, the lighter heathy soils of areas like Leith Hill having been planted with conifers and the heavier soils supporting

Walkers get a sense of seclusion walking along the sunken lanes and overgrown paths.

coppice and mixed woodland. There has been a considerable reduction in the amount of heathland since the 19th century.

The woodland provides a backdrop to the many landscaped parks of the area and has been used by designers such as Capability Brown to frame 18th and 19th century landscapes. Petworth in Sussex, Knole, Squerries Court and Leeds Castle in Kent are particular examples of the genre, together with Albury Park designed by John Evelyn, the 'father of silviculture' and many smaller gardens influenced by Jekyll and Lutyens. Artists such as Samuel Palmer, who had links with the Darent Valley, reflected the area in their paintings and Gilbert White, at Selborne in Hampshire, created his own small-scale designed landscape at his home using the dramatic hanger woodlands as his backdrop.

There are numerous quarries for local distinctive building stone, Ragstone or Bargate Stone and there is a history of disturbance to the landscape through mineral and sand abstraction. Other industry has concentrated along the river

valleys with the use of water power and charcoal. Iron workings, based on the local occurrence of ironstone, used Wealden timber and the associated hammer ponds are plentiful along the foot of the northwest escarpment. Water mills and some windmills were a source of energy and industry in the Tillingbourne and Rother Valleys.

Prosperity arrived in the 19th century with improvements in road and rail travel, turning much of the northern segment of the Wealden Greensand into a commuter belt. Original communication links ran in a strong east-west alignment along the lighter soils and ridge lines. North-south links remain relatively poor, whilst east-west links have strengthened. The south-east railway connected London to Dover in 1844 and subsequent links through the M20 and M26 have reinforced this particular transport corridor.

Small settlements are dispersed throughout the western and south-western segment of the character area, linked by historic sunken lanes. Rural buildings are typically of local tile-hung ragstone or malmstone. Continued building has left a scattering of modern houses and large gardens, introducing urban influences into rural areas.

Buildings and Settlement

In the eastern Greensand, timber-framed buildings are a feature of the local landscape, as is weatherboarding. Many of the typical Greensand cottages and houses date from the 17th century or earlier. They typically have walls of tawny-brown sandstone, laid in rubble courses, often patterned by tiny pieces of dark carrstone in the mortar between the stones. This process known as 'galletting' was imitated in the late 19th century Arts and Crafts houses which also have elaborate large chimneys and intricate corner and window details of tile creasing.

Large houses set within extensive gardens are also found all over the Greensand. The gardens, often extensively wooded, screen the houses from view and contribute to the general impression of dense woodland.

The Hythe Beds provided hard stone for local buildings whereas the Folkestone Beds are a source of sand used in building. This has resulted in numerous quarries which are visible from elevated viewpoints. Malmstone and hearthstone in the Upper Greensand have also been quarried for building stone in East Hampshire. The Hythe Beds provide hard building stone in the form of ragstone or bargate stone which is extracted from numerous quarries particularly visible from the North Downs scarp. This stone is a distinctive feature of local buildings in Kent and significant in Surrey, particularly in rural areas.

Much of the eastern linear Greensand belt is heavily dominated by modern developments including substantial urban settlements, major road and rail networks and other forms of economic activity.

Land Cover

Away from the Gault Clay, the Wealden Greensand is generally noted for its cover of broadleaved and coniferous woodland within a network of pasture with hedgerows, arable land and heathland.

The diversity of soils is reflected in a similar range of woodlands. On the Gault clay there are semi-natural ancient woodlands which were formerly traditionally managed woods. Oak standards and birch are prevalent on the lower Greensand while ash and hazel dominate the gault clays and upper Greensand with dogwood, elm, some small-leaved lime and sycamore, some oak and a diverse ground flora. Banks and ditches are frequent in these woods, together with occasional large ash stools, all evidence of the wood's age. Where the soil becomes more acid, holly, hawthorn, bramble and bracken begin to be found.

The outcrops of the Folkestone Beds produce more acidic sandy soils and the woods are generally oak and birch, associated with former heaths. Other species such as Scots pine, sweet chestnut, holly, rowan, hawthorn, bilberry and elm are also present. In all woods, wetter areas have willow and, to a lesser extent, alder, with ash, hawthorn, oak, hazel, birch and nettles.

The character and content of hedges also, to some extent, reflects their soils. On the Gault clay, hedges tend to be species-rich: dense at the base, they occasionally have a few oak trees distributed along their lengths. On more acidic soils hedges have fewer species and often consist of only blackthorn or hawthorn. These are dense and trimmed low, with occasional oak trees, but are sometimes gappy. Without management, these hedges have grown into lines of tall shrubs, often comprising belts of ash, sycamore, oak, hawthorn or hazel hedgerow trees. Few hedges and unstructured fields is the pattern discernible in the north-west of Sussex where small rough pastures are used for horse grazing.

Ancient semi-natural woodland on the Wealden Greensand survives mainly on river valley floors and on steep slopes. Ancient woodland is scarce on the Greensand plateau itself. These woodlands on the steep slopes of the scarp in the west of the area, comprise the hangers landscape for which the Greensand is renowned. The wooded commons (charts) of Kent and Surrey are also known local landscape features and can be considered ancient woodland.

Up to the early 20th century the area was much more open with extensive heathland but new conifer plantations and scrub invasion on a wide scale have reduced the area of heath. Forestry plantations are a dominant land use within the Greensands, significantly contributing to the overall wooded character.

Traditional agricultural practices in the area include the fruit growing orchard belt where fields are separated with alder and poplar windbreaks. Recent conversion to arable farmland has reduced this area. Hops and chestnut coppices producing hop poles are also traditional of the area. Mixed farming, permanent pasture and arable farming is seen amongst the woodlands, commons and heaths. It is a zone of medium- and small-sized irregular fields and enclosed strip fields with a diminished hedgerow component.

The Changing Countryside

- Loss of heath; open heathland commons are compromised by encroaching birch, oak and pine scrub due to a decline in traditional management regimes which eventually obscures the characteristic open views from tops of hills.

- Past planting of conifers in ancient woodland has altered the character of these important features.

- The visual intrusion of mineral extraction operations has significantly affected certain parts of the Greensand – for example, sand extraction above Seale is very prominent when viewed from the Hog's Back in the adjacent North Downs character area.

- Old landfill sites within former sand pits do not enhance the local landscape.

- Loss or neglect of traditional woodland coppice, fruit orchards and hedgerows.

- Localised damage from the 1987 storm.

- Potential landscape impacts arising from the development of the Channel Tunnel High Speed Rail Link and motorway widening schemes.

- Former commons and heaths associated with large military establishments have been to some extent protected from pressures often associated with public access and agricultural intensification. However, in other areas, military land use has resulted in significant landscape change.

- Fragmentation and degradation of designed parklands.

- General degradation of major river-floodplain landscapes.

- New roads and improvements often lead to the erosion of the enclosed and winding character of the local road network.

Shaping the Future

- There are opportunities for the restoration of heathland by scrub and tree removal. Land, formerly owned by the Ministry of Defence, may provide scope for increased conservation of heaths.

- The conservation of woodlands, fruit orchards, hop gardens and traditional coppice should be addressed.

- The sensitive design, layout and routes for major communications development is important within the character area.

- Many existing mineral extraction sites and landfill sites in former sand pits need assimilating into the landscape.

- The enhancement of hedgerows and other features needs consideration through appropriate agri-environmental land management schemes.

- Many historic and designed parklands are in need of restoration

Selected References

Kent County Council (1993), *Landscape and Nature Conservation Guidelines*, Kent County Council, Maidstone.

Dipper, S (1995), *Landscape Assessment of West Sussex – Section 1*, West Sussex County Council, West Sussex.

Countryside Commission (1991), *The East Hampshire Landscape CCP 358*, Countryside Commission, Cheltenham.

Landscape Design Associates (1995), *A Landscape Assessment of the Sussex Downs AONB*, unpublished.

White, J T (1977), *The South-East Down and Weald: Kent, Surrey and Sussex*, Eyre Methuen, London.

University of Sussex, The Geography Editorial Committee (1983), *Sussex: Environment, Landscape and Society*, Alan Sutton, Gloucester.

Glossary

hanger: a wood on the side of a steep hill

shaws: strip of trees or bushes forming the border of a field

Low Weald

- Broad, low lying and gently undulating clay vales underlie a small-scale intimate landscape enclosed by an intricate mix of small woodlands, a patchwork of fields and hedgerows.

- Topography and soils vary locally in relation to higher drier outcrops of limestone or sandstone, which are commonly sites of settlements.

- The Low Weald generally includes an abundance of ponds and small stream valleys often with wet woodlands of alder and willow.

- Tall hedgerows with numerous mature trees link copses, shaws and remnant woodlands which combine to give the Low Weald a well-wooded character. Field trees, usually of oak but now declining, are characteristic of the area south-east of Dorking.

- Grassland predominates on the heavy clay soils while lighter soils on higher ground support arable cropping in a more open landscape.

- Rural in character with dispersed farmsteads, small settlements often include many timber and brick-built traditional buildings where not now dominated by recent urban development.

- Historic settlement pattern was dictated by a preference for higher drier outcrops of limestone or sandstone with moated manor houses being a characteristic feature.

- Urban and airport related development sprawl in the flat plain around Gatwick, and in the Horley-Crawley commuter settlements, contrast with the pleasant, wet, woody, rural character of the area and as such are less distinctively Wealden.

- Hop growing and orchards are still a distinctive land use in the east.

- The Kentish Low Weald is traversed by numerous narrow lanes with broad verges and ditches; these are continuous with the drove roads of the North Downs.

The Low Weald is a broad low-lying clay vale which runs around three sides of the High Weald through Kent, Sussex and Surrey, bounded for much of its length by the Wealden Greensand. Topography and soils vary with higher drier pockets of land on the outcrops of limestone or sandstone - which are commonly the sites of settlements – within the often flat and wet soils of the vale.

MARTIN JONES/COUNTRYSIDE AGENCY

Many small towns and villages have been targeted for new housing development. Much is being constructed to national standards and has little in common with local characteristics.

The area is well-wooded, with many of the fields created by woodland clearance. It is also rich in ponds and small streams with riparian willows and alders reflecting its wet nature. Ponds are also evidence of a history of brickmaking, marl pits and the iron industry. Where major river valleys, notably the Arun, Adur, Beult and Medway, cross the Low Weald this wet character is accentuated by wet grazing lands with willow and sallow scrub. The Adur in particular has extensive wetland habitats in this character area, including marshes with water levels controlled by complex sluice systems.

Hedgerows are tall with many mature trees and run between small copses of oak and birch. Chestnut and hornbeam coppice is also frequent, in many places a relic of the Low Weald's industrial history of charcoal burning for iron and glass production. The area is also characterised by remnant

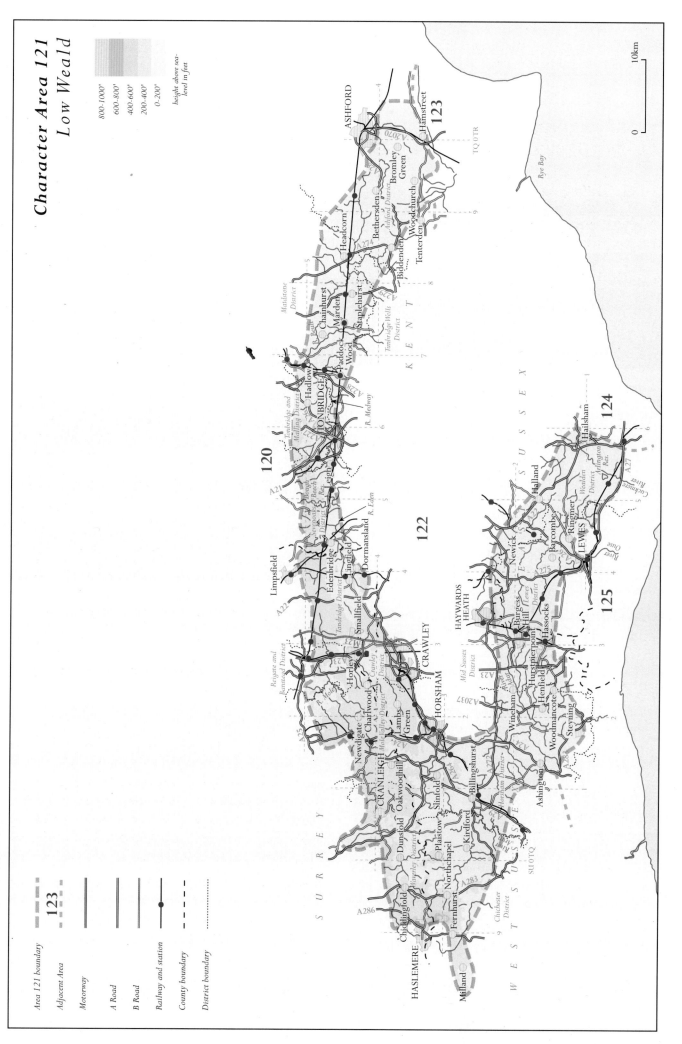

Character Area 121
Low Weald

height above sea-
level in feet

800-1000'
600-800'
400-600'
200-400'
0-200'

Area 121 boundary

123 Adjacent Area

Motorway

A Road

B Road

Railway and station

County boundary

District boundary

10km

ASHFORD
Hamstreet
123
Bromley
Green
Woodchurch
Headcorn
Bethersden
Biddenden
Tenterden
A274
A229
Maidstone
District
Chainhurst
Marden
Staplehurst
Tunbridge Wells
District
R. Beult
Paddock
Wood
Hadlow
K E N T
Tonbridge and
Malling District
TONBRIDGE
R. Medway
A228
Leigh
A21
Penshurst Beach
Res.
Bough
Sevenoaks
District
Edenbridge
Lingfield
Dormansland
R. Eden
120
Limpsfield
A22
Smallfield
Tandridge District
Reigate and
Banstead District
A25
Horley
Crawley
District
Crawley
A23
HAYWARDS
HEATH
CRAWLEY
A264
122
Newdigate
Charlwood
Mole Valley District
Lambs
Green
R. Mole
HORSHAM
A281
Horsham District
A24
A2037
River Adur
Billingshurst
A272
Wineham
A281
Henfield
A283
Ashington
A24
Steyning
Woodmancote
A283
Dupsfold
Oakwoodhill
Slinfold
Plaistow
Kirdford
Northchapel
Chichester
District
A283
Chiddingfold
A286
Fernhurst
W E S T   S U S S E X
HASLEMERE
Milland
Waverley District
S U R R E Y

Halland
Newick
A272
Hassocks
Burgess
Hill
Hurstpierpoint
Mid Sussex
District
E A S T   S U S S E X
Ringmer
Barcombe
Lewes
District
River
Ouse
LEWES
A26
A275
124
Hailsham
Wealden
District
Arlington
Res.
Cuckmere
River
A27
125

Rye Bay

107

strips of cleared woodland or 'shaws' which combine with the generally small, densely hedged field enclosures to enhance the woody nature of much of the vale. Other parts of the Low Weald to the south-west, in Sussex for instance, are often more open and exposed in character.

Traditional orange-red brick and tile hung buildings reflect the use of local Weald clays and provide vivid contrast with rich green vegetation.

Agriculture in the Low Weald is largely pastoral due to the heavy clay soils with either forage or grazed grassland. However, where there are lighter soils on slightly higher ground a more mixed farming is found, including arable and fruit growing on the drift deposits of brickearths in Kent. Arable cropping is often associated with larger fields, a much more sparse hedge pattern and fewer trees in contrast to the characteristic well-wooded pastoral appearance of the Low Weald.

Much of the Low Weald is essentially rural in character and has a pleasant wet woody character. Settlements are mainly villages or small hamlets and usually built of brick reflecting the use of local Weald clays, or more locally (as at Horsham) of stone for roofs, providing islets of very local character. Timber-framed buildings are common at the eastern (Kent) end of the Weald, with oast houses and weatherboarding in the fruit and hop growing areas close to Romney Marsh.

The most notable variation in the Low Weald character is provided by the contrast of the urban and airport sprawl in the flat plain around Gatwick, including the Horley-Crawley area. The natural character of this area is flatter and less-wooded, ie less distinctively Wealden, and the airport and associated road and rail developments have destroyed its rural feel. Major settlements at Crawley and Horley have resulted in suburban sprawl within the rural character of the Low Weald.

The clay soils produce rich green grassland and woodland vegetation which provide a vivid contrast to the intense orange-reds of the locally produced Wealden clay bricks characteristic of many of the Low Weald villages.

The well-wooded character restricts many views within the area although even small rises in terrain permit longer views. Parts of the Low Weald have an unusual remote quality, especially in Kent. Elevated landforms outside the character area such as the Wealden Greensand, the North and South Downs and the High Weald form important backdrops in many views.

Physical Influences

The Low Weald area coincides with the outcrop of the Weald Clay, lying below the irregular escarpment of the Greensand belt and the Chalk. It gives rise to a broad vale that is typically low-lying and undulating, rarely exceeding more than 30 m - 40 m AOD, with many areas as low as 15 metres. Towards the south, the undulations become rolling and larger in scale.

Carpets of bluebells are typical of the significant areas of semi-natural woodland. The characteristic oak standard over hazel coppice reflects past management.

Localised deposits of limestone and sandstone form gentle ridges and high points throughout the Low Weald. In many places, these are the sites of farmsteads, hamlets or larger settlements. The Weald Clay produces heavy, poorly-drained soils which are nutrient-poor and are largely used as pastureland, with arable crops less common. Drift deposits of brickearths in the Kent area give rise to good quality soils suitable for hop and fruit growing. It also supports a prosperous brick and tile-making industry, producing a wide range of bricks from numerous sites. As the deposits extend to deep levels, surface disturbance and visual impact caused by excavations are relatively minimal.

The Low Weald is heavily dissected by river floodplains and many small, narrow and commonly sunken streams cut into the heavy clays locally, forming flat low-lying areas, such as the plain around Gatwick. Ponds are frequent on the edges of fields and in woodlands although they tend to be small and are often silted up. Some are the result of past quarrying for brick-making, marl pits or the early iron industry. Much of the area is subject to localised flooding.

Historical and Cultural Influences

A Roman iron industry that once thrived in the Low Weald was revived from the late 15th century. It left old hammer ponds, which are now valuable archaeological and wildlife sites, and has also ensured the management and survival of large areas of woodland.

The wild and wooded appearance of the Wealden area led the Romans to call this area *Sylva Anderida* which the Saxons later amended to *Andredsweald*. Deforestation in subsequent centuries, mainly for shipbuilding and charcoal smelting, has left only remnants of the original wood in existence today. The Low Weald retained a high woodland cover until Domesday, when about two-thirds of the area was still wooded. Clearance was very piecemeal, often leaving belts of wood known as 'shaws' between fields. Today many fields are still bounded by these shaws while other fields are formed from cleared land along woodland edges (assarts), typically resulting in woods with very irregular shapes. This led to the characteristic settlement pattern of small hamlets and ancient farmsteads. Many hedges may also have originated as remnant woodland strips as reflected by their often species-rich composition, including ancient woodland indicator species.

The Low Weald has inspired poets such as Edmund Blunden and 20th century artists such as Rowland Hilder. The Low Weald landscape is also the setting for H E Bates' *Larkin* books dramatised as *The Darling Buds of May*.

Buildings and Settlement

Owing to the original wooded nature and heavy clays of the Low Weald, settlements tend to be very small and scattered and are often just linear groups of houses along roadsides following transport corridors through the Weald. Many villages are centred on greens or commons. The majority of rural buildings are traditional in character with the common use of local brick weatherboarding and tile-hung buildings. Older houses are half-timbered, locally with slate roofs. The muted colours of the soft grey of the timber, the gentle ochre or white-washed walls and the massive greeny-grey stone tiles (Horsham slabs) provide contrast with the greens of their rural settings. Black weather-boarded barns with half-hipped roofs are also common features.

Although many lanes are narrow and enclosed between hedges, with occasional views from gateways, the poor ground conditions for early travellers resulted in broad trackways to allow horse-drawn vehicles to avoid water-logged areas. This is still reflected today in the many country roads with wide verges and attendant ditches that cross the area.

Land Cover

The heavy clay soils are notoriously difficult to cultivate so that permanent pasture is the main farming use. Arable farming is associated with the lighter soils on higher ground and there is fruit farming in the east in Kent. Fields are generally small and irregular, divided by a dense network of hedges and shaws that create a small-scale landscape, except where hedges have been removed. Occasional lines of single trees mark out vanished field hedges while small copses and tree groups frequently occur within the fields and as part of the hedgerow pattern. Hedges are generally species-rich with oak, ash, field maple and holly also occurring as hedgerow trees. Many of these hedges typically occur as low, square-cut or tall, uncut hedges. Many were still woodland strips as recently as the late 19th century.

The extent of woodland cover varies depending on the original level of clearance for agriculture, yet a good deal remains. Broadleaved woodland is common and significant areas of semi-natural ancient woodland occur, particularly below the Wealden Greensand. The ancient character of many woods is reflected by their large coppice stools, banks and ditches. Oak is the principal tree of the Low Weald and the characteristic woodland often has oak standards over hazel coppice. Areas of base-rich soil on limestone outcrops support ash with field maple and hazel. In addition to these woodland types there are pockets of older coppice with mosses and sedges often invaded by birch. Coppiced woodland varies between chestnut, hornbeam or hazel, with goat willow, hawthorn and holly as shrub species. Shaws are remnants of more extensive woodland and therefore have similar species and have often been managed in similar ways. For example, the wider shaws are often coppice with standards.

The courses of the many small rivers and streams that meander across the Low Weald are marked by numerous riparian trees. In many cases, the ponds, unimproved permanent pastures, road verges, small rivers and streams of the Low Weald are habitats of high value for nature-conservation.

The Changing Countryside

- Urban influences have affected many large parts of the rural area, especially around Gatwick Airport and Horley, owing to the accessibility and popularity of the character area.

- Development pressure is focused mainly on the towns and the area on the boundary between the Low Weald and the High Weald (an Area of Outstanding Natural Beauty).

JOHN TYLER/SUSSEX DOWNS CONSERVATION BOARD

Views from the South Downs show the low lying gently undulating Low Weald with its mosaic of pasture, arable and mature woodland linked by hedgerows.

- Continuing creeping fragmentation of farmland around houses into gardens or pony paddocks, sometimes with conifer hedges.

- Past pressures on ancient woodland arising from past conversion to conifer plantations, damage through neglect, and/or damage through old consents for the working of clay pits.

- Loss and decline of hedges and hedgerow trees, and consequential fragmentation of landscape structure, due to lack of management and farm diversification.

- Riparian landscapes under pressure from decline and neglect, including loss of farm ponds, as agricultural practices have intensified.

- Loss of traditional hop gardens, orchards and associated wind-break features.

Shaping the Future

- Conservation of characteristic shaws, ancient woodlands and coppice should be considered.

- New woodland planting of shaws and hedgerows would help integrate existing and proposed developments.

- The conservation of farm woodlands, riparian landscape features and ponds would be beneficial.

- The retention of the character of rural lanes is important.

- The restoration, conservation and re-creation of hedges within the Low Weald, including new planting of hedgerow trees, would improve the landscape structure.

Selected References

White, J T (1977), *The South-East Down and Weald: Kent, Surrey and Sussex*, Eyre Methuen, London.

Kent County Council (1993), *Landscape and Nature Conservation Guidelines*, Kent County Council, Maidstone.

Brandon, P (1970), *The Sussex Landscape*, Hodder and Stoughton, London.

Surrey County Council (1994), *The Future of Surrey's Landscape and Woodlands – Part 1: An Assessment (Consultation Draft)*, Surrey County Council.

Glossary

AOD: Above Ordnance Datum

islet: little island or small piece of land markedly different from its surroundings

shaws: strip of trees or bushes forming the border of a field

STEPHEN DAVIS

Damp grassland is characteristic of the whole area, occurring on poorly drained heavy clays. Where the land has not been agriculturally improved, species such as green winged orchid and meadow saxifrage can be found. The densely hedged fields enhance the wooded character of the area.

High Weald

Key Characteristics

- A well-wooded landscape rising above the Low Weald and deeply incised in many places to give a complex pattern of ridges and steep stream valleys.

- Distinctive and scattered sandstone outcrops or 'bluffs' rise above the farmland and woodland.

- The Ashdown Forest, in contrast to the more intimate green woods and pastures elsewhere, is a high, rolling and open heathland lying on the sandstone ridges to the west of the area.

- Main roads and settlements are sited along the prominent ridge-lines with a dense network of small, narrow, and winding lanes linking scattered villages, hamlets and farms. Large reservoirs are significant features within the High Weald landscape adding to the area's interest and variety.

- The legacy of the early iron industry, based on sandstone, ore, water and timber, has left extensive areas of coppice woodland and the characteristic 'hammer ponds' which provided power.

- High forest, small woods and copses, and a network of hedges and shaws link small, irregular fields created from cleared woodland. Many of these contain flower-rich meadows bordered by species-rich hedgerows. Heavy clay soils have reduced the impact of agricultural change in the area and it is still, in the main, a quiet pastoral landscape with mixed farming predominating.

- The cultivation of fruit and hops, together with the associated distinctive oast houses and the seasonal appearance of hop poles, are still a characteristic feature of the eastern High Weald.

- Distinctive red tile, brick, local stone and timber building materials, often including hung tiles and white weatherboarding, are characteristic of the historic settlements, farms and cottages. Local building materials characterise the area but recent 'suburbanisation' of farmstead buildings is eroding the distinctive local style in many places.

JOHN TYLER/COUNTRYSIDE AGENCY

Settlements were traditionally sited on the drier ridge tops whilst the slopes and valley bottoms form a mosaic of pasture, arable and woodland linked by hedgerows and shaws.

Landscape Character

The High Weald character area lies at the core of the Wealden anticline. The Greensand, Chalk and Wealden Clay to the north, south and west surround the sandstones and clays which underlie the forested ridges of the High Weald. The central sandstone core is strongly dissected by many major rivers, the headwaters of which have cut numerous steep-sided valleys or 'ghylls', several of which are heavily wooded. From a distance, the appearance of the High Weald is one of a densely wooded landscape although closer inspection reveals a patchwork of fields, hedges and woods forming both open and enclosed landscapes along the rolling ridges and within the valleys.

Even more enclosed than the neighbouring Low Weald, the High Weald is – or feels – very secretive. The mosaic of small hedged fields and sunken lanes, together with the wooded relief and comparative inaccessibility, provides a sense of remoteness which is rare within lowland England landscapes.

Character Area 122
High Weald

Ashdown Forest consists of open rolling heathland, birch woodland and scattered Scots pine on the sandstone ridge of the High Weald. The Forest forms the literary landscape much loved by readers of 'Winnie the Pooh'.

Typically, the roads, towns, villages and farms are sited on the ridges, with the damper, wooded valleys mainly unsettled. Vernacular buildings have a strong local character influenced by a variation in locally available building materials and there is an abundance of white weatherboard, brick, tile, stone or plaster buildings. Numerous oast houses add to the local distinctiveness with stone church towers and spires located on ridges standing as major local landmarks.

Within the forested ridges and ancient countryside, hidden reservoirs constitute significant local features in the landscape. These reservoirs have a distinctive branching or winding character as a result of their creation from small Wealden river valleys.

Along the English Channel coast, the High Weald gives way to eroded sandstone and clay sea cliffs around Fairlight and disappears under the urban areas of Bexhill and Hastings to the south east. The eastern end of the High Weald is characterised by a series of broad, often flat-bottomed, river valleys opening out towards the coastal levels of Romney Marsh between Tenterden and Fairlight.

Physical Influences

The High Weald is underlaid by the Hastings Beds which comprise interbedded sands, soft sandstones and clays which give rise to the high, broken ground. Although not exceeding 240 m AOD, the High Weald is a hilly country of ridges and valleys. Numerous major ridges run mainly east to west, for example the Ashdown Forest Ridge and the Battle Ridge.

These major ridges are deeply dissected by many tributaries of rivers which rise in the High Weald producing a network of small, steep-sided ridges and valleys (ghylls). Low lines of sandstone often line these valleys, as at Eridge, where they provide the only inland rock climbing in South East England. The major rivers draining the High Weald are the

Rother, Brede, Ouse and Medway which flow in broad valleys running roughly east to west.

North-west of Battle, Jurassic Purbeck Limestone contains gypsum beds which were formerly mined.

Historical and Cultural Influences

Clearance of the Wealden forest on a significant scale did not begin until the 9th century, reaching a peak in the 13th and 14th centuries. From the mid-14th century until the first world war the High Weald was relatively unchanged and even today many of the traditional field patterns and woodlands associated with the essentially medieval landscape still remain.

Medieval farmers were responsible for shaping the present day landscape of small fields and scattered farmsteads, with woodland and shaws left amongst them. Steep valleys were left un-felled to form 'ghyll woodlands'. The river valleys and the higher, drier ridge tops were important lines of communication on which early settlements were located.

The medieval pattern of dispersed farms, small hamlets and villages is associated with the practice of cultivating small parcels of land for rent – 'assarting' – which gave rise to the pattern of ad hoc rural settlement. These early, isolated, agricultural settlements later evolved into the characteristic High Weald hilltop villages such as Mayfield, Wadhurst and Hawkhurst.

The influence of the Wealden iron industry extended over 2000 years, features of which – such as the hammer ponds – have survived to the present day. These consist of a stairway of ponds created by damming a 'ghyll'. This produced a head of water which worked the bellows for smelting and the forges' tilt hammers. From the 15th to the 17th century, the High Weald was the foundry of England. Extensive woodland management in the form of coppicing (for charcoal for the forges) accompanied the industry and little clearance was undertaken. The wealth generated by the iron industry funded grand houses and parklands, many of which still stand today.

Heathland was historically more widespread in the High Weald than it is today. Cessation of grazing, together with new conifer planting has led to the loss of open heathland, the only sizeable heathland remaining in the High Weald being Ashdown Forest, a former Royal Hunting Forest.

Buildings and Settlement

The High Weald is characterised by a dispersed settlement pattern of hamlets and scattered farmsteads dating from the medieval period, with large towns such as Tunbridge Wells, Crowborough, East Grinstead, Bexhill, Hastings and Horsham.

The High Weald consists of many examples of high-quality vernacular architecture with distinct local variation. Oak grown as standards in coppice and used green, is found in surviving timber-framed houses and barns. Stone tiles from Horsham, used for the roofs of larger homes and farm buildings, were typical before red clay plain tiles became ubiquitous. Brick and stone walls are common, usually clad in characteristic softwood weatherboarding and tile. Timber-framed barns are also a particularly notable and characteristic feature of the High Weald.

Traditional buildings reflect the use of local materials, such as redbrick and tiles.

A network of lanes, many of which are sunken between high hedges, links the numerous villages and towns. Ribbon development along the network of lanes has, in many places, brought a suburban feel to the well-wooded landscape. Typically the towns, villages and farmsteads are sited on the ridges such as at West Hoathly, Battle, Mayfield and Burwash.

Many new housing developments on the fringes of towns such as Heathfield, Crowborough and Horsham are a contrast to the traditional character of the High Weald's small villages and farmsteads.

Due to the wealth created by the Iron Industry and the intricate wooded topography, the High Weald contains many grand houses and estates, such as Repton's Bayham Abbey landscape. Gardens, such as those at Penshurst and Sissinghurst are a feature of the area and the parkland at Eridge is one of the oldest deer parks in the area.

Land Cover

The dominant land-use is grassland supporting mainly sheep grazing with some cattle and pigs. Within this complex small-scale agricultural landscape there are variations in local land use. These are due to subtle changes in the soils

and range from hops and orchards on the better soils of the Kent river valley bottoms to the sandy heaths of Ashdown Forest in the west. The generally nutrient-poor soils, all prone to waterlogging, have meant that the High Weald has retained much of its woodland cover. Remnants of former hunting forests dating back from the time of the Norman conquests are present today, surviving as ancient oak and beech pollards with associated elaborate systems of boundary banks and ditches.

The patchwork landscape of small woodlands, small fields and hedgerows dissected by river valleys, wide roadside verges, ponds and old churchyards, support a wealth of plant species across a wide range of habitats. Relic heathland, ancient semi-natural woodland, wooded ghylls and some remaining unimproved herb-rich meadows are all characteristic High Weald habitats. The overriding character of the woodland is broadleaved, often ancient in origin, with a few large blocks and many smaller woodlands interconnected by hedgerows and broad strips of woodland or shaws. Numerous conifer plantations such as at St Leonard's Forest are locally dominant features and contribute to the overall wooded character.

Heathy areas occur in open spaces and along rides in the woodlands on lighter soils in the western area. Mature hedgerow trees within the well-established hedge network reinforce the illusion of a well-wooded landscape with the notably high number of ponds, characteristic of the High Weald, creating interesting variety and contrast.

Diversification on farms has introduced features more appropriate to a suburban landscape.

The Changing Countryside

- Development around built-up areas throughout the region, but particularly in the north and west related to the location of railway lines and stations and on the fringes between the Low and High Weald areas.

- Loss of characteristic landscape features such as hedgerows, meadows, wooded ghylls, hammer ponds and parklands due to inappropriate management.

- Loss of heathland due to cessation of grazing, notably in Ashdown Forest.

- Fragmentation of agricultural holdings due to the marginal nature of farmland – renovation of farm buildings by urban-based owners and the associated introduction of non-characteristic materials, details, designs and exotic tree species – also other forms of diversification of marginal farmland to new uses such as fish farms, craft workshops, etc.

- Decline in use of vernacular building materials in new developments and introduction of urban features such as lighting and alarms.

- Decline in traditional management and neglect of small coppice woodlands, traditional orchards and hop gardens.

- An increase in road traffic above levels acceptable for the rural nature of the generally small roads and winding lanes with subsequent increase in conflicts between motorised traffic, pedestrians, horse-riders and cyclists.

- Pressures on the landscape from new main roads and improvements.

- Incipient forces for change from new land uses such as pony paddocks and associated clutter, tennis courts, street lighting and from golf courses.

- Loss of remoteness and erosion of local character by suburban type development and materials.

- Replacement of characteristic hedges with conifers, concrete or close-boarded fences around urban edges.

Shaping the Future

- Appropriate management measures would prevent a further decline in the extent and quality of coppice woodlands and shaws. New native broadleaved woodland planting should be considered.

- Heathland restoration in Ashdown Forest, St Leonard's Forest and Broadwater Forest is important.

- The conservation and restoration of traditional orchards and hop gardens where appropriate should be addressed.

- Hammer ponds, meadows and parklands are important aspects of the history of the area.

- Vernacular styles and building materials should be an important aspect of new developments.

- The replacement of conifers, concrete and close-boarded fences with new hedges would be beneficial in many areas.

- The character of more remote areas needs to be safeguarded.

HIGH WEALD AONB

The area is well wooded and contains a high proportion of ancient semi-natural woodland which usually has extensive carpets of bluebells and wood anemones.

Selected References

Countryside Commission (1994), *The High Weald: Exploring the Landscape of the Area of Outstanding Natural Beauty*, Countryside Commission, Cheltenham.

White, J T (1977), *The South-East Down and Weald: Kent, Surrey and Sussex*, Eyre Methuen, London.

Hull F (1988), *Ordnance Survey Historical Guides: Kent*, George Philip, London.

Brandon P (1970), *The Sussex Landscape*, Hodder and Stoughton, London.

East Sussex County Council (1984), *Environmental Appraisal and Strategy for East Sussex*, Unpublished Draft.

Glossary

shaws: strip of trees or bushes forming the border of a field

Romney Marshes

Key Characteristics

- A flat, open and agricultural landscape, with distinctive drainage dykes, marshes and open skies. The treeless, low-lying, reclaimed marshland is now maintained by manmade drainage and river floodplain improvements.

- A high-quality agricultural land of extensive arable fields and some traditional open wet pasture land grazed by cattle and sheep. Narrow, straight roads and widely dispersed settlements with distinctive churches combine with the overall open character to provide a sense of remoteness.

- Clumps of trees on pockets of higher ground around farmsteads, reed fringed ditches, patches of standing water and rushy pasture, all contribute to local diversity in a relatively uniform landscape.

- The area's high nature-conservation value is concentrated in the wet grazing marshes, dykes, mudflats and the less extensive but distinct sand-dunes and shingle ridges of Dungeness.

- Former sea cliffs, mainly of sandstone, mark the post-glacial shoreline and form a notable feature overlooking Romney Marshes at Rye, Winchelsea, Hythe and Pett. The Napoleonic Royal Military Canal runs along the base of this degraded cliffline for much of its length.

- 20th century development is evident in the towns along the coastal strip.

- The landscape displays a sharp contrast between the shingle coastal promontories, the extensive open, low-lying agricultural land behind and the inland backdrop of well-wooded rising ground.

Landscape Character

The Romney Marshes are an area of reclaimed open marshland, mainly in Kent but partly in East Sussex. The Marshes are bounded to the south and east by the English Channel and to the north and west by old sea cliffs cut into the Wealden and Lower Greensand beds of the Lower Cretaceous.

Romney Marshes include Romney Marsh proper, the Walland and Denge Marshes, and the Broomhill, East Guldeford, Brede and Pett Levels. In contrast to the reclaimed marshes, there are extensive storm beaches of shingle at Dungeness Point and also small areas of sand dunes such as at Camber Sands.

Dungeness power station and its transmission lines dominate the shingle landscape.

The Romney Marshes owe their present day appearance to the natural process of sediment deposition behind large shingle promontories and to the reclamation in stages of the area for agricultural use. The Marshes have a distinctive windswept feel with flat, open marshland of either pasture or arable fields often divided by an irregular network of drainage ditches and banks with few trees and typically no hedges. The sky dominates the wide open, windswept character of the Marshes, much of which have a strong feeling of remoteness.

In this extremely flat and open landscape, the only real diversity in land cover is provided by the raised ground and clumps of trees of the marshland hamlets such as Old Romney and Newchurch. The dry landscape created by the widespread conversion to arable use produces less local but more seasonal variation in land cover, textures and colours.

Within the Marshes as a whole, Walland Marsh is particularly distinctive as it contains the greatest surviving concentration of small fields, dykes and unimproved pasture. Stock grazing still persists over most of this area giving some semblance of the once more traditional appearance of the overall landscape.

Dungeness, at the southerly tip of the Marshes, is the largest shingle foreland in Europe and the extensive low-lying shingle beaches, ridges and salt marsh provide a real sense of isolation and remoteness, especially along the coast. Much of this area is dominated by the imposing power station and associated transmission lines. Past gravel extraction pits, now flooded, military uses and expanding holiday resorts add to the general clutter along the coast.

Physical Influences

The strong sea-level rise at the end of the last glaciation, about 10,000 years ago, drowned the lower reaches of rivers extending into the present English Channel area and created tidally-influenced estuaries draining into shallow marine bays. The area of Romney Marshes was one such bay into which flowed the rivers draining the Weald. The clearly recognisable ancient cliff-line which forms the backdrop to the marshes must have formed at this time.

As sea-level stabilised, about 5,000 years ago, a series of shingle and sand spits and islands grew slowly out into this bay from the west, progressively enclosing the area of the marshes. A westward-progressing 'silting-up' of partially enclosed brackish and marine lagoons ensued creating areas of saltmarsh, forest and peat accumulation marginal to the remaining extensive open water.

The early stages of the development of the cuspate shingle foreland of Dungeness, seaward of the existing shingle and sand spits, is believed to have commenced about 3,000 years ago.

By 700 to 800 years ago the Marshes were changing from saltmarsh to reed and sedge meadows and large enclosed lagoons as 'silting-up' progressed. Dungeness was approaching its full development. Since that time the development of the landscape has been mainly influenced by

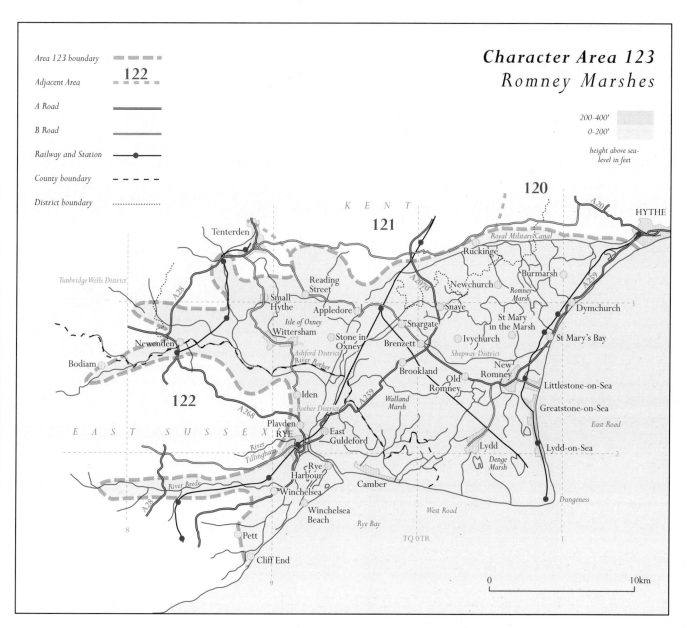

man and remnant lagoons, particularly in the Romney Marsh area itself, have been gradually reclaimed a little at a time by individual landowners (a process known as 'inning').

Prominent village churches and the widespread use of weatherboarding and hung tiles create a distinctive architectural character for the scattered Romney Marsh villages such as Lydd.

Historical and Cultural Influences

The present day landscape of the Romney Marshes is relatively young in geological and historical terms. Less than 2,000 years ago, the appearance of the landscape was radically different to that of today.

Between 43 - 100 AD, when the Romans first landed on the Kent and Sussex coast, the extensive area of Romney Marshes had not yet been fully formed by natural processes. Instead, the Romans would have been faced with a broad, open and shallow bay studded by an archipelago of upraised islands. These dry sites provided suitable locations for the first human settlement of the area. The villages of Lydd and New Romney in the Romney Marshes for instance have provided evidence of early human occupation in the form of pottery fragments dating from the 1st century.

The impoundment of the present Romney Marshes occurred earlier than at Pevensey Levels (further along the coast in East Sussex) having taken place in stages since the 8th century. An early charter of 744 AD describes reclamation being undertaken at that time in Denge Marsh probably by farmers from an early dry settlement on higher ground such as Lydd.

By the early 9th century the gradual fall of sea level meant that what is now the Romney Marshes began to develop. Impoundment of the Marshes was a piecemeal process with each landowner reclaiming small areas at a time ('inning'). The process was facilitated in around 1258 AD when the Rhee Wall was built to retain an artificial watercourse. The irregular pattern of drainage ditches, however, is an indication that no single large-scale reclamation was attempted.

By the middle of the 13th century, most of the marsh land had come into the hands of the local abbeys and thus much of the medieval reclamation was undertaken by the monks of such abbeys. Parishes outside the area would extend their boundaries to include the fine sheep-fattening pastures of the Marshes. The present day shape of the parishes, running from the uplands down the old sea-cliff and onto the Marshes, reflects this historic influence.

The remote, almost semi-wilderness character of the Marshes has been drawn upon by many notable writers such as H G Wells, Henry James, Joseph Conrad and Rudyard Kipling all of whom either worked in the Romney Marshes or used it as a setting for their novels. The strong emotional response to the Marshes is further reinforced by the interest shown by artists. Paul Nash is one artist among many who have depicted the coast at Dungeness in their paintings, while many others have used the views of sheep and marshlands as the subject of their paintings. The artistic inspiration of the Marshes still captures the imagination of photographers, such as Fay Godwin, and the film director, the late Derek Jarman, who lived at Dungeness.

Measures to reduce tidal flooding of the rich agricultural land of the Romney Marshes include early defensive works using brushwood and wooden stakes of the 13th and early 16th centuries and concrete sea walls, first constructed in the early 19th century and then again in the mid-20th century.

Sea kale brings a splash of summer colour to the extensive storm and shingle beaches of Dungeness and Rye. The shingle foreland at Dungeness is the largest in Europe and is of international nature-conservation importance.

Buildings and Settlement

The nature of the scattered settlements and the long, straight, open roads linking them together reflects the piecemeal influence of the reclamation process. The pockets of higher ground provided dry sites for small settlements to develop, while the immediate marsh land was 'inned' by the local inhabitants with little co-operation from the neighbouring settlements. Roads tended to be raised above the surrounding land forming visual divisions in the landscape.

The low lying arable and pasture land is dissected by an irregular pattern of drainage dykes, canals and ponds, reflecting the piecemeal reclamation of the marsh. Clusters of trees around settlements offer some relief from the open, windswept spaces.

JOHN AND IRENE PALMER

The distinctive architectural character of the settlements revolves around the widespread use of weatherboarding and hung tiles, with some fine churches set among the buildings. Particular built structures of note are the defensive Martello towers along the coast and the Royal Military Canal lying at the base of the former sea-cliffs, both relict features of the Napoleonic Wars. The power station is a dominant feature in many local views.

Land Cover

Sheep grazing was the traditional land use in the Romney Marshes up until the second world war but, since that time, most of the land has been subject to widespread drainage and improvement with much arable conversion. Much of the reclaimed marshland is of high agricultural quality due to the productive loams formed during the creation of the Marshes from alluvial deposits.

Small fields, dykes and unimproved pasture are less common than they once were due to the increase in arable production marked by a decline in sheep grazing. Remnants of the once more traditional appearance of the Romney Marshes can be seen in the landscape around Walland Marsh.

Tree cover is generally limited to clumps and belts around the settlement on the slightly higher ground and to the random lines, groups and individual trees set within the wider landscape. The wet, waterlogged conditions typically support tree species such as willow and ash.

Extensive areas of open water exist around Rye Harbour and Denge Marshes. This is the result of flooding of past gravel pits in the area.

Other land uses include power stations and associated transmission lines, gravel extraction and expanding holiday resorts along the coasts.

The Changing Countryside

- Widespread arable cultivation has replaced traditional wet grazing marsh.

- Drainage and improvement works resulting in the loss of characteristic dyke, marshland and wet meadow vegetation cover.

- Golf course development.

- Pressures from tourism-related activities and developments on the coast including large and quite prominent caravan parks such as around Camber Sands.

- The open landscapes are particularly vulnerable to landscape change arising from the development of large new agricultural buildings and from military land uses.

- Past extensive gravel workings are particularly visible around Rye Harbour as is the dominating feature of the Dungeness Power Station with associated transmission lines.

- New roads and improvement schemes.

- Suburban influences.

119

- Possible de-commissioning of power station and resultant lack of beach nourishment measures.

- Erosion of fishing industry has led to a loss of distinctive shoreside character in places.

Shaping the Future

- The maintenance and enhancement of the distinctive network of ditches should be addressed, together with less frequent and intensive dredging of the channels, and the control of water levels.

- The re-creation of wetland, seasonal flooding and areas of damp pasture should be considered.

- Planning and design guidelines would discourage inappropriate developments which might impinge on the remote, undeveloped quality of the Marshes and shoreline.

- The restoration of gravel workings for landscape, wildlife and recreational uses is important.

Selected References

Kent County Council (1993), *Landscape and Nature Conservation Guidelines*, Kent County Council, Maidstone.

Millward, R and Robinson, A (1973), *South-east England - The Channel Coastlands,* Macmillan, London.

Hull, F (1988), *Ordnance Survey Historical Guides: Kent*, George Philip, London.

Eddison J and Green C (eds), (1988), *Romney Marsh: Evolution, Occupation and Reclamation*, Oxford University Committee for Archaeology, Oxford.

Glossary

cuspate: cusp shaped

The flat and windswept nature of the marsh with its wide open skies creates a strong sense of remoteness, in contrast with the neighbouring wooded and undulating land.

STEPHEN DAVIS

Pevensey Levels

- Low-lying tract of largely reclaimed wetland, actively maintained by purpose-built drainage systems and river floodplain improvements.

- A predominantly open landscape with extensive grazed wet meadows and some arable fields with characteristic dykes, wetlands and wide skies. The open windswept feel is further enhanced by the scarcity of trees and hedges in the landscape.

- Widely-spaced roads and isolated settlements combine with the overall open character to provide a sense of remoteness.

- Local landscape diversity is added by 'eyes' – islands of higher ground, many with farmsteads – and also by reed-fringed ditches, scattered willows and patches of standing water with adjacent rushy pasture.

- Views out of the area to the south-west are framed against the dramatic and distinctive backdrop of the South Downs.

Landscape Character

Pevensey Levels are the largest tract of wetland in East Sussex. Lying between Bexhill and Eastbourne they mark the short transition between the Low Weald and the English Channel and are bounded on the north and east by the higher ground of the High Weald while, to the south-west, the steep scarp of the South Downs dominates the view.

The present day appearance of the Pevensey Levels results from a combination of natural sediment, depositional processes and extensive reclamation of the wetland for agricultural use.

The Levels are extensive tracts of low-lying reclaimed wetland with pockets of raised land typically associated with farm buildings and settlements. A distinctive windswept feel characterises the large-scale open landscape of predominant pasture. Large fields are set within an irregular network of drainage ditches and banks, with a few hedges (often associated with old silted dykes) and trees except on areas of higher ground where isolated groups of trees associated with small settlements add variety and interest. Ditches are typically fringed with reeds while patches of standing water and rushy pasture further reinforce the wetland character. Although intensively farmed, much of area is still wet pasture and is managed for grazing.

The Crooked Ditch, a 14th century sea defence and its embankment, follows the ancient irregular pattern of the individual fields. A chequerboard pattern of ditched fields in the landscape has remained virtually unchanged. The upper course of the ancient Mark Dyke, although no longer a major drain, is still visible today as a reed-filled, silted channel. Pevensey Castle overlooks the Levels near the coast, further adding to the historic interest of the area.

Power lines and isolated trees are prominent features of the extensive areas of flat rushy pasture and standing water.

Physical Influences

At the end of the last glaciation, about 10,000 years ago, rising sea-levels flooded the lower reaches of the numerous coastal river valleys resulting in the creation of a tidal estuary. The present Levels were under water and consisted of a wide, shallow bay backed by the rising ground of the High Weald inland. By the 1st century the wide bay was partly sheltered by storm beach shingle spits which gradually developed across the bay allowing vast quantities of marine and estuarine alluvium to be deposited behind.

These sediments give rise to the present day loamy soils which, when drained, produce high-quality agricultural land. The Levels gradually changed from saltmarsh to reedy meadows although much of the area was still under water as recently as 700-800 years ago. In the course of succeeding centuries, more of the wetland was reclaimed for agricultural use and the former bay ceased to exist.

Historical and Cultural Influences

The present day Pevensey Levels landscape is relatively young in geological and historical terms. During the Roman period the Pevensey Levels was a broad shallow bay punctuated by numerous small clay islands, founded on the underlying Wealden beds, which provided suitable dry sites for Roman settlement of the area. These were later protected by the development of shingle along the coast affording natural protection to the first settlements located on the raised islands. The origins of many modern day settlements within the Pevensey Levels such as Chilley, Northeye and Rickney are reflected in the use of the suffix *eye* – Old English for island.

Pevensey Levels may still have been a tidal inlet as recently as the 11th century. At the time of the Norman Conquest much of the present area was under water, the tide having full access for several kilometres inland. Evidence from Domesday points to numerous salt-works where the sea-water was evaporated to make salt. These salt-works have resulted in distinctive low mounds of residues, 1-2 metres high and 15 metres in width. These form visible features in the present day landscape, such as the mounds at Wallers Haven.

The first arable fields appeared in the Pevensey Levels during the 13th century. Reclamation or 'inning' was largely undertaken and financed by local abbeys such as Battle Abbey. Individual farmers also carried out reclamation of the wetland which surrounded their farmsteads. The latter were built on the dry, isolated low hills sheltered by clumps of willow. The reclamation of the Levels involved the construction of meandering drainage channels such as the Mark Dyke which ran across nearly 4.5 kilometres of the lowest part of the Levels. The upper course, although no longer a major drain, is still visible today as a reed-filled, silted channel.

Farm buildings and settlements traditionally of brick and flint construction, are situated on pockets of raised land.

Extensive floods and inundation by the sea in the late Middle Ages led to the abandonment of much of the Pevensey Levels. As the continued inning of the wetland reduced the tidal flow, the outfall of the Levels became blocked resulting in widespread flooding as the discharge of land drainage into the sea was prevented. Early sea defence works, of the 13th century, using brushwood and wooden stakes, were followed by the 14th century Crooked Ditch. Further wooden sea defences constructed in the early 16th century were followed by concrete sea walls, first in the early 19th century and then again in the mid-20th century.

Buildings and Settlement

The pattern of scattered settlements and the open roads linking them together reflects the piecemeal influence of

Character Area 124
Pevensey Levels

600-800'	Area 124 boundary	
400-600'	Adjacent Area	**122**
200-400'	A Road	
0-200'	B Road	
height above sea-level in feet	Railway and Station	
	District boundary	

122

121   EAST SUSSEX

125

Hailsham   Wartling   Hooe
Wealden District   BEXHILL
Rother District
Polegate   Hankham
Pevensey Bay
Westham
Willingdon   Langney
Eastbourne District
Willingdon Hill
659'   Langney Point
TQ
TV
EASTBOURNE

0   10km

Beachy Head

the reclamation process. The pockets of higher ground provided dry sites for small settlements to develop, whilst the nearby wetland was 'inned' by the local inhabitants with little co-operation from the neighbouring settlements. Roads tend to be slightly raised above the surrounding land forming visual divisions in the landscape.

Particular built structures of note include the Martello towers along the coast and a number of fine churches set amongst the small settlements. The walls of the buildings, typically of brick and flint, also included weatherboarding or hung tiles, with plain tiles commonly used as a roofing material.

Land Cover

Much of Pevensey Levels, in contrast to Romney Marshes further along the coast in Kent, is still predominantly open cattle-grazed wet pasture. Although the Levels have been subject to extensive drainage and improvement for agricultural use, relatively little has been subject to arable conversion. The often old drains that divide the fields are typically reed-filled, their channels forming barriers to grazing stock movement within the levels. Apart from along roadways, fences and hedgerows are infrequent features.

The Pevensey Levels have remained primarily as grazed pasture, arable areas being confined to a few drier locations.

Woodland is restricted to areas of higher ground associated with settlements while the Levels are largely devoid of any significant tree cover, save for a few small windswept specimens that mark the line of silted dykes and the roads and lanes that cross the area raised on low embankments. Willows and hawthorn are common species along some wet ditches.

Electricity transmission lines and pylons form dominant vertical features in the flat and open landscape.

Fields are drained by an irregular network of minor dykes and the area is crossed by long straight raised roads linking settlements.

The Changing Countryside

- Drainage and improvement works resulting in the loss of characteristic dyke, wetland and wet meadow vegetation cover.

- New roads and improvement schemes form visual divisions in the landscape.

- Conspicuous new agricultural buildings and associated structures.

- Power lines are particularly prominent features in the open landscape.

- Expansion of urban development on fringes of Levels has impinged in some places on the open character of the landscape.

- Pressure from large developments along the coastline.

- Scrub invasion of dry ditches.

Shaping the Future

- The development of planning and design guidelines would discourage inappropriate developments which might impinge on the remote, undeveloped quality of the Levels.

- The establishment of new areas of wetland and wet meadows, and the encouragement of seasonal inundation, should be considered.

- Tree planting on the edge of farm buildings and settlements would help minimise their effect on the open Levels landscape.

- The nature and scale of sea defences should be addressed.

Selected References

East Sussex County Council (1984), *Environmental Appraisal and Strategy for East Sussex*, unpublished draft.

Millwood, R and Robinson, A (1973), *South-east England - The Channel Coastlands*, Macmillan, London.

University of Sussex, The Geography Editorial Committee (1983), *Sussex: Environment, Landscape and Society*, Alan Sutton, Gloucester.

MARTIN JONES/COUNTRYSIDE AGENCY

Modern development around the fringes of the levels is often unsympathetic to local character. Here at Normans Bay it has impinged on the historic setting of the Martello tower.

South Downs

Key Characteristics

- Prominent Chalk outcrop rising gently from the South Coast Plain with a dramatic north-facing scarp and distinctive chalk cliffs formed where the Downs end abruptly at the sea. A chalk landscape of rolling arable fields and close-cropped grassland on the bold scarps, rounded open ridges and sculpted dry valleys.

- Lightly settled landscape with scattered villages, hamlets and farmsteads – flint is conspicuous in the buildings, walls of villages, farms and churches.

- Roman roads and drove roads are common and characteristic features and the area is rich in visually prominent prehistoric remains, particularly Neolithic and Bronze Age barrows and prominent Iron Age hillforts.

- In the east, rivers from the Low Weald cut through the Downs to form river valleys and broad alluvial floodplains with rectilinear pastures and wet grazing meadows – a contrast with the dry uplands. Above these valleys, the high, exposed, rounded uplands of white chalk have a simple land cover of few trees, an absence of hedgerows, occasional small planted beech clumps, and large arable areas and some grassland.

- The eastern Downs have a distinctive escarpment which rises prominently and steeply above the Low Weald. It is indented by steep combes or dry valleys.

- Woodlands – both coniferous and broadleaved – are a distinctive feature of the western Downs.

- In the west, large estates are important features with formal designed parkland providing a contrast to the more typical farmland pasture.

Landscape Character

The South Downs are a long prominent spine of chalk which stretches from the chalk downland of Hampshire, eastwards across West Sussex until it is sheared off at precipitous coastal cliffs in East Sussex. The steep, northward-facing chalk escarpment of Sussex overlooks the patchy mosaic of fields, woods and heathlands of the Low Weald and, further west in Sussex, the Wealden Greensand. The western edge of the Downs flows into the chalk of the Hampshire Downs and, to the south, the Downs dip giving way to the narrow wedge of coastal plain and farmland which separate them from the English Channel.

JOHN TYLER/SUSSEX DOWNS CONSERVATION BOARD

The white cliffs of the Severn Sisters, Beachy and Seaford Heads mark the spectacular eastern end of the South Downs where they join the sea.

The Downs are a dramatic and well defined Chalk outcrop with an elevated, open and expansive character. Traditionally the Downs have been an important arable asset with, now in limited places, a sweep of rolling close-cropped chalk grassland or woodland on many of the scarp slopes. This uniform and informal landscape is often covered in a large-scale pattern of grass leys and cereals, giving a regular but often fragmented appearance. The Downs still have a 'wild', exposed, and remote character, greatly valued in the heavily populated south.

Within this simplified overall pattern there are important contrasts. In the west in Hampshire, the landscape is open and dominated by agriculture and grassland. The steep

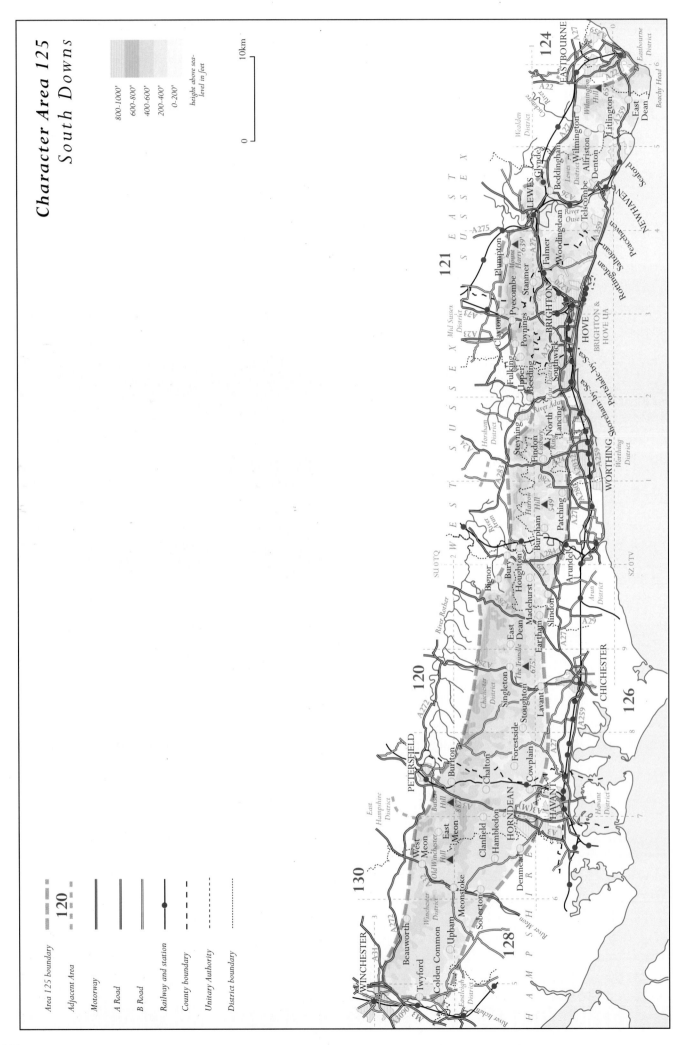

Character Area 125
South Downs

Area 125 boundary

120 Adjacent Area

Motorway

A Road

B Road

Railway and station

County boundary

Unitary Authority

District boundary

800-1000'
600-800'
400-600'
200-400'
0-200'

height above sea-
level in feet

0   10km

scarp slopes fade in prominence beyond Beacon Hill to St Catherine's Hill and Twyford Down where they meld into the open chalk landscape of the adjoining Hampshire Downs. The axis here of the ridge is less noticeable and the east/west alignment is visibly lost and becomes more complex as the Downs diminish. Moving east, extensive woodland creates a more enclosed character as the Downs pass into West Sussex. Further east still, the dry, rolling uplands are cut through with major valleys as the rivers from the Low Weald meander through wet meadow pastures to the English Channel.

On the main scarp in the east, mature woodland sits on the lower slopes while the rough texture of chalk downland turf, often patchy with scrub, dominates the landform and contrasts strongly with the pastoral low-lying patchwork pattern of the Low Weald. The scarp face has few articulating features (although Mount Caburn and Beddingham Hill are noted exceptions) and dominates in southerly views from the Low Weald. In the west the scarp is often clothed in continuous woodland which enhances the linear landform and disguises undulations in landform. The trees on the skyline give scale and definition to the scarp face which means that the deceptive sense of great height is lessened.

Physical Influences

The east-west Chalk ridge of the South Downs is the southern remnant of a once extensive dome of Chalk. The central Wealden portion was eroded during the Tertiary period leaving two ridges – now known as the North Downs and the South Downs. The South Downs have a gentle but broad rolling dip-slope inclined to the south, with a dramatic north-facing escarpment.

Butser Hill, Beacon Hill and Old Winchester Hill form prominent ridges in Hampshire before the South Downs gradually diminish to the west. The escarpment in Sussex forms an undulating ridge along the northern margin of this character area, broken only where the principal river valley systems have eroded a route through to the coast. In other places, steep combes, as at Devil's Dyke, slice into the scarp. It is a steep but rounded slope, with combes cut back into the ridge line, whilst in other places spurs and chalk outliers protrude into the Low Weald below. Southwards from the main scarp, lines of hills and ridges form an intermittent but prominent secondary escarpment which result from variations in the resistance of the different Chalk outcrops. Ancient wave platforms, features of the dip slope, are also common and finally at the Seven Sisters - a range of white chalk cliffs between Eastbourne and Brighton - the South Downs drop abruptly to the sea.

The mass of Chalk in Sussex has been cut into separate blocks by the valleys of the principal rivers – Arun, Adur,

Ouse and Cuckmere – which flow through to the sea. Flat valley bottoms and a meandering river course enclosed by steep-sided slopes with minor cliffs are, in many places, typical features of these river valleys. The valley floors provide a strong contrast to the surrounding open fields on the higher ground. The river Meon in Hampshire follows a similar course and cuts through the South Downs, the valley broadening in the adjoining coastal plain, until it reaches the sea.

Broad alluvial floodplains, such as the Cuckmere Valley pictured here, consist of fertile pasture used for dairy cattle. Other river valleys such as the Ouse, Arun, Meon and Adur cut through the Downs and provide contrasting narrow belts of flat land within the rolling landscape of the chalk.

Historical and Cultural Influences

Extensive clearance of forest for grazing, and the first introduction of domestic animals and crops, occurred during the Neolithic period. The Chalk Downs were favoured for their light, easily cultivated soils, defensive advantages and relative accessibility as shown by evidence of Neolithic tracks. Clearance was aided by the locally available flint (from the chalk) for tools as evidenced by the Neolithic flint mines at Cissbury Ring and evidence at Old Winchester Hill. The Trundle, a causewayed camp of concentric rings and ditches prominently sited on the dip slope, is one of the best examples of Neolithic enclosure in the country used for holding stock, for ceremonies and trading.

There is evidence to suggest that, during the Bronze Age, there was a temporary change to a nomadic pastoral system, before a return to general mixed farming. The increase in woodland clearance and active management would have created open landscapes and extensive grasslands on the ridge of the Downs. The round barrows of the Bronze Age are among the most common archaeological features found on the Downs including, for example, the burial mounds of the Devil's Jumps near Hooksway and those on Bow Hill above Kingley Vale and at Old Winchester Hill.

As agricultural communities became more nucleated and widespread in the Iron Age, the south facing dip-slope became covered with well-defined field systems (of small geometric fields bounded by lynchets), managed woodlands and pasture. Hillforts sited prominently in strategic locations, such as Cissbury Ring and Old Winchester Hill, reflected political and economic centres while other remaining earthworks such as cross dykes represented boundary demarcations or stock enclosures.

JOHN TYLER/SUSSEX DOWNS CONSERVATION BOARD

The South Downs consist of an archetypal chalk landscape of rolling hills, steep scarp slopes with dry valleys and a rich archaeological character. Centuries of sheep grazing on steep slopes have produced a network of tracks following the contours of the hills.

The Romans, further exploiting the light soils, created large arable estates and agricultural trade increased. By the 10th century, the availability of pasture on the Downs coupled with the fertile soils of the South Coast Plain enabled further enrichment of the estates. In some cases, these early estates gave rise to the large and rich estates of later centuries. The latter included impressive country houses, which were to share in the influencing of the English Landscape Movement, and the spread of parkland with its expansive pasture, clumps and follies.

By the 19th century, beech plantations had begun to appear and prosperous mixed farming of cereal and fodder together with sheep pasture characterised the Downs. However, this period was followed by a depression caused by cheap imports from abroad which led to a decline in grazing and cereal production. Farm buildings, hedgerows and woodlands all became neglected.

The present day concentration of woodland in the central part of the Downs is partly due to land ownership by large estates, coupled with the more sheltered inland location. Large-scale timber production had historically been linked to the navy at Portsmouth and had tended towards the thinner soils of the upper slopes, thus changing the inherent vegetation pattern.

Buildings and Settlement

With the exception of the major north-south routes which cut through the open Downs, there are few roads within the Downs themselves and, where they do occur, they are small and rural. Settlement is sparse, being confined to scattered villages, hamlets and moderately large, isolated farms with traditional barns.

The eastern end of the Downs is hemmed in by the coastal plain conurbations; these are less intrusive in the west, but pylons, telecommunications masts, road traffic, glass houses and recreation grounds are widespread throughout the area. The urban area itself is visually very intrusive in the east, along the southern edge of the dip slope, particularly where there are densely built-up areas on relatively elevated land.

On the lower parts of the Downs there are scattered groups of modern farm buildings tucked into the dry valleys of the dip slope, or clustered along the foot of the escarpment. The remainder of the Downs has limited settlement and few buildings.

The traditional buildings are of brick or flint, with brick quoins and window details and roofs of tile or slate. Apart from the large flint barns on the open sites in the Sussex Downs, there are generally few buildings or roads on the open spurs and the often isolated farm buildings are reached by long chalky tracks.

Many villages nestle in the valleys, alongside a stream. They tend to be small clusters of traditional flint and brick buildings set within mature trees and sometimes surrounding a village pond. Such villages are commonly associated with the parkland estates which are evidenced by the presence of well-built enclosing walls of flint. Single farmsteads, many with large modern buildings, are common here. On the south margins of the dip slope, villages tend to have a more diverse mix of buildings, the traditional flint interspersed with rendered and brick houses.

Notable exceptions to the traditional built character include the urban extension of Worthing, Brighton and Peacehaven, and the dual carriageways of the M3, A24, A3 and A23. One of the more recognisable recent developments in the area is the ridgetop grandstand of Goodwood Racecourse which breaks the saddle of the skyline above Goodwood. Arundel Castle is an imposing building, sitting high above the Arun floodplain, it is one of the most distinctive landmarks in the area. Much of it is a relatively new structure, though the original castle was a Norman motte and bailey.

Windmills with huge white sails were once a regular feature in the South Downs landscape. Now only a few remain such as the Jack and Jill windmills perched on the crest of the Chalk near Clayton and also the prominent Halnaker Windmill, above Goodwood, which can be seen from parts of the South Coast Plain.

The A27 cuts through the downland on the northern fringes of Hove, introducing development pressures from the encroaching town.

Land Cover

The land use pattern of the South Downs is predominantly centred on cereals and sheep, and also woodland that has survived on the steeper slopes which were traditionally difficult to clear. However, extensive plantations exist on the enclosed uplands of the dipslope in western Sussex. Cereals are grown predominantly on the deeper soils of the less exposed lower slopes. The vivid colours of the crops and the texture of the chalk fragments in ploughed soils are a particularly noticeable feature on the Downs.

The grazing of sheep maintains open and homogeneous semi-natural chalk grassland habitats that are noted for their particularly rich botanic diversity. The chalk downland turf is seen as the traditional clothing of the Downs, especially those steeper scarp slopes in the east and far west where it has developed over centuries without cultivation or chemicals. The appearance of naturalness is enhanced by the diversity of plant species, some of them rare flowering herbs, which combine to form the soft springy turf. However, due to a decrease in sheep farming, chalk grassland now only remains in small areas which are often isolated and difficult to manage. As a result, downland farming is now mainly a combination of arable crops and improved grass leys. The lack of grazing has led to the invasion of scrub in most of the chalk grassland areas which detracts from the traditional smooth appearance of the South Downs landscape.

There are scattered copses on the skyline but generally there are few trees or woods in the eastern Downs. Hedgerows are rare but, where they occur, they tend to be sparse, narrow and sporadic, with a few stunted trees. They tend to be near isolated upland farmsteads or alongside ancient chalky tracks.

Tree cover creates a much more enclosed atmosphere in the centre of the Downs with intensive farming, enclosed by hedgerows with hedgerow trees, and scattered woodland. A number of designed parklands, sometimes altered by cultivation, are also found to the west.

The present day tree cover is either broadleaved woodland, with beech, ash and sycamore, or is mixed with conifers. There are also some large plantations of Corsican pine and western red cedar and isolated remnants of yew forest. The chalk ash or beech hangers on the escarpment of East Hampshire are notable features. English elm is now largely confined to areas around the coastal towns of East Sussex and the Cuckmere Valley.

The vegetation of the river valleys is markedly different. There are permanent semi-improved pastures providing grazing for cattle in late spring and summer. The pasture at the edges of the valleys is often enclosed by hedges and copses, lines of alder, and willow and poplar, some of which are pollarded. The alluvial soils – some of the most productive in the area – support crops and intensive dairying.

Many of the Downland footpaths and bridleways follow drove roads and transport routes which have been used for centuries along the accessible downland tops. The high parts of the Downs, including the South Downs Way, are the most important recreational features of the Downs. The escarpment tops and the coastal headlands are particularly popular places due largely to the panoramic views, ease of access and apparent sense of remoteness.

The Changing Countryside

- Past expansion of arable cropping, improved grass leys, intensive livestock systems and scrub encroachment have reduced the extent of chalk grassland since 1945. Most of what remains are isolated remnants restricted to the steep scarp slopes.

- More recently, there has been a reversion of significant arable areas to grassland and restoration of sheep grazing. Also fencing of significant areas of the Downs under the South Downs Environmentally Sensitive Area scheme.

- Afforestation, both coniferous and beech, has occurred since the 19th century but is less of an issue today.

- Loss and decline in quality of beech hangers/woodland in the central part of the Downs landscape due to lack of management and storm damage.

JOHN TYLER/SUSSEX DOWNS CONSERVATION BOARD

Brick and flint cottages are characteristic of the few scattered villages and hamlets to be found in the South Downs.

- Modern drainage of the river valleys alters the traditional character, producing a more formal, regularly patterned landscape of arable fields – for example, significant areas of wet grassland in the Cuckmere, Arun and Ouse valleys are under pressure from drainage and lowering of the water table.

- The open landscape is vulnerable to change from new farm buildings, urban edge pressures extending from the heavily built-up coastal fringe onto the Downs and from prominent communication masts on exposed skylines.

- Pressures for road improvements often associated with major cuttings and/or tunnels in the Downs.

- Increasing recreational pressures including greater demands on public rights of way by walkers, horse riders, mountain bikes and from off-road vehicles. Visitors to honey pot sites and demand for formal recreation such as golf courses, are also increasing within the Downs.

- Damage to, and loss of, archaeological remains from agricultural and recreation uses.

- Winterbournes are becoming increasingly dry from continued over-abstraction of the chalk aquifer and lack of recharge due to successive dry years.

- Disused chalk quarries are visually prominent features within the downland slopes and have been utilised as major landfill sites.

- Loss of traditional boundaries such as hedgerows and flint walls to the increase in use of different types of fencing.

Shaping the Future

- The management of wetlands and river valleys, possibly by use of natural processes, needs to be addressed.

- The protection of existing chalk grassland from agriculture or scrub invasion can be achieved through sympathetic grazing and scrub management regimes. This might include targeted reversion of arable to permanent pasture, in particular the creation of species-rich chalk grassland on the upper and the steeper slopes of the Downs and in parkland.

- The conservation and restoration of beech hangers and valley woodland on the escarpment needs to be considered.

- There is scope for tree planting on the edge of settlements adjacent to downland farms.

- There are opportunities to protect archaeological remains within their setting.

Selected References

Landscape Design Associates (1995), *A Landscape Assessment of the Sussex Downs AONB*, unpublished.

Countryside Commission (1991), *The East Hampshire Landscape CCP 358*, Countryside Commission, Cheltenham.

Brandon P (1970), *The Sussex Landscape*, Hodder and Stoughton, London.

Dipper S (1995), *Landscape Assessment of West Sussex - Section 1*, West Sussex County Council, West Sussex.

White J T (1977), *The South-East Down and Weald: Kent, Surrey and Sussex*, Eyre Methuen, London.

Sussex Downs Conservation Board and Countryside Commission (1996), *The Landscape of the Sussex Downs Area of Outstanding Natural Beauty*, CCP 495.

MAFF (1995), *South Downs Environmentally Sensitive Area Landscape Assessment*, (unpublished).

Glossary

hanger: a wood on the side of a steep hill

leys: land put down to grass or clover for a limited period of years

South Coast Plain

- Major urban developments including Portsmouth, Worthing and Brighton linked by the A27/M27 corridor dominate much of the open, intensively farmed, flat, coastal plain.

- Coastal inlets and 'harbours' contain a diverse landscape of narrow tidal creeks, mudflats, shingle beaches, dunes, grazing marshes and paddocks. From the Downs and coastal plain edge there are long views towards the sea and the Isle of Wight beyond.

- Trees are not a dominant feature – there are some small woods and a few windswept individual trees in the farmland or the occasional poplar shelter belt.

- A pattern of large arable fields, defined by low hedgerows, are often interspersed by horticultural glasshouse 'estates' and isolated remnants of coastal heath.

- The complex series of creeks, mudflats and shingle beaches along the coastal edge becomes less apparent to the east with the intensively-farmed plain increasingly dominated by disordered seaside towns and leisure developments.

Landscape Character

The South Coast Plain lies between the dip slope of the South Downs and the waters of the English Channel, Solent and part of Southampton Water. The Plain stretches from Southampton Water in the west, widening to about 10 miles across to form the Manhood Peninsula and Selsey Bill, before tapering eastwards towards Brighton. The coastline includes several inlets such as Chichester and Langstone Harbours which are particularly distinctive local landscapes.

The flat coastal plain has, in part, an intricately indented shoreline and, although rather exposed to south-westerly winds, temperatures are relatively warm, soils are high quality and the growing season is long. The area is thus intensively farmed and includes a prosperous horticultural industry with glasshouse development and tourist trade.

The area exhibits one of the longest and most concentrated stretches of shoreline ribbon development in Britain and each coastal town or village has developed almost to the high water mark.

The Plain is broadly divided into the coastal margins which are heavily influenced by the sea, the expansive lower coastal plain which occupies most of the area, and the upper coastal plain. The latter forms the transitional area between the lower plain and the Chalk dip slope of the South Downs to the east and with the South Hampshire Lowlands further west.

Mud flats and salt marshes with characteristic inlets fringe the undeveloped harbours.

While large parts of the coastal margins have been urbanised by the spread of seaside towns and budget holiday accommodation, the remaining open coastline contains secretive inlets and enclosed harbours. The exposed shoreline is an exhilarating, open, linear landscape of shingle and sand with the great expanse of the sea itself as a backdrop. This shoreline is intermittently indented with inlets and estuaries where broad expanses of sheltered water are edged by an attractive mix of mudflats, marshes, wetland scrub and low-lying fields occasionally interrupted

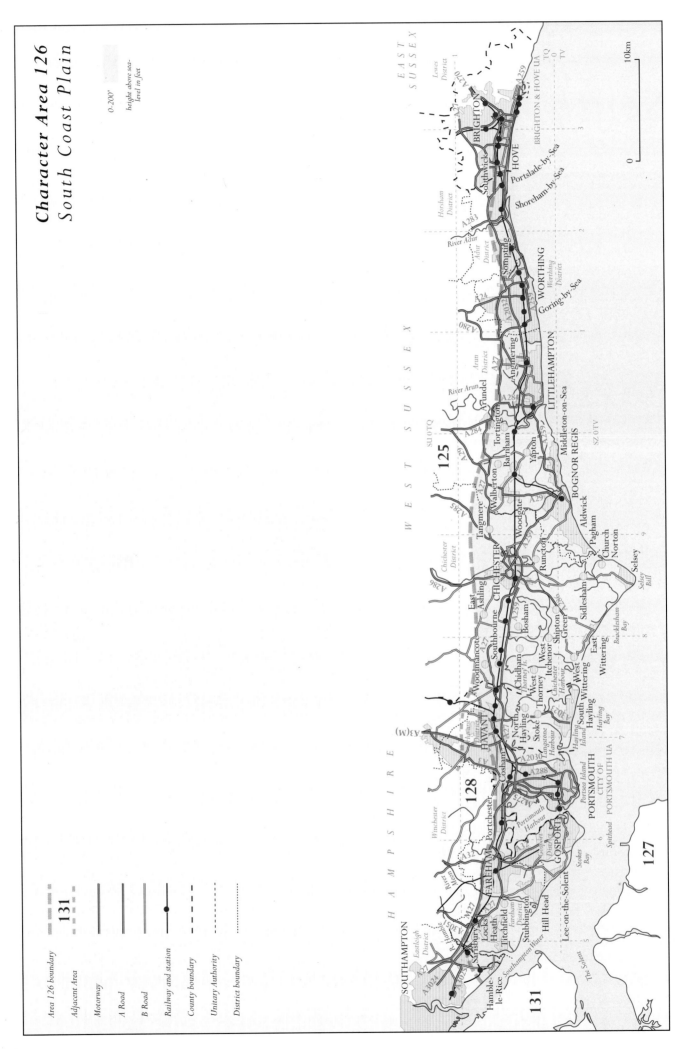

Character Area 126
South Coast Plain

by small creeks. Chichester Harbour, for example, is one of the largest natural harbours along the South Coast Plain with a diverse landscape of numerous inlets interspersed with fairly open agricultural peninsulas and wind-sculpted woodlands. Picturesque harbourside settlements are typically clustered around small boatyards and marinas while numerous moored sailing boats dot the harbour edge. Other inlets provide contrast to this scene such as Pagham Harbour which retains an overriding sense of remoteness. This is due in no small way to the extensive tidal mudflats fringed by marsh vegetation and populated by large numbers of migratory birds. In contrast to the relative peace and remoteness of the Sussex harbours, the highly developed and historical Portsmouth Harbour is constantly busy with sailing boats, Cross channel ferries and naval warships.

In the lower plain, the wide scale and treeless farmed landscape is dominated by large arable fields. Views north are contained by the rising dip slope of the Downs, but views seaward are without definition and tend to lack depth and perspective. The urban fringes of the sprawling seaside resorts are pronounced, as is all urban development in this flat landscape. Some smaller-scale landscapes also exist within this part of the Plain such as the quiet hamlets, traditional village centres, pastures, and minor roads. The chalk quarries of Ports Down are notable features and can be seen from some distance, both from the adjoining land and at sea.

To the north and east of the area, the upper coastal plain combines the flat, regular patterns of large fields with the gentle forms and patterns blending into the openness of the lower dip slope of the South Downs. The landscape is varied, incorporating both open arable farmland and low density settlements, with a more well-wooded and semi-enclosed (somewhat surburban) character locally, particularly to the west of Chichester. Hidden, intimate valleys and woods are a distinctive characteristic of the upper coastal plain to the east, such as the valley of Binsted with its steep slopes and winding lane, and the ancient woodlands of the Tortington and Titnore Lane area. The latter are on the southernmost flanks of the Chalk outlier of Highdown Hill which in itself is a unique and prominent feature on the plain.

Even where the plain is enclosed by a mixture of woodlands, the presence of windswept trees and occasional glimpses of the Isle of Wight reflect the generally open and exposed coastal location.

Physical Influences

Geologically, this landscape is part of a broad plain of flinty marine and valley gravels extending several miles inland to the dip slope of the South Downs and the South Hampshire Lowlands. The plain slopes gently southwards towards the coast becoming almost imperceptible; at Hayling Island the landscape is flat, save for the undulating sand dunes. The continuity of the Plain is interrupted by many streams and rivers which flow to the sea – in the case of the river Hamble through a wooded valley. The superficial gravel deposits give rise to deep and well-drained brown earths which occur widely over much of the area while thinner chalky soils have formed over the distinctive Chalk outlier of Highdown Hill.

The coastal plain comprises essentially two units, a lower plain between 10 and 15 metres AOD and an upper plain between 30 and 40 metres. Each of these plains is underlain by clayey, sandy and gravelley deposits of raised beach, head gravel and brickearth deposits laid down when relative sea levels were higher than at present. The Upper Raised Beach Deposits contain unequivocal evidence of 'Boxgrove Man', his artifacts and an extensive mammalian fauna indicative of pre-Anglian glaciation (>450,000 years ago) age. Boxgrove Man therefore provides evidence for the earliest known human occupation of the British Isles.

Long linear shingle beaches and sand dunes are dominant features which are enjoyed by residents of the highly developed hinterland.

The wave-cut benches underlying the upper and lower coastal plains are cut into folded Chalk and Tertiary strata preserved in a series of en-echelon synclines and anticlines. One of the latter forms Ports Down which makes a prominent backdrop to the coastal plain in the west.

The lower plain is cut by southward-facing streams, locally termed 'rifes', each of which have dry headwater extensions over the upper plain and on into the Chalk dip slop of the South Downs. Towards the west, the lower coastal plain grades into terrace flats attributed to the 'Solvent river', present in the area during low sea-level events of the Ice Age.

The plain is crossed by rivers such as the Arun, Adur, Hamble and Meon which locally form wide alluvial floodplains. Now flooded, gravel pits comprise some of the largest areas of freshwater in the region. Over the superficial deposits lies a range of fertile soils which combine with the flat terrain and favourable climatic conditions to result in high-quality agricultural land.

Picturesque waterside settlements are attractive features of the less developed harbours.

The sand and shingle beaches have been shaped by the complimentary processes of erosion and deposition since the last major change in sea level, forming spits across river mouths and inlets. Loose sand has gradually formed modest sand dune systems in some places. Around Selsey, outcrops of brickearth and chalk have been eroded to form low cliffs. Chichester and Pagham Harbours are submerged shallow valleys, dominated by mudflats built up through the deposition and stabilisation of silt and mud transported by streams.

The three harbours of Chichester, Langstone and Portsmouth are interconnected by narrow channels and together form the largest intertidal area on the south coast.

Historical and Cultural Influences

The coastal area (particularly in and around Langstone Harbour) has disclosed extensive palaeoenvironmental evidence of early exploitation. It was, however, the Neolithic forest clearance and grazing, with the introduction of domestic animals and crops when the climate was warm and the land lightly wooded and accessible, that began to open the landscape.

The Romans recognised the agricultural potential of the coastal plain as reflected by their establishment of Chichester between 43 and 61 AD as an important new market town and military centre. Important villa sites, now inland but once on the coast, are still evident as is the Roman fort at Portchester.

By the 10th century, a system of rich agricultural estates was established to exploit the coastal plain's fertile soils, along with the pasture on the adjacent Downs and the timber and stock rearing of the Wealden fringe further north. By this stage the South Coast Plain would have been developing its reputation as one of the most fertile and intensively cultivated areas of Britain; the prevalence of market gardens and smallholdings on the coastal plain today in Hampshire bears witness to this long history of cultivation.

From 1066, the Norman period saw inland Saxon towns develop outports at New Shoreham and Littlehampton, from which goods could be traded more effectively. Agriculture was prospering and allowed the economy to diversify and the number of market towns to expand.

After an agricultural 'golden age' in the 19th century, cheap imports from America and southern Europe led to a decline in local cereal production and sheep grazing. The establishment of the railways brought new access to the coast and the seaside towns doubled in size by the end of the 19th century. Between 1837 and 1939 large parts of the coastline were built over as the tourist trade grew following the lead of Brighton. This had been prompted by contemporary writings on the health benefits of sea air and bathing. Originally served by paddle steamer from London, Brighton promoted the development of the railway and excursion fares from the capital. As demand increased so the smaller resorts such as Worthing, Littlehampton and Bognor Regis developed along with the rail link in the latter half of the 19th century.

Buildings and Settlement

Within the coastal margins, building materials were traditionally mixed largely reflecting the proximity of the sea for importing raw materials. Timber frames, flint, cob and thatch are all common. The medieval churches around the harbours are of flint and stone. Today, the character of settlement is mixed with traditional harbourside hamlets providing contrast with the recent holiday and residential villages that have sprung up along the shoreline and fringes of villages. Modern marinas and boatyards have also added to the harbour landscape. Urban expansion, industrial paraphernalia and caravan accommodation associated with the edges of seaside towns is prominent along the coastal margins.

On the lower coastal plain, settlements are dominated by suburban villages and the extensive seaside towns between Brighton and the edge of Southampton. Large reflective glasshouses, advertisement signs for farm shops, nurseries and equestrian facilities, golf courses, horse paddocks and industrial and institutional buildings all bring a suburban character, which confuses the definition between the urban centres and their rural hinterland.

The ancient market town and compact cathedral city of Chichester sits at the centre of this character area, with its distinctive spire forming an important landmark. To the east, numerous villages form a fairly continuous residential sprawl, although this pattern includes some traditional flint hamlets and farm buildings. Along Southampton Water, smallholdings and bungalows are scattered but merge with the increasingly suburban outreaches of Fareham towards the Solent. Several large offices and residential tower blocks and gas holders in the larger towns dominate long-distance views.

PORTSMOUTH COMMERCIAL PORT

The natural harbours have lent themselves to development leading to a thriving maritime trade.

To the north at the base of the Chalk dip slope, settlement is more dispersed. A network of typically-winding secondary and minor roads, usually hedged or wooded, links together small flint villages, isolated dwellings and farm buildings and the mixed housing styles of village fringes.

Many villages have retained their attractive medieval and late medieval core often arranged around a green or market area and the varied vernacular architecture displays strong relationships with its region.

Land Cover

Along the coastline itself, the vegetation is typified by a scanty covering of low growing, often mat-forming, specialised plants which can tolerate the saline conditions and mineral substrate. The shifting, dry shingle, mud and sands of the shoreline are particularly hostile to the establishment of vegetation and are generally devoid of cover, except where shingle-loving species and sand dune grasses have colonised naturally or by introduction. On the newly-formed ground of the mudflats in the inlets, pioneering intertidal marsh communities have colonised and these demonstrate a well-defined succession of plant types and species towards the land. Although not a dominant characteristic, scrub and small areas of wind-sculpted woodland persist on some coastal fringes, particularly around the sheltered inlets. Oldpark Wood, near Bosham Hoe, is a significant example.

Semi-natural communities occur almost as 'islands' within the arable land which project into the peninsulas from the lower coastal plain. This is a fertile area which supports intensive arable farming and horticulture, with some dairy, beef and poultry. Areas of medium-quality agricultural land where soils are shallow, stony and poorly-drained, often support good quality permanent grassland such as the Arun floodplain.

The thicker gravel deposits support a mixture of high and medium quality soils which are intensively farmed where the soils are flintier. The area also supports mixed farming, including pig rearing, with horse paddocks and grazing on the poorer land.

The lower coastal plain, particularly in the west, is typically a homogeneous landscape of large open fields with few trees or hedgerows. Drainage ditches, wire fences or low banks are more usual as field boundaries. The sense of exposure within this open landscape is heightened by the odd stunted and wind-swept oak that stands along the lines of former hedges. A small number of isolated coastal heaths and woodlands occur on the open plain, with shelter belts of pine, oak or poplar shielding buildings from exposure to the wind.

In the upper coastal plain, tree cover varies. There is a strong network of small and medium-sized broadleaf woodlands, including some which are ancient and semi-natural, well-linked by hedgerows and garden exotics to provide an enclosed field framework. The landscape pattern comprises coniferous plantations, some ancient woodland, and a strong frame of small fields, woods and hedgerows. This quite high degree of vegetation cover is especially notable in contrast to the relatively treeless open lower coastal plain. In many places woodland accentuates the prominence of elevated towns, as in the case of Arundel where the well-wooded landscape separates the town from the suburban villages to the west.

The Changing Countryside

- Mineral extraction, landfill and flooded gravel pits.

- Small villages engulfed by the expansion of urban coastal developments.

- Possible pressure for new service areas along A27/M27 in the future.

- Ribbon development, holiday camps and caravan parks.

- Pressures for recreational uses and marina/harbour developments along the coast.

- Development of large modern glasshouses.

- Construction of rock islands as coastal protection measures immediately off the coast have a major visual influence.

- Coastal dredging operations may exacerbate erosion of the coastal edge resulting in the loss of distinctive landscape features such as coastal marshes.

- Future changes in sea level may become an important issue given that the South Coast Plain's flat low-lying nature makes it particularly vulnerable to rises in relative sea level.

- Loss of hedges and hedgerow trees owing to field enlargement.

- Recent significant loss of tree cover due to Dutch Elm disease and storm damage.

Shaping the Future

- The conservation of woodlands and new planting should be considered where appropriate.

- There are opportunities for the reversion of arable fields to grazing pasture.

- The conservation of wetlands – including those of the intertidal zone – is important to the area.

- There is scope for further restoration of field hedges and hedgerow trees under appropriate agri-environmental land management schemes.

- Coastal zoning and management would balance nature conservation, landscape and recreational interests.

IAIN McGOWAN PHOTOGRAPHY

Fertile soils are intensively farmed, with a prosperous market garden and horticultural trade reflecting the relatively warm temperatures and long growing season.

Selected References

Millward R and Robinson, A (1973), *South-east England – The Channel Coastlands*, Macmillan, London.

Dipper S (1995), *Landscape Assessment of West Sussex – Section 1*, West Sussex County Council, West Sussex.

Hampshire County Council (1993), *The Hampshire Landscape*, Hampshire County Council, Hampshire.

Hinton D A and Insole, A N (1988), *Ordnance Survey Historical Guides: Hampshire and the Isle of Wight*, George Philip, London.

Countryside Commission (1992), *The Chichester Harbour Landscape CCP 381*, Countryside Commission, Cheltenham.

Brandon P (1970), *The Sussex Landscape*, Hodder and Stoughton, London.

Langstone Harbour Board – Langstone Harbour Management Plan – February 1977.

Glossary

AOD: Above Ordnance Datum

en-echelon: arranged in a stepped formation in parallel lines

substrate: surface on which organism grows

Isle of Wight

Key Characteristics

- A small-scale island landscape with an often intimate feel and an overwhelming sense of discovery. There is a juxtaposition of varied and distinctive landforms, diverse land cover types and often sudden and dramatic views of the sea. The close relationship of the area to the sea is a vital ingredient of the island's cultural heritage from prehistoric times.

- The island exhibits, at a small-scale, the key characteristics of many southern English landscape character areas: from intensively farmed arable coastal plain to wooded dairy pasture; from steep Chalk downs to diverse estuarine seascapes and dramatic sea cliffs and stacks.

- The southern coastal plain constitutes an open, intensively managed, arable farmland with large open fields, few trees, and relict hedges. The open character and maritime influence give an exposed windblown feel.

- The Chalk downs are characterised by open rolling arable lands with remnant unimproved grassland on the steeper and usually higher areas. There are few hedgerows or trees here but beech and ash woodland and coppice are supported on the northern slopes of the open downs and some coniferous plantations on the southern slopes. Some remnant heathland/acidic pasture exists in a vale on a band of Greensand between the two ranges of Chalk downs.

- The character of the northern pastures is determined by dairy farming which has created the predominantly lush, green, irregular fields bounded by mature hedgerows. Woodland, much of it coppiced, is a common feature and the occasional orchard adds variety. On the north coast the numerous harbours, creeks, salt marshes and tidal mudflats are fringed by woodland. Formal estates, defined by exotic evergreen planting, dominate parts of the coast whilst Victorian urban seaside settlements are concentrated on others.

- Local limestone and sandstones are the main traditional building materials although differing geologies have determined variations. These stone buildings have dominated the older 'church and manor' settlements which are scattered across the landscape. Local brick buildings are common and indicate a strong Victorian influence within the towns.

- The Undercliff and the coastal chines are particularly unusual and distinctive landscape features.

PATRICK EDEN/COUNTRYSIDE AGENCY

Dramatic coastal views across Freshwater Bay and Compton Cliffs, showing the valued coastal grasslands.

Landscape Character

The Isle of Wight is a diverse island landscape exhibiting at a small-scale the key characteristics of many southern English landscape character areas. It is separated from the South Coast Plain and New Forest character areas by the Solent; its insularity providing a characteristic maritime quality. The dominance of the sea and sky in many views gives unity to the varied landscape features that make up this small land area.

Chalk downland provides an impressive and hilly backcloth for the open rolling countryside of the southern coastal farmlands. The central spine of Chalk supports open, windswept downland rising above sandstone hills and ridges. This provides a sense of enclosure to the southern half of the island – the scrub and yellow gorse of the sandstone hills and low gravel ridges adding interest and variety to the scenes. The varied topography strongly influences the views, many of which are restricted, particularly so north of the Chalk spine where the mosaic of small pasture fields, woodland and dense hedges, with mature oak hedgerow trees, provides a distinct sense of enclosure.

In contrast, the coastal plain to the south offers sweeping views across the low and intensively farmed arable landscape of large, regular, open fields. These are bounded by a sparse, scrubby network of hedges with sporadic wind-profiled trees. This open windswept landscape is broken by three short, south-flowing rivers, their valleys marked by associated wetlands and reedbeds. These rivers are often fringed by low willow scrub bounding the unimproved pasture and relic drainage channels. Where these meet the sea on the southern coast, steep coastal valleys or 'chines' occur. The 'chines' are often well-wooded in contrast to the almost treeless nature of the surrounding arable farmlands. Creeks and inlets marking ancient drowned valleys dot much of the northern coastline, providing many tranquil landscapes of great antiquity.

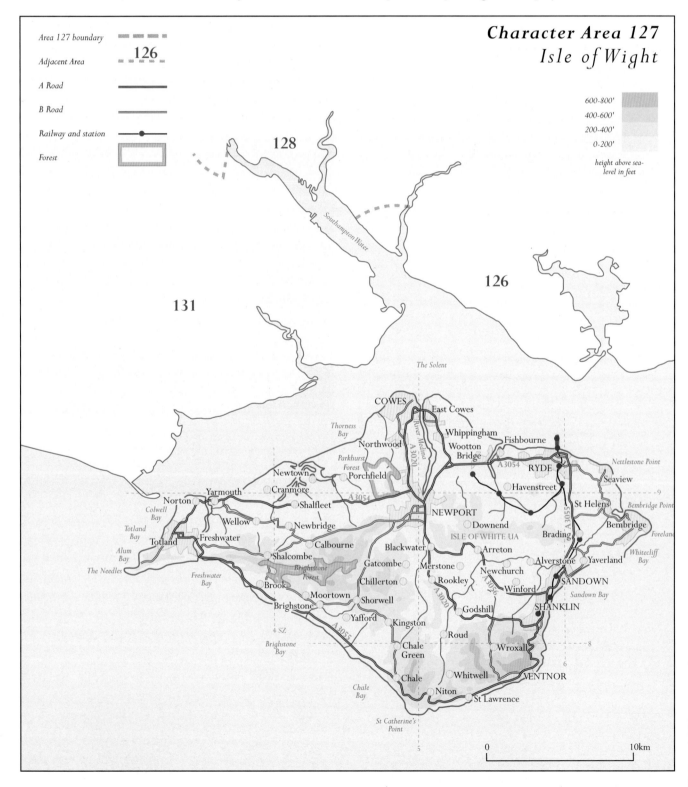

Character Area 127
Isle of Wight

Physical Influences

The geology of the Isle of Wight mirrors that of the Hampshire Basin across the Solent. The northern claylands of the island have a strong geological similarity to the New Forest and, indeed, the island was connected to this region before rising sea levels created the Western Solent.

A central Chalk ridge of steeply inclined strata divides the island on an east-west axis. This spine reaches a maximum height of 214 m AOD at Brightstone Down, an area of deeply dissected dry valleys with generally thin and infertile soils. At Tennyson Down, the advancing sea has carved the ridge into the precipitous cliffs and distinctive stacks known as the Needles. The southern Chalk downs are higher, reaching 240 m AOD at St Boniface Down which, being capped with Plateau Gravel, supports a rare example of relict heathland.

The northern half of the Isle of Wight is characterised by low-lying Tertiary clays overlain in places by gravel capped ridges. In some areas, coastal erosion has caused slumping resulting in heathland dominated cliff edges and gorse or wooded slopes giving way to sections of bare, unstable clay.

To the south of the central Chalk scarp, ridges of the Upper Greensand overlie Gault, the Lower Greensand and the Wealden Beds whose clay gives rise to a dissected plain. Short, south flowing streams arise from the foot of the Chalk scarp and cross the plain to the south-west coast where they have cut deep ravines or 'chines' in the soft Wealden and Lower Greensand beds of the unstable cliff-line.

The Undercliff of the southern coast of the Isle of Wight is the largest area of rotational landslip in Western Europe. Here, Greensand and chert topped cliffs tower above a series of terraces running down to low coastal cliffs; a particularly British landscape comparable with Lyme Regis and Folkestone Warren.

The island's main rivers – the Medina and Eastern Yar – rise near the southern coast and flow northwards to the Solent through deep gaps in the central Chalk ridge. In each case the downstream section has been submerged by post-glacial sea level rise to form a drowned river valley or *ria*.

Historical and Cultural Influences

After the close of the last Ice Age, 10,000 years ago, the sub tundra landscape of the Isle of Wight gave way to birch, pine and hazel scrub. An improved climate led in turn to much of the island becoming covered in deciduous forest. Evidence suggests that woodland clearance was begun sometime after 4,000 BC by New Stone Age communities. Clearance had become greatly accelerated by the Bronze and Iron Ages (c1000 BC to 43 AD). The lighter soils of the Chalk and Greensand along the coast, plus the freely draining gravel caps in the north of the island, attracted many early settlements. As the population expanded, large areas of woodland were cleared for agriculture. Prehistoric clearance on the downs created pastoral grassland whilst clearance and over-farming on the sands and gravels commonly created heathland.

The influence of generations of holiday makers cannot be escaped on the island – here the impact of a caravan site on the coast.

In post-Roman times, the oak woods of the north of the island came to be managed for timber through a need for coppiced poles, fencing and firewood. By the Middle Ages, the island had become a mixed agricultural landscape; a mosaic of woodland, pasture, meadows and arable fields with sheep and farmed rabbits grazing the open pasture of the Downs. By Tudor times, seven deer parks had been created, including the King's Park of Watchingwell (considered to be one of England's oldest deer parks). During and following the Tudor period, land was enclosed by Parliamentary Enclosure Acts. In the 19th century, many fields were enlarged and hedgerows straightened as improvements in drainage allowed heavier soils to be worked. More recently in the 20th century the agricultural pattern was further diversified as market gardening and pig-rearing played a significant role in the agricultural economy.

Tourism has been important to the island's economy since the mid-19th century; its success has relied on the special visual qualities of the landscape. The development of the railways enlivened interest and was directly responsible for the growth of 'new' towns such as Ryde, Sandown, Shanklin and Ventnor. The decision by Victoria and Albert to live at Osborne promoted further Victorian development. The array of Victorian villas and gardens, particularly along the Undercliff and at Ryde, are evidence of this enthusiasm.

Buildings and Settlement

The island's patterns of settlement and varied styles of building are as varied as its landscapes. Small, intimate villages are connected by narrow, winding lanes. Greensand is the most common building material and it characterises the villages which are to be found at the base of the Chalk downs. Many of the settlements tend to be small and linear, developed originally as cottages along streets. The southern half of the island is less intensively developed than many other areas. The exception to this is the Undercliff, an area on the southern coast where a mild microclimate, fine views and secretive landscape made it a popular place to live during Victorian times. There are many grand Victorian houses and grounds with a scatter of exotic plants.

The traditional use of local materials has had a significant influence in enhancing the appearance of the built environment. The stone-built villages, constructed from locally quarried sandstone and limestone, commonly use tiles as a traditional roofing material. A few ancient buildings are roofed with a combination of limestone slabs and tile upper courses. Elsewhere, brick is the principal building material. Important buildings within the landscape include Carisbrooke Castle, Osborne House and an array of medieval churches.

The Victorian influence is evident throughout the island – particularly here at the Osborne Estate.

Land Cover

The Isle of Wight – the Garden Isle – is characterised by mixed agricultural use. Farmland forms a patchwork of small enclosed fields and copses on the northern clays. On the Wealden and Lower Greensand Beds arable farming is intense. The central Chalk ridge and the high Chalk southern downs support some stretches of sheep-grazed downland.

Permanent grassland with established hedgerows still dominates the heavy clay soils of the northern Wight. Here there are numerous small woodland blocks and a few large plantations such as the extensive Parkhurst Forest. Relict wood-pasture of ancient origin is also a notable feature of this area.

A view of the island from the distinctive 'Needles' illustrating the dominance of chalk and the maritime influence.

The more varied geology of the fertile southern lowland part of the island supports a patchwork of large open fields often distinguished by their reddish brown soils. The land use gradually shifts from mainly pastoral in the east to an intensive arable regime with very large open fields in the west. The Chalk downs support a variety of land uses including chalk grassland pasture, open intensive arable production, ancient hanger woodlands, scrub and commercial forestry. Where the Chalk or Greensand is capped by gravels, heathland type communities (gorse, bracken and heather) thrive. True heathland, however, is scarce on the island and is largely concentrated at Golden Hill and Headon Warren.

The coastline supports a mixture of intertidal mud-flats and marshes, ancient woodland, chalk turf and coastal heath. Grazing marshes and reedbeds stand in stark contrast to high, vertical cliffs and stacks that dominate the coastline.

Horticulture – largely concentrated in East Wight – plays a major role in the island's economy with fields of vegetables, bulbs and flowers interspersed by a small number of orchards.

Mineral extraction on the island includes chalk for agricultural lime and for construction fill, gravel and building sands.

The Changing Countryside

- Loss of trees, unimproved grassland and historic hedgerows due to agricultural intensification.

- Increase in tourism-related developments, particularly on the coast and visual impact of semi-derelict caravan parks in other areas.

- Loss of chalk downland due to intensive arable production, afforestation and to scrub growth.

- Loss of unimproved meadows.

- Decline in area of heathland and damage to wetland landscapes (marsh, bog and wet meadows) from agricultural and drainage improvements.

- Demand for new structures such as television masts and wind farms on elevated sites.

- Significant visual impact of chalk extraction on high land and exposed slopes, plus resulting damage to ancient chalk grassland or archaeological sites.

- Demand for landfill sites for waste disposal outstripping supply of suitable, exhausted, mineral working sites.

- Degraded historic parks and gardens.

- Erosion of settlement character due to use of new building materials and styles.

- Coastal erosion affecting chines, coastal habitats and archaeological sites.

- Ploughing and denudation of ancient monuments.

Shaping the Future

- There are opportunities for the restoration and re-creation of chalk downland pasture via reinstatement of traditional grazing regimes and reduction in ploughing or application of herbicides and fertilizers.

- The management of riverside features and adjoining land, including re-establishment of wetlands and traditional grazing and hay-cutting regimes, is important.

- The reversion of arable land to grazing plus restoration of characteristic coastal vegetation around the island's coast should be considered.

- The conservation of significant parks and gardens should be addressed.

- The identification of threatened ancient monuments and appropriate action would help protect and conserve archaeological sites in their setting.

- The conservation and management of existing woodlands and identification of new areas for planting should be considered.

- Integrated coastal zone management is important.

Selected References

Basford H V (1980), *The Vectis Report*, Isle of Wight County Council.

Basford H V (1989), *Historic Parks and Gardens of the IoW*, Isle of Wight County Council.

Countryside Commission (1994), *The Isle of Wight*, CCP 448, Countryside Commission, Cheltenham.

Hinton D A and Insole, AN (1988), *Ordnance Survey Historical Guides: Hampshire and the Isle of Wight*, George Philip, London.

Isle of Wight Joint Advisory Committee (1994), *Isle of Wight AONB Management Plan Summary, Isle of Wight AONB Project*, Newport, Isle of Wight.

Jones, J and J (1987), *The Isle of Wight: An Illustrated History*, The Dovecote Press, Wimborne, Dorset.

Margham J N (1982 & 1983), *Isle of Wight village morphology (parts 1&3)* Proceedings of the Isle of Wight Natural History and Archaeology Society 7 475 - 487, 601 - 608.

White H J O (1921), *A short account of the geology of the Isle of Wight*, The Geological Survey of Great Britain, HMSO, London.

BRIAN MANBY

Settlements such as Ventnor saw development as coastal resorts in Victorian times, the mainland seen in the background shows its proximity.

Glossary

AOD: Above Ordnance Datum

chert: hard dense rock of amorphous silica

chines: fissures or cracks

hanger: a wood on the side of a steep hill

South Hampshire Lowlands

Key Characteristics

- The gently undulating landscape is characterised by a diversity of features and land uses which reflects changing soil types and local variations in topography.

- Predominantly mixed farmland and woodland, a patchwork of small, intimate and irregular fields defined by hedges, winding lanes and scattered farmsteads.

- Wide lush river valley bottoms, with water meadows and riverine vegetation, afford open views in an otherwise small-scale and intimate landscape.

- The rural character, defined by well-managed farmland and a few historic estates, is being diminished by urban expansion and the busy M27/M3 corridors.

- A dispersed settlement pattern of villages and scattered farmsteads is linked by winding roads and lanes.

- Oaks prevalent within hedgerows and woodlands help to create an impression of a well-wooded landscape.

- Small pockets of horticulture within extensive pasture, with some arable use, are confined to the higher drier ground.

Landscape Character

The enclosed landscape of the South Hampshire Lowlands extends across southern Hampshire, nestled between the Chalk downs and the more open South Coast Plain. The Lowlands blend into the New Forest character area west of Southampton and Romsey and tail off in the east at the open Chalk ridge of Ports Down which contrasts strongly with the low-lying enclosed farmland beyond.

The low-lying undulating plain of the South Hampshire Lowlands is characterised by its varied composition of landscape features and land uses reflecting the changing soil types and local variations of topography. A varied small-scale agricultural landscape, the lower ground is generally used for grazing on the heavy, difficult to work clay soils with some arable use confined to pockets of better drained higher ground. The predominantly pasture farmland is set within a patchwork of small, intimate and irregular fields typical of an ancient landscape. A winding network of small roads and lanes links the surrounding villages and farming settlements. Typically, settlements have a loosely clustered pattern with many villages often distinctly nucleated. Between the village settlements, numerous small farmsteads and cottages are dotted along roadsides.

Open views of the wet pasture with its riparian vegetation found in the wide valley bottom of the Itchen Valley.

Much of the South Hampshire Lowlands landscape is dominated by mixed farmland within a well-wooded setting. Rich field and roadside boundary hedges, numerous hedgerow trees, ancient semi-natural woodlands and remnant wood-pasture combine to create an impression of a secluded, enclosed and well-treed landscape. Many of the hedgerows, widely occurring as hedgebanks, are old and species-rich with large characteristic oak trees helping to sustain the well-wooded character.

In contrast to the predominantly wooded farmland character, an intensively cultivated landscape occurs as small pockets within the surrounding farmlands on the light, well-drained loams mainly around the Meon Valley. These soils support intensive levels of market cropping with the associated land uses of garden centres, nurseries and

smallholdings or allotments. This land use gives rise to a field pattern of regular, medium-sized open fields divided into typically unfenced plots and linear strips with a fragmented, skeletal hedgerow network – evidence of neglect and widespread removal. Tree cover is sparse although occasional shelter belts of pine, cypress, poplar and alder form distinct vertical features within the open landscape. Wet pasture and riverine vegetation, commonly associated with fast-flowing chalk rivers, are characteristic of the major valleys which transect the area such as the Meon, Itchen and Test. Such valleys offer open views in contrast to the otherwise enclosed and secluded landscape while the swift rivers offer a great sense of movement within the landscape.

The overall feel is one of calm prosperity, with well-managed farmland and some large estates, although pressure from urban expansion and the busy M27 and M3 corridors detract from the essentially rural character of the landscape.

Physical Influences

The varied South Hampshire Lowlands landscape owes its diversity to the complex relationship between the underlying rocks, soils, drainage and landform. The area is part of the extensive broad belt of low-lying Tertiary clays and sands capped by sands and gravels deposited by the rivers of the area. They fringe the lower slopes of the Chalk to the north. These Tertiary deposits support a variety of soils including widespread, seasonally-waterlogged, heavy, clay soils, with small areas of light, well-drained loams and free-draining acidic former heathland soils. The gently undulating landform is low-lying with a few localised areas of better-drained higher ground. A geological and topographical contrast is provided by the spine-like Chalk ridge of Ports Down, just over one kilometre wide, which rises steeply above Portsmouth Harbour and the surrounding low-lying expanse of Tertiary deposits. Numerous small watercourses drain the South Hampshire Lowlands forming tributaries of the lower reaches of the rivers Test, Itchen, Hamble and Meon which transect the area en route to the sea.

Historical and Cultural Influences

It was about 7000 years ago that the first Hampshire farmers began to utilise the rich deep soils of this area and started to clear the heavily-wooded land that was later known as the Forest of Bere. Bronze Age barrows remain as witness to activity in the area in the period 2000 - 3000

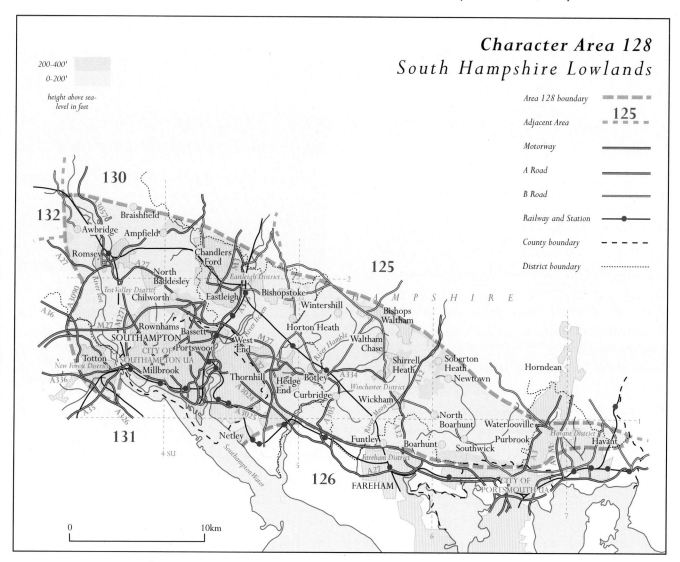

Character Area 128
South Hampshire Lowlands

BC and the fertile soils and woods still drew attention from Roman colonists millennia later. The confluence of the rivers Test and Itchen in Southampton Water has always been a strategic defensive and trading area. It was here that the Romans built a large fort (Clausentum – now part of Southampton) as the nearest coastal point to Winchester – the area's administrative centre.

The fast flowing river Itchen is typical of the rivers found in the South Hampshire Lowlands.

By the end of the 7th century, under the rule of the West Saxons, a major port was flourishing at Southampton. Many of the first village sites and churches remain from this period. In the 9th century Viking raids disrupted the expanding economy and the port of Southampton faded in importance, not reviving until the 11th century. Domesday Book, which was compiled at this time, described this zone as a county of rural settlements.

The 12th and 13th centuries saw the expansion of settlements with a growing population. Deer parks and castles were built by the nobility and new towns were set up by the Kings and Bishops. The Black Death of the 14th century helped stem this population increase and saved Hampshire's remaining woodland from clearance for crops.

The whole of the rich coastal hinterland has always been at risk from raids and invasion and the landscape retains evidence of defence which spans from the Hundred Years War, where threat of French raids on Southampton led to the construction of defensive walls, to the Napoleonic Wars which led to the string of Palmerston Forts (also known as Palmerston's Follies) on Portsdown Hill built as a protection for the ports from land-based attack.

By the 16th century, Southampton's share of trade had decreased and the iron smelting and salt working along the shore had ceased but, by the 17th century, it was buoyant once again, with arable production increasing. Water meadows, particularly along the main rivers and stream networks, were flooded early in the season to keep off frosts and provide an early 'bite' for stock. They were a common feature of the landscape. Paper and silk making

took advantage of water mills, explaining the location of many settlements near watercourses.

The Industrial Revolution brought improvements to roads and the development of the railway. New seaside resorts were developed at Hayling Island and Southsea. Towns expanded, constructed from bricks of local clay. Poor soils were used for dairying, pigs and market gardening and there was an increasing return to sheep farming due to less competition from abroad.

A number of artists were familiar with the area: one of Turner's paintings now hangs in Petworth House and John Millais, when resident in Southampton, drew his fishing expeditions on the Test and Itchen. Botley will always be connected with the writer William Cobbett who lived and wrote of the area between 1804 and 1810 and, of course, Isaac Walton's classic, *The Compleat Angler* contemplated life and fishing on the Itchen.

Buildings and Settlement

Major urban centres such as Southampton, Eastleigh and Havant with their mid-19th century housing, recent housing estates and associated industrial and commercial developments, dominate parts of the area and pressure for urban expansion has affected the rural nature of those areas in proximity.

The influence of modern housing estates 'backing into' the countryside is evident from this view of the north east of Southampton.

Villages and scattered farming settlements are generally at a low density, the villages commonly loosely clustered together, some with clear nucleii. Dispersed throughout the area are small farms, cottages and a few large houses with pony paddocks dotted along adjoining roads and lanes. These minor roads and narrow lanes form a quite dense, often busy, network linking the rural settlements with the local main roads and the busy M27 and M3 corridors which form discordant features in the landscape.

Large estates and their houses are evidence of the historical prosperity of the South Hampshire Lowlands with a prominence of riding schools and horse grazing. In contrast, the scattered pockets of mainly horticultural land use give rise to distinctive glasshouses, polythene tunnels and storage buildings, mainly associated with mid-19th century houses and bungalows.

The visual dominance of high rise buildings in Southampton is apparent for long distances.

Land Cover

The characteristic pattern of land cover found on the broad belt of heavy clay soils which dominate the South Hampshire Lowlands is a combination of mixed arable but predominantly grazing land within a well-wooded setting. Oak and ash are particularly characteristic, with oak especially widespread within the rich network of field and roadside hedgerows and also in the numerous areas of ancient semi-natural woodland or remnant wood pasture.

Some former heathland areas exist which support mainly horse grazing. Further contrast is provided by sporadic shelter belts of pine, cypress, poplar and alder in an otherwise sparsely wooded area associated with the market gardening on the pockets of lighter, better-drained soils especially in the vicinity of the Meon Valley. Coniferous plantations occur in parts of the Forest of Bere.

Parts of the Lowlands remain as evidence of the Enclosure Acts, where a regular and largely intact hedgerow network, with roadside hedges, defines the fields. The low trimmed roadside hedges allow good views across the grazed patchwork landscape of small to medium-sized and regularly shaped fields and woodlands. In contrast, horticultural areas have fields which are typically larger and much more open, and the fragmented and gappy hedgerows provide evidence of neglect – many have been removed entirely.

The Changing Countryside

- Woodland and hedgerow loss has increased field sizes throughout sections of the South Hampshire Lowlands.

- Pressure for urban developments and associated infrastructure within the landscape.

- Neglect and/or poor management of ancient, semi-natural woodlands.

- Abandonment of traditional water-meadows management and grazing.

- Loss of mature willows, alder carr coppice and associated ancient field systems within river valleys.

Shaping the Future

- The preservation of remnant field systems needs to be addressed.

- Opportunities exist to conserve degraded ancient woodlands and to manage many other woodlands.

- There is scope for re-establishing traditionally grazed water-meadows along river valleys, pollarding of mature willows and coppicing of alder carr along river banks.

- Restoration of field hedgerows and boundaries through appropriate agri-environmental land management schemes should be considered.

- Good design in keeping with character of area through Planning Guidance, together with landscaping, would decrease visual intrusion of urban development in more rural areas.

Selected References

Hampshire County Council (1993), *The Hampshire Landscape*, Hampshire County Council, Hampshire.

Hinton D A and Insole, A N (1988), *Ordnance Survey Historical Guides: Hampshire and the Isle of Wight*, George Philip, London.

Broadleaved woodlands are a significant feature of this area.

Thames Basin Heaths

- Particularly diverse landscape unified by the high incidence of heathland and coniferous forestry, the open unenclosed nature of which is unusual within the context of the south-east region.

- Heavily populated and developed area characterised by large towns plus numerous smaller settlements along transport corridors interspersed by open land.

- Important occupation area from Mesolithic to modern times based on exploitation of the rivers with numerous Prehistoric, Roman and medieval settlements, the latter of which extended along valley bottoms.

- Fragmented but often connected blocks of largely neglected remnant heathland as a result of early agricultural clearances and widespread development, with most heath retained on large commons or as Ministry of Defence training areas.

- The western part of the area is fairly well-wooded with grazed pasture but retains a heathy character due to the dominance of oak/birch/bracken/pine and remnant heath on small unimproved pockets of land.

- Variety and contrast is given by the wide grazed floodplain, drainage ditches, restored gravel workings and lush wetland vegetation associated with the Kennet Valley.

- Cultivated farmland and pasture is typically enclosed within small and irregularly shaped fields divided by hedgerows with small areas of wood and heath heavily used for horse grazing.

- Large tracts of coniferous plantations or mixed wood with beech and birch are typical of much of the area, with significant areas of ancient woodland in the west.

JOHN TYLER/COUNTRYSIDE AGENCY

Small towns and villages, such as the Roman settlement of Silchester, nestle discreetly amongst the gently sloping plateaux of the Reading and Bagshot Beds. Use of local materials is reflected in the buildings and flint wall.

Landscape Character

The Thames Basin Heaths comprise a distinct area of commonly unenclosed heathland and coniferous forestry developed on the acidic soils in the west of the Thames Basin. The Heaths extend from the Thames Basin Lowlands in the east, across north Hampshire north of the Downs and through south-east Berkshire towards the dip slope of the Berkshire and Marlborough Downs.

The once extensive heathland is now largely fragmented and degraded but the landscape still maintains its open and 'heathy' character. The area still contains large areas of rolling unenclosed heathland where the varying seasons and weathers change the character of the open landscape from colourful and exhilarating to sombre and bleak. The distinctive and widespread occurrence of oak/birch/bracken/pine reflects the poor acidic soils and heathland origins of this area.

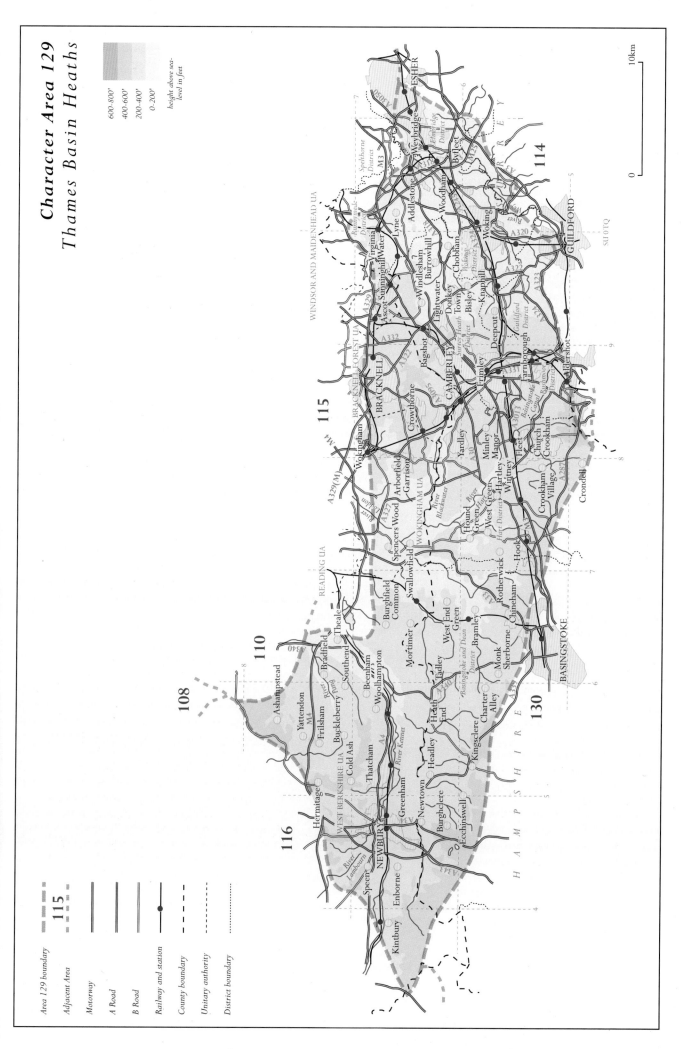

Character Area 129
Thames Basin Heaths

height above sea-level in feet
600-800'
400-600'
200-400'
0-200'

Area 129 boundary
115 Adjacent Area
Motorway
A Road
B Road
Railway and station
County boundary
Unitary authority
District boundary

10km

Blocks of remnant heathland on acidic soils are often open and unenclosed, which is rare in the south eastern landscape. Their bright purple patches make a distinct impression on the character of the Thames Basin Heaths.

The Heaths have experienced rapid and intensive residential development in the last 50 years with large towns such as Ascot, Camberley, Farnborough and Woking comprising major focal points within the wider landscape. The M3, M4, M25 and A34 are major transport routes that cut through the area adding to the generally developed character of much of the heathlands. Within the wider rural landscape, farming is generally small-scale and enclosed, primarily restricted to pasture with widespread horse grazing and very little productive arable land due to the poor soils.

Trees are a significant feature of western Surrey. Fields, gardens and houses appear to be set within all-enveloping woodland; an illusion partly created by large wooded gardens and by belts of woodland along roadsides, together with substantial areas of woodland and forestry. Broad heaths and a subtle mosaic of grassland, bogs, ponds and fringes of encroaching scrub combine with the woodlands and forestry to give the essential character of the area.

At the western end of the Thames Basin Heaths, a landscape of mixed farmland and woodland forms most of the boundary with the Hampshire Downs to the south. This is largely a landscape of small to medium-sized irregular fields and woodlands as well as hedgerows and hedgebanks with large trees. Views are constrained by the many woodlands and hedgerows. The chalklands are visible from areas of higher ground but, generally, this is an intimately enclosed landscape, valued for its sense of remoteness and seclusion.

Large areas are under private ownership, including sizeable tracts owned by the Ministry of Defence. Barracks, areas of army housing, camps, military signs and notices give much of the landscape an inescapable military tone.

This is an ancient landscape with many small well-hedged, irregular fields set in winding, locally sunken lanes with hedgebanks, hedgerows and oaks. Small farms, cottages and straggling roadside settlements are dispersed throughout. A more regular field pattern also occurs, with a network of typically straight roads and small hedged fields or small to medium-sized fields, often internally fenced. Roadside settlements, smallholdings, market gardening and garden centres also tend to occupy this recently enclosed landscape. Bracken and gorse, typically prominent along the fencelines and in the hedgerows, reinforce the impression of a 'heathy' character.

Contrast and variety is provided by the Kennet Valley south of the Berkshire and Marlborough Downs. Generally, the valley sides rise gently, in places in a series of terraces, encompassing an area of gentle character which is quintessentially English lowland river and vale. Over quite large areas the valley bottom is still undrained and damp in character with a complex pattern of river, canal, drainage dykes and linking channels, with associated wet pasture, reed beds and woodland.

The Kennet Valley has also borne the impacts of recent development, in particular the rapid growth of Newbury and Thatcham, and some substantial sand and gravel extraction. From Theale towards Reading, for example, the extensive lakes of wet workings have completely transformed the original character of the landscape.

South of the Kennet, the land rises to a plateau of mixed woodland with extensive conifer plantations, heath, farm and parkland. This area includes the famous defence establishment at Aldermaston, which is a distinct feature at night when lit.

Physical Influences

The dominant landform is generally flat to gently sloping plateaux commonly incised by broad or, in places, steep-sided river valleys. The plateaux are generally underlain by Tertiary deposits including clays, silts, sands and gravels of the Reading and Bagshot Beds, with London Clay in the valleys. These give rise to nutrient-poor acidic soils with a mainly light or slowly permeable character which are a major factor in the land use. Localised areas of more fertile loamy soils support arable farming within the predominantly heathland, woodland and pasture land use.

Where the Chalk scarp of the Hampshire Downs meets the lower lying Heaths, water from within the higher Chalk strata produces many spring lines. These are commonly associated with ecologically important habitats and also with distinctive linear settlement patterns. Many valley areas are affected by gravel extraction. Elsewhere, drift deposits contribute to the variety of land cover elements within the area. Plateau deposits consisting of acidic sands and gravels give rise to heathland, whereas valley deposits including fertile silt as well as gravels have created lush water meadow landscapes.

Numerous watercourses drain the Heaths including the rivers Enborne, Kennet, Pang, Loddon (and its tributary the Lyde), Blackwater (and its tributary the Whitewater), the Hart, the Windle Brook and the Bourne. The Basingstoke Canal is also an important element in the hydrological balance.

Historical and Cultural Influences

The development of the heathland character began with prehistoric clearance of the natural woodland for grazing or cultivation. The characteristically light soils, assisted by the slight natural acidity and permeability of the underlying sands and gravels, were leached of nutrients and became more acidic and thus better suited for acid-tolerant species such as heather and gorse. Much of this heathland survived well into the 18th century when it was one of the largest and most continuous areas of lowland heath in England.

JOHN TYLER/COUNTRYSIDE AGENCY

The wide grazed floodplain of the river Kennet is a distinctive feature. Regular flooding in winter restricts land use to permanent pasture.

The last 150 years has seen the extent of heathland greatly reduced due to cessation of stock grazing resulting in encroachment by 'pioneer' species such as birch and the invasive bracken. More recently still, further areas of heathland have been lost through piecemeal housing development, commercial forestry plantations, scrub woodland, nurseries and other suburban developments.

The whole area has a complex history of human intervention containing many known and many more potential sites of archaeological interest. Henges, long and round barrows, Roman settlements, traces of ancient field systems and evidence of lynchets are all frequent and characteristic features of the historic landscape. Some areas reflect wider historic land uses: for example, the influence of early medieval hunting forests such as the Forest of Evesley or Bracknell Forest which are extensive tracts of

largely undeveloped land within a generally heavily developed area. Other historic land uses, such as those resulting from the use and harnessing of river water, eg as flood meadows and mills, add to the typically diverse historic landscape associated with the Heathlands.

During the 18th century the Thames Basin Heaths became a major focus for new development in the region due largely to the perceived scenic qualities of heathland coupled with the rapid growth of London. This led to a major increase in the number of people moving to the area. Park estates, modest country houses and villages grew up in the more open parts, generally surrounded by woodland, which were fairly close and accessible to London.

Buildings and Settlement

Large areas of the Thames Basin Heaths within easy reach of London are dominated by extensive residential suburbs, intermixed with golf courses and parkland. On many areas of former heathland the developing woodland has created a mature and enclosed setting for large houses at low density, associated in many places with a network of small fields, usually used as paddocks.

Away from the influence of London and the main commuter routes, the area is characterised by a network of winding roads and lanes throughout which villages and scattered farming settlements are generally at a low density. Villages are commonly linear but locally there is a clear nucleus, typically associated with a village green. Within the Kennet Valley the settlements of Newbury and Thatcham dominate the area having grown extensively and almost coalesced in recent years.

Military installations are significant built structures within the Heaths landscape such as the Atomic Warfare Establishment at Aldermaston, Farnborough Airfield and also Greenham Common airfield. These military installations generally coincide with areas of heathland or former heath surrounded by an alternating landscape of medium-sized farms, large houses in extensive grounds and small villages. Some villages such as Aldermaston, located on the site of a former Saxon settlement, have managed to retain a large part of their traditional character. In contrast other villages, such as Burghfield or Mortimer, have experienced major expansion as commuter settlements during this century. Red brick housing is generally the norm for much of the Heaths.

Land Cover

An internationally rare habitat with a high conservation value, heathland forms extensive pockets of uncultivated land within the Thames Basin Heaths character area. These distinctive landscape features form open tracts of seasonally

Woodlands, coniferous and broadleaved, are major features of the character of the Thames Basin Heaths. Much is secondary woodland with oak, birch and sweet chestnut being common constituent species.

colourful land, dominated by various types of heathers, gorse, beech and birch. Many of the smaller grass-dominated heathlands are in local authority ownership allowing public access while the generally larger but comparatively fewer areas of heather-dominated heathlands are within restricted areas owned by the Ministry of Defence. A notable exception is Chobham Common owned by Surrey County Council.

Farmland is generally of traditional scale, extensively hedged and, in some places, intercut with small woods and relict heathland. Improved grasslands dominate the agricultural scene with some small areas of arable on the localised areas of more fertile soils. In addition to the widespread grazing of farm livestock, grazing by horses is a notable and common feature within the small paddocks that are a particular feature of the farmland in the urban fringes. Riding schools and stud farms provide small paddocks and medium-sized fields, typically defined by a network of hedges, although often these are reinforced or supplemented by distinctive post and rail fencing.

There is little ancient semi-natural woodland, except in the west part, with most woodland planted over the last 200

years. The main woodland type is oak-birch secondary woodland with beech, rowan, holly and rhododendrons frequent in many woods. Many smaller woodlands or wooded strips near the edge of settlements are often used for informal recreation. Increases in the size of fields within arable areas, at the expense of hedgerows and woodland, have left many woods isolated, contributing to the erosion of the patchwork landscape that gives the Heaths their essential character.

Throughout the area, scattered isolated pockets of ancient semi-natural woodlands and some areas of wood-pasture provide significant nature-conservation value. A diverse range of significant landscape features such as streams, meadows, commons and some ancient field systems are also important wildlife habitats. Typically, hedges consist of oak, holly, ash or hazel.

Commercial nurseries are a common land use within this area, for example around Chobham and Bisley where light free-draining soils support a distinctive landscape pattern of regular blocks of tightly spaced young trees. Some areas of neglected and overgrown former nurseries have led to unusual woodlands which provide new and varied habitats. Golf courses are also a common land use in the Heaths.

These are generally well-wooded between the fairways and are commonly either formed within woodland or on open heathland.

Secondary woodland, and sometimes also semi-natural woodland, adjacent to areas of suburban housing is often subject to the increasing influence of non-indigenous plants within their understorey and ground layers. Where gardens have extended into established woodlands, ornamental shrubs and grasses combine with woodland species such as laurel, holly, sweet chestnut, beech and oak to give many areas a gardened appearance.

Forestry plantations are common on former heathlands. They are mainly coniferous, usually Scots pine, and are often edged by broadleaved trees such as birch, oak or sweet chestnut. Bracken is common beneath the trees and in open areas while heather also re-colonises where the canopy has not closed. Many of the forestry areas are owned and used by the Ministry of Defence, alongside active forestry management and public access. Some areas are typified by their distinctively dense crop of young trees grown for the Christmas tree market.

Open riverside meadows are a distinctive characteristic of the river valleys with alder, willow and poplar as typical tree species. Extensive gravel extraction activities are a common feature in these areas, such as in the Kennet Valley where current workings and large lakes, important for their recreation and wildlife value, are highly prominent features.

The Changing Countryside

- Poor management of existing woodland and tree belts is diminishing the character of the landscape and making development more intrusive.

- Planting of extensive conifer plantations since 1945 has dramatically altered the traditional appearance of the heathlands.

- Loss of characteristic features such as hedgerows in small pockets of farmland.

- Ministry of Defence activity has restricted development and public access.

- Mineral extraction along rivers.

- Decline in commons grazing.

- Agricultural diversification pressures on the landscape giving rise to inappropriate land uses, such as Christmas tree nurseries and golf courses.

- Development pressures from the continuing rapid growth of towns in the area and from pressures relating to transport infrastructure and road improvements.

Shaping the Future

- The conservation of remaining areas of heath should be considered through the management of woodland scrub encroachment by the restoration of grazing. This might also include the reversion of woodland (in particular coniferous plantations) to heath.

- The restoration and management of sand and gravel workings and waste disposal sites should be addressed.

- The reversion of arable to permanent pasture in remnant unimproved valley floors, and the management of willow and alder along watercourses, are important.

- There is scope for the restoration and conservation of hedgerows.

- Former Ministry of Defence landholdings might present opportunities for restoration and conservation of remnant heathlands, as at Greenham Common.

Selected References

Hampshire County Council (1993), *The Hampshire Landscape*, HCC.

Surrey County Council (1994), *The Future of Surrey's Landscape and Woodlands – Part 1: An assessment (Consultation Draft)*, SCC.

Babtie Public Services Division (undated), *A Landscape Strategy for Berkshire: Consultation Proposals*, Berkshire County Council.

JOHN TYLER/COUNTRYSIDE AGENCY

Farming is generally small-scale and restricted to intensive pasture, with widespread horse grazing and little productive arable land due to the poor soils.

Hampshire Downs

Key Characteristics

- Strongly rolling downland with scarps, hilltops and valleys which have an overall open and exposed character.

- Scarps and hilltops are characterised by extensive open tracts of large arable fields and some ley pasture, sporadically interrupted by woodlands. In contrast, within the sheltered downland valleys, the network of mixed-species hedgerows interspersed by numerous oak/ash or hazel woodland coppice gives a strong sense of enclosure.

- Clay-with-flints overlying Chalk mainly on higher ground supports a mix of arable farms, former commons, wood-pastures and ancient semi-natural woodland. A network of distinctive and ancient droving roads and track ways are a particular feature, as are numerous large estates with formal parkland.

- Distinctive appearance of chalk cob and flint in traditional rural buildings and walls surrounding farm courtyards, with thatch surviving in many places.

- Widespread prehistoric settlement and burial mounds with visually prominent Iron Age hillforts, Roman estates and nucleated medieval village settlement patterns.

- The Test and Itchen are significant and distinctive Chalk river valleys cut into the broad downland landscape.

Landscape Character

The Hampshire Downs are part of the broad belt of Chalk linking the Dorset Downs and Salisbury Plain in the west with the South Downs in the east, and the Berkshire and Marlborough Downs to the north. In stark contrast to the Hampshire Downs, adjacent character areas are dominated by the heaths and coniferous forestry of the Thames Basin Heaths to the north and the Wealden Greensand to the east. The South Hampshire Lowlands form the landscape immediately to the south separating the Downs from the south coast.

JOHN TYLER/COUNTRYSIDE AGENCY

The clay tops of the downland often support areas of deciduous woodland.

Characterised by a complex landform consisting of strongly rolling chalk downland, dissected by both deep and shallow sheltered valley landforms with numerous distinct hilltops, ridges and scarps, the Downs are both striking and conspicuous. The landscape is large in scale with a predominantly rural character typified by often extensive views and widely dispersed settlements.

Many of the higher parts of the Downs are capped by a shallow deposit of clay with flints. In places this is in the form of a flat or gently domed plateau. The plateau is predominantly a landscape of arable farmland with varying degrees of enclosure. Hedgerows or the edges of numerous ancient woodlands frequently define the field pattern, although some areas of former common or open field system are more open with fenced fields and long views.

Away from the clay plateau on the lighter chalk soils, intensive arable production is typical in the largely open landscape. Low, trimmed hedgerows, post and wire fences or coniferous shelter belts define the large fields. There are few woodlands. Throughout the Downs on the steeper uncultivated slopes, woodland or unimproved chalk grassland occurs.

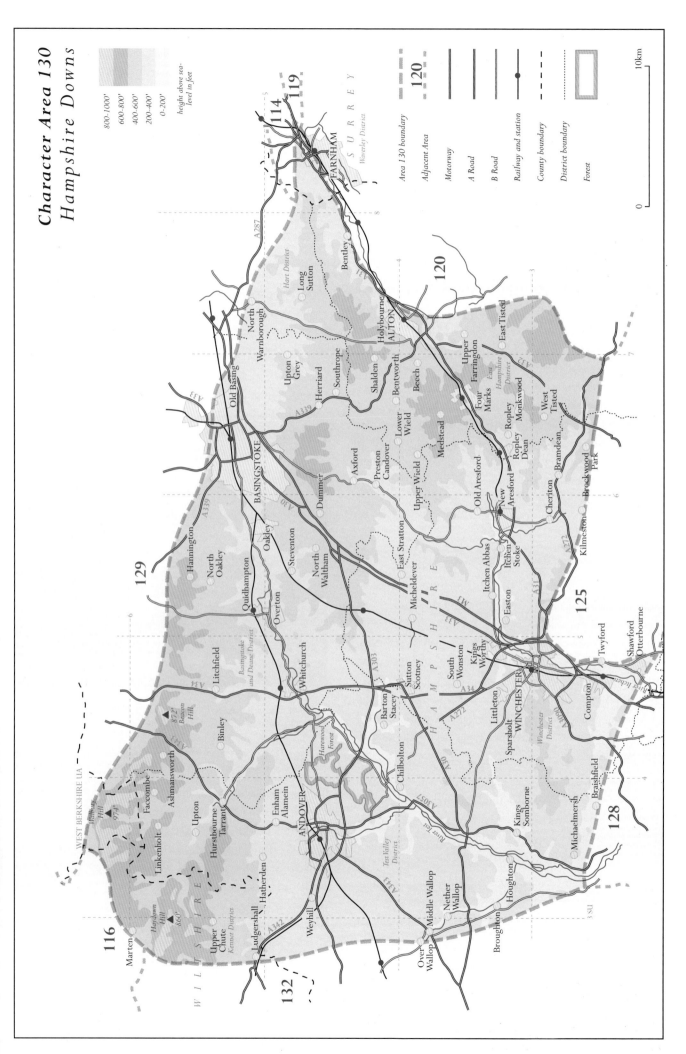

Character Area 130
Hampshire Downs

height above sea-level in feet
- 800–1000'
- 600–800'
- 400–600'
- 200–400'
- 0–200'

- Area 130 boundary
- 120 Adjacent Area
- Motorway
- A Road
- B Road
- Railway and station
- County boundary
- District boundary
- Forest

0   10km

116

129

132

114
119

120

125

128

WILTSHIRE

WEST BERKSHIRE UA

SURREY

HAMPSHIRE

Waverley District

Hart District

East Hampshire District

Basingstoke and Deane District

Test Valley District

Winchester District

Kennet District

FARNHAM

Bentley

Long Sutton

North Warnborough

Upton Grey

Herriard

Southrope

Holybourne
ALTON

Shalden

Bentworth

Beech

Upper Farringdon

East Tisted

Old Basing

BASINGSTOKE

Dummer

Axford

Preston Candover

Lower Wield

Upper Wield

Medstead

Four Marks

Ropley

Ropley Dean

Ropley Monkwood

West Tisted

Bramdean

Brockwood Park

Hannington

North Oakley

Oakley

Steventon

North Waltham

East Stratton

Micheldever

Old Aresford

New Aresford

Itchen Abbas

Itchen Stoke

Cheriton

Kilmeston

Quidhampton

Overton

Easton

Litchfield

Whitchurch

Sutton Scotney

South Wonston

Kings Worthy

WINCHESTER

Twyford

Shawford

Otterbourne

Binley

Ashmansworth

Faccombe

Harewood Forest

Barton Stacey

Chilbolton

Littleton

Sparsholt

Compton

Braishfield

Upton

Linkenholt

Hurstbourne Tarrant

Enham Alamein

ANDOVER

Kings Somborne

Michaelmersh

Marten

Upper Chute

Ludgershall

Hatherden

Weyhill

Middle Wallop

Nether Wallop

Over Wallop

Broughton

Houghton

River Itchen

River Test

Inkpen Hill
974

Haydown Hill
860'

872'
Beacon Hill

A287

A33

A339

A339

A30

A303

A34

A34

A272

A272

A31

A3057

A343

A342

A303

A31

A272

A32

A31

M3

A30

A30

A303

A343

A34

A30

M3

A31

A272

A3090

5

8

4

3

7

6

5

4

3 SU

6

5

4

3

153

The hedgerows of the lower valleys give a sense of an enclosed landscape contrasting with the open arable land outside the valleys.

JOHN TYLER/COUNTRYSIDE AGENCY

Numerous wooded valleys are particularly characteristic features. Within them, ancient semi-natural woodlands are seemingly interconnected by a dense and well-trimmed network of mixed-species hedges with oak hedgerow trees that frequently mark field and road boundaries. These pockets afford a degree of enclosure and seclusion within the more open and exposed areas of higher ground more typically characterised by large fenced fields and extensive views.

Physical Influences

The underlying Chalk gives rise to a variety of contrasting landforms including broad strongly rolling downland, both deep and shallow valleys, and distinct hilltops and ridges with minor steep scarps in places. On the plateau and ridge areas the Chalk is typically overlain by a shallow but virtually continuous deposit of clay-with-flints. This stony clay cap creates damp heavy soils amongst the generally free-draining thin chalky soils, supporting former heaths and oak wood-pastures mixed in with the surrounding arable farming.

The rivers Test and Itchen have cut significant valleys into the Chalk and their swiftly flowing rivers are notable features within the landscape. The vast majority of other valleys within the Downs are generally dry, although some support winter streams or 'bournes'.

Historical and Cultural Influences

Flint, with its remarkably hard crystalline structure and strong planes of fracture, played a significant role in the prehistoric and cultural development of the Hampshire Downs. Using flint tools to clear substantial areas of woodland, early Neolithic farmers began to cultivate the light chalk soils. The land cleared for cultivation and pasturing had, by the Middle Ages, become dominated by sheep grazing. Grazing sustained the chalk grassland or 'sheepwalks' which were often defined by long boundary banks.

Settled agricultural communities became more widespread during the Bronze and Iron Ages within the Chalk valleys and along the ridges of the Hampshire Downs. Towards the end of the Iron Age, and through the Roman periods, the Downs were noted for their exports of cereals and wool, an economy that boomed until the end of the Roman occupation when some cultivated areas were abandoned.

Successive settlers exploited the Downs according to their own socio-economic needs. Of particular note were the Saxon infield-outfield and later open-field systems surrounding medieval settlements. Between the 15th and 19th centuries, open-field downland became increasingly enclosed following successive Parliamentary Enclosure Acts which helped create much of the present day hedgerow and field pattern.

Amidst this downland and agricultural landscape, parklands and large estates feature widely, among them Chawton House, providing rural inspiration for the novels of Jane Austen.

RAY SMITH

The flint, found naturally in the chalk, has been used over time — more recently as a building material in the area.

Buildings and Settlement

The predominantly agricultural landscape of the Hampshire Downs is characterised by a widely dispersed settlement pattern of villages and hamlets linked together by a complex network of remote and narrow lanes, often with steep hedgebanks. The occasional settlements are generally of brick, or brick and timber in the valleys, or of brick and distinctive knapped flint in the hills. Thatch roofs survive in some buildings, although plain tiles are a more typical roofing material. Chalk is used infrequently as a building stone due to its inherent softness and solubility, although chalk cob is used in walls surrounding some farmsteads.

Major routes, such as the M3 motorway, pass through this area, linking Winchester and Basingstoke with London.

Land Cover

Some parts of the steeper, uncultivated slopes are covered by short, grazed turf on chalk soils which have been generally exempt from agricultural 'improvements' such as the application of herbicides/pesticides or ploughing. These traditional areas of chalk grassland or 'sheepwalks' are a scarce landscape feature with only comparatively small areas remaining among the predominantly arable landscape.

The river Test flows along the edge of the area and gives rise to a range of significant wildlife habitats from the river channel to floodplain grassland.

Oak is the dominant tree species, particularly on the clay-capped ridges, with infrequent but characteristic occurrence of beech on the lighter valley soils. Ash, hazel and field maple occur widely while yew, holly and whitebeam are restricted to the thinner, chalky soils. Oak is also found as a hedgerow tree within the frequent mixed-species hedges that follow the remote and narrow lanes in the area. The hedges tend to be either low and well-trimmed, or high, overgrown and unmanaged. In many areas, hedges are non-existent.

The Changing Countryside

- Many hedgerows and woodlands have been removed in recent years as field sizes have been increased for arable crop production, thus causing the more traditional patchwork pattern of the landscape to be eroded.

- Significant development pressures arising from expansion of major settlements such as Andover and Basingstoke.

- Development of major new roads and improvements has significantly diminished the character of the landscape, such as the M3 cutting at Twyford Down.

- Over-abstraction of water resources and ground water pollution has affected the viability of the Chalk aquifer under the Hampshire Downs leading to detrimental effects on Chalk streams and rivers.

- Strong past and future pressures for large golf course developments within the Downs.

Shaping the Future

- The landscape and nature-conservation interest of ancient woodlands, former wood pastures and relic commons should be addressed.

- There is scope to conserve and manage neglected and fragmented hedgerows.

- The protection of archaeological features and their settings is important.

- The protection of the Chalk aquifer from pollution should be addressed, together with the management of water resources and the conservation of rivers and their landscape setting.

- There are opportunities to conserve Chalk grassland by the reinstatement of traditional management regimes.

Selected References

Countryside Commission (1991), *The East Hampshire Landscape*, CCP 358, Countryside Commission, Cheltenham.

Hampshire County Council (1993), *The Hampshire Landscape*, Hampshire County Council, Hampshire.

Hunton, D A and Insole, A N (1988), *Ordnance Survey Historical Guides: Hampshire and the Isle of Wight*, George Philip, London.

Glossary

ley: land put down to grass or clover for a limited period of years

The impact of the cutting for the M3 through the chalk grassland at Twyford Down.

New Forest

- An extensive and complex mosaic of broadleaved and coniferous woodlands, unenclosed wood pasture, heath, grassland, and farmland.

- A constant presence of numerous grazing ponies and cattle, both a strong visual element and a significant impact on the land cover.

- Open and exposed plateaux and small valleys dominated by heath, with heather, gorse and grassland with scattered birch and pine. Bog vegetation in valley bottoms.

- Pockets of farmland and widely dispersed settlements with large isolated dwellings, bounded by high hedges, contained within the woodland.

- Wood-pasture of mature oak woodland, patches of bracken interspersed with glades and heavily grazed 'lawns', verges and commons.

- Large woodlands of mature broadleaves and an understorey of holly and bracken, contrasting with dark blocks of coniferous plantations.

- Fringe areas of farmland with villages. Small fields lined by full hedges, opening out to larger arable fields, with contrasts between the more intimate features of the Avon Valley, and the salt-marshes and shingle beaches on the southern coastal plain.

Landscape Character

The New Forest character area comprises a raised plateau and surrounds, defined in the east by Southampton Water and in the south by the Solent. To the west it includes the valley of the river Avon, flowing south to enter the Solent, which forms the boundary with the Dorset Heaths. To the north-east the valley of the river Test, in the South Hampshire Lowlands, forms the boundary while, to the north, the land drops gently before rising again to form the higher Salisbury Plain and West Wiltshire Downs.

ROBERT CADMAN/COUNTRYSIDE AGENCY

Woodland of great variety occurs in the New Forest: here, mixed woodland on the western edge.

Its distinctive character arises from its unique combination of ancient woodland, wood-pasture, heath, grassland, small-scale pastoral farming and low density of settlements, forming a rich mosaic both visually and ecologically.

This is a landscape of contrasts: of wide, open sweeps of heather moorland with dense dark plantations; of the high canopy of large oak woodlands with open, close-cropped grassy commons; of the occasional long, straight road with narrow lanes contained by banks and hedges; of unenclosed heath and common, with the hedged gardens of scattered dwellings. In woodlands, sunny glades of grass and bracken break up the canopies of large, mature oaks, while stretches of open heath are interrupted by clumps of self-seeded pine or birch. These stretches of informal, unrestricted landscapes contrast markedly with the urban areas to the south and east.

Colours and textures play an important part in constructing the overall landscape character and even here there are contrasts – the dark greens of the conifers; the light greens of freshly sprouting broadleaves; the bright green of the bracken, turning to russet in the autumn and winter; the purple of the heather, turning to a dark, textured brown in the winter; and the sweeps of yellow gorse, turning a rough dark green during the summer.

The heathland areas are in themselves mosaics on a smaller scale, of rough heather, acidic grassland, swathes of bracken, clumps of gorse, boggy valley bottoms and groups of self-sown birch and pine.

The woodlands, many protected by Inclosure fences, also vary greatly in character, according to the age and spacing of the dominant species. In places the canopy comprises large, mature oaks, or oak with beech and sweet chestnut, with an open understorey of holly and patches of bracken.

Other woods are denser, of younger oak, with an understorey of holly and hazel, on the limey clays. In some places large mature firs and pines have been left, whilst there are also dense, dark plantations of pine and spruce.

The Forest area is sparsely populated and those settlements that do occur are dispersed, each dwelling with its garden or paddock protected by fences and hedges against the grazing animals. Smallholdings, forming irregular patterns of small fields, bounded with hedges, are associated with these forest villages. A particular feature is the siting of pubs or hotels overlooking large, close-cropped village commons with picturesque groupings of grazing livestock.

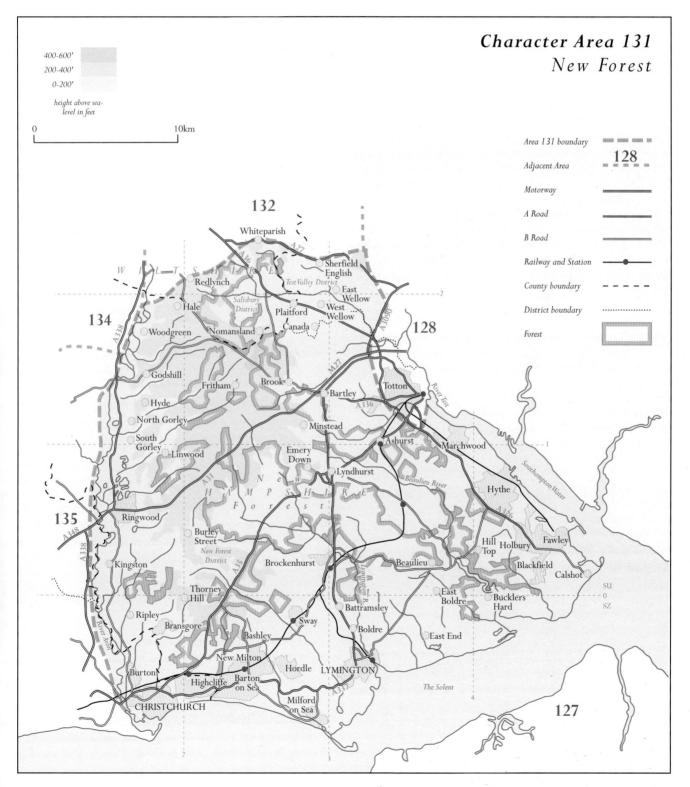

Character Area 131
New Forest

Throughout, there is the sense of history, of continuity of woodland and heath and the influence of the ever-present grazing animals. Ponies gather to graze road verges and commons, while groups of cattle shelter nearby. Deer are occasionally glimpsed moving through woods or across heaths. Everywhere the impact of grazing is visible through the close-cropped swards, tightly nibbled clumps of gorse and the consistent browse line of trees and hedges.

The landform is nowhere dramatic, rather a slightly raised plateau, going up to only 120 m or so but, rising as it does from sea level, this gives an impression of being elevated and exposed on the open plateaux. Much of the area comprises shallow ridges between pleasant, undulating and sheltered valleys, dropping down to more gently sloping land around the Forest edges.

The heather moorland, open in character, offers a sense of exposure in many areas of the New Forest.

The fringes of the Forest contain several small villages, characterised by the linear development of detached cottages along roadsides and linked by a network of narrow, winding lanes often lined with banks and hedges. Mature hedgerow oaks, some pollarded, give these fringe areas a wooded feel. Strongly pastoral, and providing back-up grazing for stock, all these fringe areas retain a strong sense of historical association and identity with the Forest.

The influence of the Forest is less evident along the coastal plain in the south. Here the landscape is somewhat featureless, a well-managed arable landscape with neat, low hedges and occasional plantations. The few oak or pine hedgerow trees that do occur reveal the proximity of the sea and are stunted and windblown.

Along the coastal plain in the east are larger towns, of almost coalescing urban areas with extensive recent development, and, in the case of Fawley, industrial complexes. The tall chimneys of the oil refineries here are visible from many stretches of heath and forest in the locality. The urban fringe effect extends all along this stretch of coastal plain, with mixed uses such as garden centres, caravan parks, light industry and farming. Similarly, the urban fringe effect extends along the coastal plain in the south-west, where fences tend to replace hedges. Towns front onto the wide sweep of shingle beach running from the spit at Keyhaven to Christchurch.

Less affected by development is the south-east stretch, with the attractive creeks and estuaries of the Lymington and Beaulieu rivers. There are quiet but bleak and exposed salt-marshes and rough grazing along this part of the coast line and the sense of openness is enhanced by the views out over the Solent, to the hills and cliffs of the Isle of Wight. Even here, however, one is aware of the constant presence of woodland on higher land to the north.

The small river valley of the Avon to the west is flat-bottomed, clearly contained for much of this stretch by the landform rising up to the New Forest plateau to the east and to the Dorset Heaths to the west. On the floodplain are low-lying pastures, and groups of large water bodies where sands and gravels have been extracted. In places these fields and lakes have a rich riparian vegetation of willows but, on drier stretches, there are open arable fields with low hedges. The valley contrasts strongly with the free-draining, sandy, heather-covered hills which are visible to the east.

The whole character area, being located away from main routes and centres of development, has a relatively low population and is strongly influenced by its unique history so that it retains a feel of remoteness and a distinct sense of place.

Physical Influences

The New Forest character area is dominated by a raised and eroded plateau which is at its highest in the north and drops down to the south-east. The plateau is formed from Triassic bedrocks, of varied soft sedimentary deposits of sands and clay lain down by a succession of shallow seas, freshwater lakes and rivers.

Following the laying down of these sedimentary rocks, changing sea levels formed broad terraces stepping down to the south-west. Subsequent river erosion cut small valleys through to the underlying clays; these valleys tend to be narrower and steeper in the north, while in the centre and to the south the valleys are shallower and separated by gentle flat-topped ridges. In the south are broad coastal plains of gravel deposits.

Complex patterns of variable soils and local drainage thus occur. The sands and clays give rise to poor, infertile and acidic soils although the ones of marine origin tend to produce slightly better, less acidic soils. Peat and alluvium occur in the valley bottoms. Throughout there are close links between landform, soils and vegetation, with enclosed and farmed land on the better quality soils, and heath on the most acid and impoverished soils.

The plateau is drained by a few small rivers, the main ones being the Lymington and Beaulieu rivers which flow south-east down to the Solent, draining much of the central Forest area. In the west, the river Avon runs south to Christchurch and a number of small tributaries run into it from the plateau to the east. In the north the land drops down to the valley of the river Blackwater, which flows east to join the Test above Southampton.

Historical and Cultural Influences

There is evidence that woodland cover was cleared for agriculture in prehistoric times but, as nutrients leached out quickly from the free-draining acid soils, the impoverished land was abandoned for the more fertile soils of the valleys. As a result, areas of heath developed within a thinly wooded landscape. There are a number of Bronze Age round barrows and Iron Age field systems and defensive hillforts still visible in the area. The Romans used the area for the resources it offered, notably fuel wood, sand and clay. A thriving pottery industry was established, with several kiln sites located within the area. Pottery from here was distributed to Roman sites throughout southern Britain, until the 5th century AD.

Originally known as Ytene, the place of the Jutes, the extensive area of heath was appropriated as a royal hunting ground, with communal rights over the land, from at least the time of Edward the Confessor. William the Conqueror claimed the area as Royal Forest, and the Perambulation (the area subject to Forest Law) comprised Crown owned lands together with private land. The primary concern was the protection of deer for the benefit of the King — smallholders were prevented from enclosing land and were given rights of common instead. These included rights to graze ponies, cattle, donkeys and sheep, to run pigs out to eat beech mast in the autumn, to collect wood and peat for fuel and to take marl as a soil improver. Over time the Forest Law became more concerned with the needs of the Commoners than of the Crown.

By the 15th century, however, the tree cover had diminished to such an extent that an Act of Parliament had to be passed to permit the enclosure of land to protect the regeneration of trees. The extensive oak woodland, and proximity to the sea, had resulted in exploitation of the woods for timber for both shipbuilding and fortifications. Timber felling on a large scale began in the 17th century to supply the demands of the navy for shipbuilding and further Acts were passed to encourage tree regeneration. Over time the numbers of stock put out to graze by Commoners changed considerably, reaching a peak during the 18th century when there were an estimated 7,000-9,000 stock, with similar numbers of deer. However, the extent of enclosed land increased through the 19th century, until 1877 when the New Forest Act limited the amount of land the Crown could enclose.

Along the coast a salt-making industry grew up, the evidence of which can be seen in sea-walls built up to contain salternes, and in the salt water boiling houses and associated windmills along the southern coast.

During the second world war a number of airfields were built on the heathy plateaux but these have now been abandoned and are returning to heath.

From 1924 the (then) Forestry Commission has administered the Crown lands. Formal Forest Law was rescinded in 1971, being replaced by the Verderers' Court, which was elected to protect the rights of Commoners, along with Agisters who were employed to oversee the welfare of the Commoners livestock. In 1989 a New Forest Committee was formed, comprising all those organisations with an interest in the balancing of needs and management within the New Forest Heritage Area and, in 1994, the New Forest was given planning protection similar to that of the National Parks.

Thus the landscape of the New Forest and its surrounds is a manifestation of the centuries of changing balance between the land management needs of hunting interests, commoners' grazing interests and the production of timber, with the recent addition of recreational use.

R. CLEGG/COUNTRYSIDE AGENCY

The autumn colours of the New Forest make this an ideal time to visit the area.

Buildings and Settlement

Over much of the area settlements are few and the population low. The few settlements are dispersed, in loose clusters or strung out along roadsides, without a clear centre or structure.

Materials are eclectic, with brick and slate, or brick and tile, commonly used. Less frequent, but a notable feature, are the small thatched cottages, with steep pitches and the thatch brought down close to the ground. The size of dwellings is varied – there are many large isolated houses with extensive gardens but also many scattered small cottages, each with its garden and paddock, and occasional small workers' cottages or terraces. Within the Perambulation, each dwelling has a high fence or hedge to contain and protect it from the grazing animals.

Of particular note is the well-ordered estate village of Beaulieu. This neatness, and the obvious affluence of many of the larger houses, is in contrast to the nature of outbuildings and fences elsewhere where wire, corrugated iron and bits of timber are used to patch and mend, giving in places a slightly run-down air. Around the fringes of the Forest, some villages are characterised by the linear development of dwellings along roadsides, each with its own garden, some with paddocks and outbuildings. These arise from relatively recent encroachment of the commons and tend to lack mature trees.

Attractive Forest cottages with Forest ponies grazing.

The larger settlements such as Brockenhurst and Lyndhurst also have a variety of materials and a dispersed building pattern. Along the eastern edge, adjacent to Southampton Water, settlements are large, with extensive 20th century residential development. Fawley is notable as an industrial development, with chimneys and structures of the oil refineries visible from afar.

The settlements adjacent to Solent Water are large and sprawling. Some have attractive centres focused upon an estuary, as with Lymington and Christchurch, while others are spread along the sea front as typical seaside towns of the 20th century, with boarding houses and blocks of flats looking out across the water, the latter notably at Milford on Sea.

The major A31 road, which crosses the plateau, has been upgraded and now forms a road of almost motorway standard cutting through the area. Other main roads, particularly in the south, are straight and busy but otherwise roads are few within the Forest. On the fringes the roads form a network of narrow winding routes, contained by banks and hedges.

Land Cover

Some two-thirds of the Forest area is lowland heath, dominated by heather, often in mosaics with gorse and bracken, open patches of closely grazed grassland, and scattered birch and pine. Some stretches of heath are dominated by gorse, with birch and bramble.

The woodlands form one of the largest tracts of semi-natural woodland in southern England. They are dominated by large oaks, with an understorey of holly and patches of bracken. Where grazed, a wood-pasture is formed, with patches of grass and bracken under the canopy of oak. The Inclosures have a much denser woodland canopy, largely of oak, with beech and some sweet chestnut. Just over half of the Inclosures have now been planted with conifers.

The open lawns, and grassland areas within the woodlands and heaths, are maintained by close grazing. Most are rich in species, which vary according to the exact nature of the substrate, and some are relatively fertile.

The central area is dominated by this combination of forestry and common rights grazing – of ponies, donkeys, cattle, pigs and sheep – but within the Forest are small enclosed fields and paddocks used for livestock rearing and increasingly for horses. The emphasis on livestock rearing extends its influence beyond the Perambulation. On the fringes of the Forest, field sizes remain small, and pastures provide back-up grazing for the Commoners livestock. There is however more mixed farming, with cattle, occasional dairying and root crops. On the gravel plains to the south, and on the drier parts of the low-lying Avon valley, arable crops predominate.

The Changing Countryside

- Variations in the grazing pressure have led to subtle changes in the balance between open and enclosed habitats. There has been a steady encroachment of heathland by self-sown pine. Planned intervention has included the agricultural improvement of lawns through draining and re-seeding, cutting and burning of heathland and clearance of bracken and pine.

- Many broadleaved woodlands in the Inclosures have been replaced by conifers.

- There have been continuous development pressures, in particular for housing, to meet the demand from commuters to the Southampton area. This has meant that some settlements, particularly on the Forest fringe, have grown and lost their dispersed character, whilst the towns on the coast have expanded.

- In recent decades the area has grown enormously in popularity as a place to visit for recreation. Volumes of traffic and numbers of visitors have steadily increased, as have the facilities provided for them. This has resulted in minor but widespread changes, for instance through signs, waymarking, gates and car parks which tend to clutter the area.

- The widening and fencing of the A31 road has allowed more people to gain access to the area but it also effectively divides the northern part of the Forest from the southern.

- Gravel extraction in the Avon valley has resulted in a local landscape of open water divided by willows and scrub, with new schemes continuing to create immature local landscapes. Construction of large structures connected with the oil refineries and a power station at Fawley has introduced prominent industrial elements that are visible from many places.

The A31 – the heathland character extends right up to the road.

Shaping the Future

- The New Forest character area is an important historical landscape, as well as having high nature-conservation value and high intrinsic aesthetic value. The Forestry Authority is in a primary position to influence the management of both woodlands and open land through the preparation of ongoing management plans drawn up in consultation with the Verderers, English Nature and other interested parties which should address the balance between all the interests.

- The impact of stocking levels on the mosaic of open and wooded habitats is critical and the balance between heath and woodland needs to be constantly monitored. In the fringe areas, an agri-environment approach could include the restoration of arable land back to pasture, to retain the predominantly pastoral quality of the landscape.

- The provision of further recreational facilities, as demand increases, should be addressed to avoid any loss or damage to the character of the landscape.

- The management of woodlands is of overriding importance in the area.

- Developments such as the exploitation of oil reserves underlying the area, further gravel extraction or a bypass round Lyndhurst, need to be handled particularly carefully to prevent undue impact on the complex landscape.

Selected References

Countryside Commission (1986), *The New Forest Landscape*, CCP 220, Countryside Commission, Cheltenham.

Hampshire County Council (1993), *The Hampshire Landscape*, Hampshire County Council, Winchester.

Land Use Consultants (1991), *New Forest Heritage Area: proposed boundary*, LUC, London.

Tubbs, C (1968), *The New Forest: an ecological history*, David & Charles, Newton Abbot.

Glossary

salternes: salt works

substrate: surface on which organism grows

Salisbury Plain and West Wiltshire Downs

Key Characteristics

- Extensive open, rolling Chalk plateau dominated by large arable fields.

- Scattered copses and shelterbelts.

- Woodland confined mainly to valleys and steep slopes.

- Unimproved chalk grassland of high nature-conservation value.

- River valleys with frequent settlements and narrow floodplains, dominated by former floated flood meadows and meandering rivers.

- Steep scarps with unimproved grassland and woodland.

- Abundant older buildings of cob, thatch, brick, Chilmark Stone, flint and clunch.

- Outstanding prehistoric ritual landscape with widespread earthworks and monuments prominent in an open landscape, including Stonehenge.

- Military structures, airfields, tracks and signs.

Landscape Character

Salisbury Plain and the West Wiltshire Downs are bounded by the chalk downland of the Hampshire Downs and the Berkshire and Marlborough Downs on the eastern and northern sides and by the Dorset Downs and Cranborne Chase in the south west. On the southern margin, where they abut the heaths and woodlands of the New Forest, and in the west and north west, where they abut the greensands, clays and limestone of the Blackmoor Vale, Vale of Wardour, and the Avon Vales, the predominance of chalk landscapes is broken. Within this large and varied area, the dominant and unifying features are the rolling chalklands, the steep escarpments and the attractive sheltered and populous valleys of chalk rivers flowing southwards and eastwards to Salisbury.

Much of Salisbury Plain is a vast, rolling landscape of seemingly endless arable fields and unimproved grassland

punctuated only by small hilltop woodlands of beech and conifer. There are also areas of pasture with very few hedges and low post and wire fences which maintain the feeling of openness. It is an upland grazing country, with spacious far horizons. The long and round barrows and dykes, commonly sited prominently on the low ridges, give a very special sense of an ancient landscape which is nowhere greater than in the views of Stonehenge across the open downs. Indeed, the Plain is of international significance, not just for the immediate World Heritage Site and Stonehenge, but for its other extensive 'ritual' landscapes and evidence of prehistoric activity. The sense of historical continuity is perhaps greatest when looking at the banks, trackways and strips of scrub and woodland which mark present-day parish boundaries. These extend up from the valleys onto the open downland and mark Saxon estate boundaries and Bronze Age land divisions. Apart from the intensive farming, the main modern influence on this landscape is military activity in the form of buildings, airfields, waymarking for tanks, the vehicles themselves and their tracks.

Chert, flint, render and thatch cottages are characteristic, as in the Salisbury Avon valley here at Fittleton.

To the south and west of the Plain, the West Wiltshire Downs are gently domed, broad hills separated by shallow, dry valleys. Only in the extreme west have they been eroded by the headwaters of the Wylye to form dramatic hills and deep chalk combes. Arable cultivation dominates,

Character Area 132
Salisbury Plain and West Wiltshire Downs

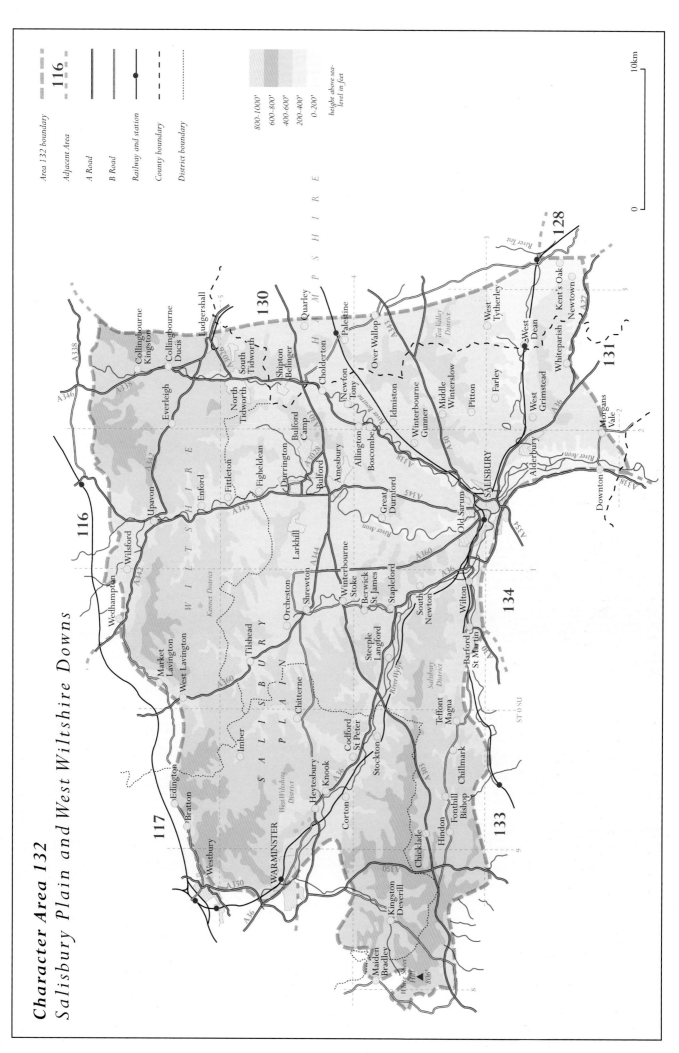

with copses around farms and barns. Ridgeways, field systems and hillforts emphasise the prehistoric significance of this part of the area.

Cutting through these spacious rolling landscapes with their long views and broad sweeps of arable farmland are the more intimate landscapes of the Wylye, Avon and Bourne Valleys. The river Wylye has cut a fairly straight course, forming a valley with gentle northern slopes and small, dry, side valleys but with more convoluted southern slopes. At the edge of the floodplain, low hillocks are the sites of compact villages, clustered around spired limestone churches. There is a great variety of materials in the older buildings but a particular characteristic is the use of Chilmark Stone and a chequered pattern of clunch and napped flint. Unimproved chalk grassland and woodland is found on the steeper slopes and there are abundant willows and alders along the water courses. The low ridges of the abandoned floated flood meadows are characteristic of all the valleys, including the Avon, which is narrower and more densely populated. Here, there are frequent settlements and a strong influence of modern development around the small towns of Durrington, Amesbury and along the A303.

Stonehenge, on Salisbury Plain, is the best known of the ancient monuments for which the area is famous.

The valleys lead to Salisbury, dominated by its cathedral spire, where 20th century settlement has spread from the old riverside city centre up the surrounding hillsides and towards Wilton. A pleasantly remote area of meadows along the river Avon provides a fine setting for the ancient core of Salisbury. This character continues along the river Nadder to Wilton, which is dominated by the grand mansion of Wilton House and the surrounding parkland. There are well-timbered historic parks like Boyton and Wilbury in similar valley-side settings.

In contrast to the densely-settled character of the valleys and the remote and austere landscape of the downland and Plain, the Chalk scarps are abrupt and dramatic. This is particularly the case, for instance, with the scarp overlooking the Vale of Pewsey with its patches of unimproved grassland and clusters of woodland above closely-spaced scarp-foot villages.

Physical Influences

The Chalk margins to the Plain in the north and west are dominated by a near-continuous scarp. There is, for instance, a steep scarp along the northern boundary overlooking the Vale of Pewsey and along the western edge overlooking the Upper Greensand. During the Quatenary, Clay-with-flints deposits were laid down over at least part of the Chalk and these high-level deposits survive today, generally supporting woodland, in contrast to the thin, dry soils of the Chalk. Scattered across the Plain and Downs are Sarsen stones – weather-worn blocks of grey sandstone ('greywethers') derived from the former cover of Tertiary deposits.

The rivers, forming the principal valleys of the Wylye, Till and Avon, flow south and south-eastwards to form the Hampshire Avon. The valley bottoms are lined with gravel and alluvium. Most of Salisbury Plain is, however, without surface water.

Historical and Cultural Influences

The Plain and Downs are one of the major lowland prehistoric landscapes in England. By Neolithic times, there was extensive occupation and it seems likely that much of the original covering of vegetation had been cleared. The Neolithic culture was centred on the causeway camps of Whitesheet Hill and Robin Hood's Ball but long barrows are also conspicuous features. By about 2200 BC, a complex of features had developed in the Stonehenge area and much of the land had been exploited for pasture and cropping for a long time. There were ritual complexes at Durrington and Stonehenge, the latter serving as the symbolic focus of the great ridgetop barrow cemeteries of the second millennium. As the Bronze Age progressed, the landscape was divided up by boundaries which formed the basis of later territorial units and, from about 600 BC, major hillforts were built either on new sites like Scratchbury and Battlesbury or as enlargements of Bronze Age enclosures.

Roman roads are conspicuous features of the landscape, possibly serving a town near Old Sarum, but villa sites are sparse and it may be that part at least of the area was a grain-producing imperial estate. Certainly, the Anglo-Saxon placenames indicate an ancient, substantially cleared, landscape. The earliest Anglo-Saxon incomers, perhaps in the 6th century, occupied the most favourable valley sites and, by the middle Saxon period, most settlement was concentrated within the valleys, a process that accelerated as the Middle Ages progressed. Planned villages, surrounded by strip fields, were laid out in the river valleys and much of the downland was given over to sheepwalks, a pattern which remained until the present century. The later medieval prosperity of the area, largely from the wool and cloth trade, is most obviously reflected in the 13th and 14th century grandeur of Salisbury Cathedral but also in its parish churches.

During the post-medieval period, the system of floated flood meadows was developed and the earthworks of the now abandoned meadows are amongst the most characteristic features of the area. Very large estates were formed and large country houses were built, notably those clustered around Salisbury, Wilton, Longford, Standlynch and Clarendon. However, in general, the period down to the present century was one of out migration and decline: throughout the 19th century, Wiltshire was one of the poorest counties in England. Much of the landscape was dominated by open sheepwalks. Whitlock writes of his father in the 1880s taking the sheep on the 15-mile journey from Tilshead to Pitton – 'he walked them over the downs for the whole distance, never encountering a face, never using a hard road … and always treading the soft, springy virgin turf'.

The large patchwork of rectangular fields from the chalk scarp.

In the 20th century, the two major trends have been the expansion of the Ministry of Defence training areas and agricultural change. Military camps were established at Tidworth, Larkhill and Bulford and have become substantial settlements: airfields are also conspicuous. Sheep farming has disappeared over most of the area in the post-war period, replaced by the large, commonly hedgeless, fields of arable farms.

The deeply rural qualities of much of the landscape are celebrated in the novels of A G Street, in the writing of W H Hudson, and in Hardy's novels, whilst Salisbury's fine setting has attracted many artists, most notably Constable.

Building and Settlement

The pre-20th century settlement pattern was one of nucleated villages lying on the edges of the valley floodplains and at the foot of the scarps. In this area of strong landlordship, groups of estate cottages in uniform style are quite frequent. The oldest cottages are in cob with thatch roofs but brick and tile became common in the villages in the 19th century and are also the dominant materials of the small towns. In some places, flint has been used in combination with brick edging and banding. Locally, a porcelaneous chalk from the base of the Upper Chalk has been used for houses and farm buildings. In the south, the greenish, grey-brown Chilmark Stone has been used, while the Wylye Valley has distinctive buildings in a chequered pattern of napped flint and clunch. Amidst this great variety, the churches are usually imposing buildings in grey limestone. Wide boundary walls of cob or brick and flint with tile or even thatch coping are a typical feature around parks, farmsteads and larger houses. Although many villages are compact, they are sometimes rather strung out along the valleys and some have stone-lined streams flowing through them.

There are scattered farmsteads on the more sheltered sites on the downs and between the villages along the valleys, with large isolated barns on the open downland.

There has been extensive 20th century development around the edges of many villages. Salisbury has a fine riverside and water meadow setting to the old centre but 20th century development has spread up the hillsides towards Old Sarum and Westwood. Fortunately, the long views of the Cathedral's magnificent spire have been unaffected by post-war changes.

Military housing at Tidworth, Larkhill, Durrington and Amesbury has a considerable impact on the landscape although Amesbury itself is an attractive riverside settlement. Military buildings can be intrusive, particularly on the open Plain, where they are usually the only structures of any kind and the military settlements can hardly be expected to lie as inconspicuously in the landscape as the older villages.

The principal roads connect the valley settlements, and only a few roads and unenclosed trackways rise over the open downland. However, the A303 and some north-south roads lie on ridges for considerable sections and can be prominent in the open landscape.

Land Cover

Flat chalk downland on the plain has been saved from the plough by military use and now contains one of the largest remaining areas of calcareous grassland in north-west Europe. The surrounding cereal cultivation within very large fields with few, if any, hedges dominates much of the Plain and Downs. In some areas, and particularly on the high Plain, the only other land-cover is shelterbelts, small plantations of beech or conifers and occasional patches of scrub. Only a small proportion of the formerly vast sheepwalk survives but it nevertheless comprises substantial areas of high nature-conservation value.

One of several 'White Horses' of the chalk downs seen from across productive arable land.

Below the high downland and plain, the landform becomes more intricate. There is more common woodland and a predominance of pasture within small to medium-size fields, particularly in the Hampshire section of the area. Along the valleys, tree cover increases around the villages and alongside streams and rivers. Here too, the land is mainly pasture but arable extends down the valleys on the more gentle gradients.

Woodland is common along the scarp above the Wylye Valley, along the Great Ridge and on the steepest parts of the northern scarp. In these areas, as the landform becomes more irregular, arable landcover changes to pasture and small irregular fields with patches of scrub on the steepest places.

A final land cover element is landscape parks, which are generally well-maintained and some of which, like Wilton, are extensive.

The Changing Countryside

- There are several trunk roads across the Plain and the A303 runs directly past Stonehenge. There are strong pressures to upgrade the road to dual carriageway at this point and other road improvements could have significant impacts.

- The impact of the army on the Ministry of Defence lands has continued for decades and the damage caused by tanks to the Ancient Monuments has been severe. This is apparently now under control. It could decline with the reduction in the defence programme although there could be an increase in activity if troops are brought back to bases in the area. The MOD has been planting trees on the plateau which are at odds with its otherwise open character.

- The general decline in grazing is damaging the remaining areas of unimproved grassland and there is some scrub encroachment.

- Hedgerows, which are only a recent feature of the downland in many places, have largely disappeared. On the scarp slopes and along the valleys, they have more historic significance and there has been some neglect, mismanagement and removal.

- Arable farming and pressures for development are a potential threat to archaeological features that do not have statutory protection.

Shaping the Future

- The targeted use of a number of management initiatives offers the chance to create grassland of nature-conservation interest.

- Many of the villages still retain their historic pattern and are still dominated by older buildings in very localised materials like Chilmark Stone and clunch. Such villages would benefit from local design initiatives.

- The area contains some of the country's outstanding prehistoric monuments. There is scope for their continued management in conjunction with landscape and nature-conservation objectives and increased public education and interpretation.

- The chalk grasslands and valley bottom wetlands, particularly the flood meadows, are an important characteristic of the area.

Selected References

Whitlock, R (1955), *Salisbury Plain,* Robert Hale, London.

Countryside Commission (1995), *The Cranborne Chase and West Wiltshire Downs Landscape*, Countryside Commission, Cheltenham, CCP 465.

Countryside Commission (1994), *The New Map of England: A Celebration of the South Western Landscape*, Countryside Commission, Cheltenham, CCP 444.

Glossary

clunch: type of soft limestone

Cattle grazing in smaller fields divided by small areas of broadleaved woodland in the valley.

Dorset Downs and Cranborne Chase

Key Characteristics

- A rolling, chalk landscape with dramatic scarps and steep-sided, sheltered valleys.

- Scarp slopes with species-rich grassland, complex combes and valleys, spectacular views, prominent hillforts and other prehistoric features.

- Open, mainly arable, downland on the dip-slope with isolated farmsteads and few trees.

- Very varied valleys with woodlands, hedged fields, flood meadows and villages in flint and thatch.

- Distinctive woodlands and deer parks of Cranborne Chase.

Landscape Character

The steep scarp slopes of the Dorset Downs rise steeply above the Upper Greensand of the Blackmoor Vale and Vale of Wardour to the north and west. To the south and east, the broad, rolling dip slope, cut by intricate river valleys, falls to a landscape of low-lying valley bottoms. Beyond this lie the Dorset Heaths.

The many attractive viewpoints at the top of the scarp slopes and its outliers, like Win Green, Fontmell Down and Hambledon, give fine views over this typical Chalk landscape. The highest points of the steep, sometimes wooded, scarp slopes abound with prehistoric features, especially round barrows and hillforts. The remaining unimproved calcareous grassland, typically associated with the thin, chalky soils of the scarp, is frequently rich in wild flowers and downland wildlife. Below, ancient villages cluster around the springs which emerge at the base of the scarp.

To the south and east the chalk dip-slope provides long views across a rolling landscape of large regular fields dominated by arable. Although largely devoid of individual trees, there are occasional blocks of woodland. As the edges of the valleys are approached, fields tend to become smaller and pasture more common. Within the more sheltered secluded valleys, the recurrent elements of linear villages, streams and rivers, flood meadows, valley side woodlands and narrow lanes

combine in different ways to impart local character to individual valleys. Indeed, within the simple overall structure of scarps, slopes and valleys, there is great variety.

JOHN TYLER/COUNTRYSIDE AGENCY

Downland landscapes: Cerne Abbas, Dorset. The river Cerne, a chalk stream, flows due south through the remarkably straight Cerne Valley.

The area extends westwards with a deeply-indented scarp which is rather like a headland jutting out into Blackmoor Vale. Streams like the Cheselbourne have cut through the scarp to form very steep, intricate valleys but, outside the valleys, the landscape is bold and broad scale with woodland on the steepest slopes. To the west, the scarp breaks down into a slumped, uneven profile adjacent to the Greensand with extensive woodland, rough grassland and patches of scrub. Between the Stour Valley and Shaftesbury, the scarp runs near to the outlier forming Hod and Hambleton Hills with its two fine hillforts and then continues in a rather more uniform character to the prominent landmark of Melbury Hill. On the northern edge, there are scarps above the Nadder and Ebble valleys which, towards Salisbury, have been sculpted into a series of north-facing bowls. On the dip-slope, there are generally few trees but woodland becomes increasingly important to the east of the Stour valley where there are remnants of the

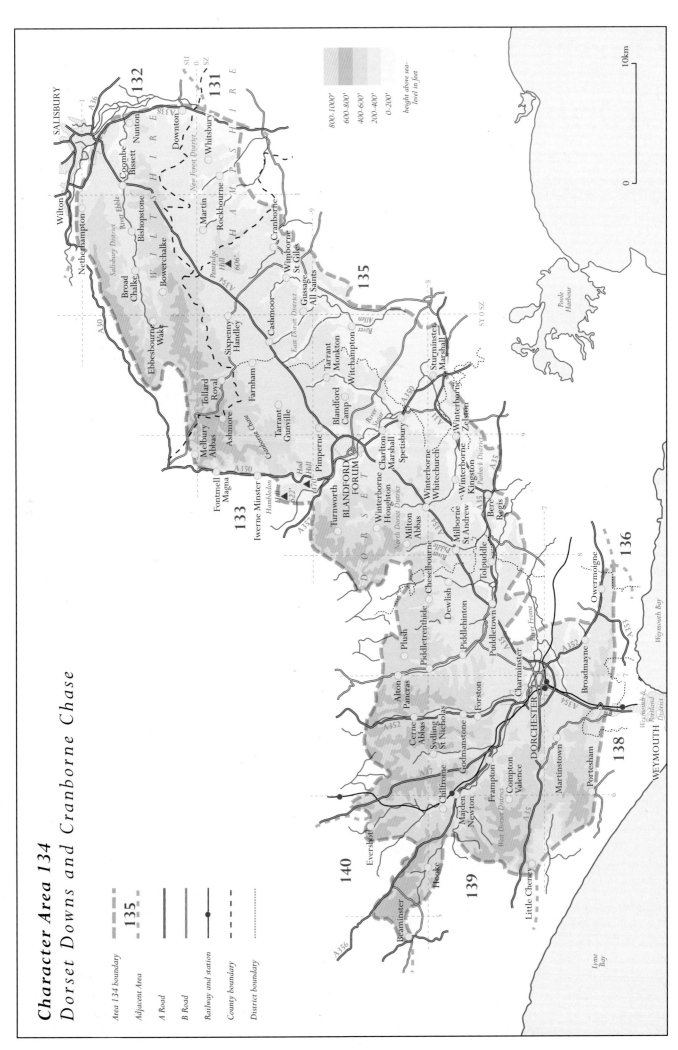

Character Area 134
Dorset Downs and Cranborne Chase

Area 134 boundary — — **135**

Adjacent Area — — **135**

A Road ——

B Road ——

Railway and station ——•——

County boundary — — —

District boundary ·········

800–1000'
600–800'
400–600'
200–400'
0–200'

*height above sea-
level in feet*

10km

ancient hunting ground of Cranborne Chase. Locally, natural regeneration and hill top planting has created distinct landmarks, while to the south the occurrence of yews just off the low ridges is evident from names like 'Great Yews' and 'Nine Yews Farm'.

Cranborne Chase is characterised by woodlands, shelterbelts, clumps and copses containing ancient hazel coppice and by enclosed areas of arable pasture and parkland. In contrast to the thinly-scattered farmsteads of the dip-slopes, the Chase has quite common settlement comprising villages within the valleys and a scatter of hamlets linked by ancient lanes. Within the substantial parks there are large mansion houses. They are a contrast to the modest vernacular buildings elsewhere on the Downs and add to the Chase's unique character.

The valleys of the Frome, Piddle and Stour are all different in character. The river Frome and its tributaries form a branching network of valleys. These probably have the most deeply eroded and enclosed landforms, especially in the Cerne and Sydling Water valleys, where the distinctive character is emphasised by the Cerne Abbas Giant carved out of the chalk high above the valley floor.

In contrast, the valleys of the Piddle system typically have V-shaped upper valleys which wind through narrow gaps to open out dramatically. The Stour valley is the least remote, with a wide flood plain, large villages and the attractive town of Blandford Forum within its parkland setting.

Perhaps the strongest characteristic of the Dorset Downs are the numerous focal points within the broad pattern of slopes and valleys. There are vast hillforts, like Maiden Castle and Hambledon Hill, particularly dramatic where their thick ramparts are emphasised by low winter or summer evening lights, there are barrows on hill and ridge tops and there are the grand houses of Cranborne Chase framed by ancient limes and chestnuts.

Physical Influences

The Chalk has been shaped to its present form of scarps, dip-slopes and valleys by water erosion. Much of the erosion probably took place by increased run-off from the melting of semi-permanent ice-caps on the Chalk crest, at the end of the penultimate glaciation. The bounding escarpments are erosional features. They are capped by partially dissected, south-easterly inclined dip-slopes.

The highest parts of the Downs represent the remains of a once-extensive Chalk platform. They are locally capped with Clay-with-flints and this gives rise to the soils most likely to support woodland. Away from the Clay-with-flints, the soils are generally thin and strongly calcareous. Deeper soils have accumulated at the base of the scarp and in the valley bottoms.

The major drainage pattern runs south-eastwards, forming the upper parts of the Piddle, Frome, Stour and Avon catchments but the Nadder and Ebble drain eastwards into the Avon.

Downland landscapes: the Dorset Downs near Toller Fratrum, Maiden Newton.

Historical and Cultural Influences

There was certainly Mesolithic activity in the area of the Downs but the first major imprint on the landscape is that of the Neolithic and there is a notable concentration of Neolithic ritual/ceremonial monuments around Dorchester. The causewayed camps of Maiden Castle, Maumbury Rings and Hambledon Hill are examples of important monuments of this period. Other concentrations of Neolithic and Bronze-Age sites are found in Cranborne Chase, including the Dorset Cursus which seems to have been used for excarnation or exposure of the dead. It is likely that the clearance of woodland on the Downs and the steady downwashing of downland soils had begun early in prehistory although there may well have been early valley settlement obscured by later settlement and cultivation. During the Bronze Age, the Downs seem to have been quite densely settled and groups of round barrows are still common features. Large areas were divided up by early field systems which, together with boundary dykes like Grimm's Ditch and Bokerley Dyke, are evidence of highly-organised societies. Defended hilltop sites for which the Downs are rightly famous, were developed during the Iron Age although the most celebrated, Maiden Castle, has its origins in the Neolithic.

The civitas capital (or regional administrative centre) of Dorchester was the main settlement of the Roman period. The roads radiating from it are still prominent features in the present day landscape but the main Roman influence was a long period of peace in which settlements multiplied and in which there was increasing exploitation of the valleys around the high downland. The gradual Saxon takeover of the area seems to have maintained a continuity of settlement. The numerous *tons* and *bournes* are evidence of Saxon farmsteads and waterside settlements and the Saxon charters show that much of the landscape was divided up into small estates which embraced valley bottoms, valley sides and access to the open downland. Domesday Book shows that much of the present pattern of settlement had been established and in the Middle Ages it was more common than it is today. The loose ribbons of farmsteads and cottages that make up many of the valley villages were originally laid out in potentially much denser planned form, and the landscape is littered with deserted settlements. Open field systems developed along the valleys sometimes lapping up to the edge of the open downland crests but, from the mid-14th century onwards, there was piecemeal enclosure and expansion of sheep grazing.

Maiden Castle: the well-known prominent hill fort on the Dorset Downs south of Dorchester.

In the east, Cranborne Chase was a royal hunting ground from at least the time of William the Conqueror until the 17th century. Its conservative landlords kept it substantially in its medieval character until it was disenfranchised in 1829. The medieval religious houses in and around the Chase formed the basis of the later parks and mansions like Tarrant Crawford and Iwerne.

During the 17th century, an elaborate system of flood meadows was developed in the valleys and the economy of the Downs was dominated by sheep rearing. This continued in the succeeding centuries, with the downlands being enclosed within strongly rectilinear fields in the 18th and 19th centuries. During the 20th century, there has been large-scale conversion of the downlands to arable.

Today many perceptions of the Dorset Downs and Cranborne Chase have been coloured by the writing of Thomas Hardy: Cranborne Chase was the 'venerable tract of forestland' in *Tess of the d'Urbervilles*. Maiden Castle featured in *Far from the Madding Crowd*.

Downland landscapes: Crow Hill on the Dorset Downs north of Abbotsbury.

Buildings and Settlement

Apart from the attractive town of Blandford Forum in the Stour Valley and Dorchester at the southern edge, the main settlements within it are the villages strung out along the narrow valleys or in more compact form in the wider valleys. They are linked by narrow roads following the valley bottoms, with more sinuous tracks extending to the farmsteads on the valley sides.

On the higher ground, there are only a few farmsteads and the road pattern is dominated by straight enclosure and turnpike roads. The farmsteads on this higher ground are mostly of modern construction but, in the valleys and in the villages that cluster at the foot of the scarps, a wide variety of building materials have been used. Timber framing, often disguised by more recent additions, is a particular feature. Flint with brick dressing and banding is common and clunch (chalk) is sometimes used with brick to give chequered patterns. Low, rendered buildings are common and there are many pre-18th and 19th century brick buildings. Although thatch is the traditional roofing material, there are many tiled roofs and some slate. This mixture of materials reflects the lack of a consistent supply of building stone and dressed stone is largely confined to the churches and manor houses.

Land Cover

The dip-slopes are dominated by large tracts of arable cultivation. Hedges are typically low and sparse. The few hedgerow trees and shelterbelts of beech, ash and sycamore are found mainly near the scattered farmsteads and there are small blocks of woodland, mainly plantations dominated by beech, oak and ash. In contrast, Cranborne Chase has extensive woodland cover, with a mixture of ancient woodlands, plantations, shelter belts, clumps and copses interspersed with arable, pasture and parkland.

On the steep scarp slopes, unimproved chalk grassland survives and woodland cover varies from one section to another. Between Melbury and Blandford, for instance, it spills over from Cranborne Chase, crowning spurs and filling the steep combes. To the east and west, it is sparser, comprising many ridge-top copses and scarp-foot hedges.

Within the valleys, the land cover is more mixed. Arable farming is widespread in the shallow slopes and hedges tend to be more frequent. The valley floors are occupied by former water meadows with common willows and poplars along the boundaries. There are woodlands on some of the steepest slopes and the knolls are often emphasised by tree clumps, mainly of beech. In some valleys, the land cover forms an attractive mosaic and setting for the many villages.

Cranborne Chase near Melbury Abbas: a typical downland view; combes cut into the northern scarp. Chalk grassland remains on the valley slopes but the downs are ploughed across Breeze Hill and, in this case, planted at Melbury Wood.

The Changing Countryside

- The economics of modern farming are resulting in the establishment of non-farming uses, including golf courses, and other alternative enterprises.

- The geometric shape and species composition of some game coverts depart from the overall character of this area.

- New crops such as linseed and brassicas alter the appearance and are often highly visible in this very open landscape.

- There has been an increase in outdoor pig-rearing in some locations.

- Scrub encroachment on the scarp slopes is reducing floristic and landscape interest, as has past arable conversion.

- Several major roads pass through the area. The associated earthworks, lighting and signs are likely to be particularly prominent in such an open landscape.

- Lowering of the water table and low flows in the chalk streams such as the river Piddle may affect wildlife and landscape interest.

- New housing around and within existing settlements is often 'suburban' in character and does not respect local styles and materials.

- Scattered, isolated, archaeological features are prone to damage by arable cultivation.

- There is a general lack of management of woodland, coppice, copses and parkland features.

- Continuing loss of ancient floated water meadow systems is occurring in the Chalk valleys.

Shaping the Future

- The Chalk landscape has been strongly influenced by the drive for efficient arable farming. Subject to economic feasibility and grant regimes, there is potential for conversion of arable fields back to chalk grassland. This could re-create something of the character of pre 1940s downland. A range of agri-environmental schemes represent an important opportunity to restore the historic open, rolling grasslands for which the chalklands have traditionally been known. Ideally, the new downland landscapes should create unified and large-scale chalkland scenery, rather than small-scale patchworks.

- There is scope to conserve the usually small and geometrically shaped woodlands to form new outlines, reflecting the flowing contours and composed on a grand scale. The existing woods tend to be on hillside slopes and there is potential to create new woods, and occasional carefully placed clumps on ridgetops and summits to enliven the horizon and create landmarks along ridgetop roads. These would need to be carefully planned to take account of local character, landform and existing features, including maintaining the integrity of planned landscapes.

- Hedgerows and hedgerow trees are locally important. Replacement trees should not disrupt important open vistas and areas of distinctive sweeping landform.

Selected References

Landscape Design Associates (1993), *Dorset County Landscape Assessment*, Countryside Commission, Dorset County Council, Purbeck District Council.

Taylor, C (1970), *Dorset*, Hodder & Stoughton.

Countryside Commission (1993), *The Dorset Downs, Heaths and Coast Landscape: a landscape assessment of the Dorset AONB*, Countryside Commission, Cheltenham CCP 424.

Countryside Commission (1994), *The New Map of England: A Celebration of the South Western Landscape*, Countryside Commission, Cheltenham CCP 444.

Dorset Heaths

- An exposed, open, broad-scale landscape forming a strong contrast with the adjacent character areas.

- Undulating lowland heath with tracts of heather, stunted pines and gorse scrub.

- Blocks of conifers forming locally-prominent landmarks.

- Mosaics of heathland, farmland, woodland and scrub.

- Much is sparsely populated with scattered settlements and a few small villages and towns but the extensive conurbation of Poole-Bournemouth forms a major influence in the south and east.

- Flat-bottomed, open valleys with floodplain pastures and willows.

- An outer edge of low, rolling hills with an irregular patchwork of pasture, woodland and dense hedges marking the transition to the chalk.

Landscape Character

The Dorset Heaths lie to the south of the Dorset Downs and extend south of Poole Harbour to the prominent Chalk ridge of the Isle of Purbeck. To the east the boundary with the New Forest is formed by the Avon Valley.

Most of the area forms a shallow basin around Poole Harbour and is drained by the rivers Piddle and Frome. The sandy infertile soils were once covered almost entirely by heathland – the Egdon Heath of Thomas Hardy – which, although fragmented by reclamation, modern development and tree planting, remains the dominant and unifying feature. The larger areas of heather have an open, wild character, in which even subtle variations in landform are clearly revealed. Minor breaks in slope are emphasised in many places by changes in vegetation, such as the heather, purple moor grass, bracken and gorse, which carpet the area. The pattern is broken locally by steep-sided sandstone hills and patches of exposed chalk where the vegetation has eroded on the steepest slopes. The changes in the weather,

captured so evocatively in Hardy's novels, are strong influences: the heathlands can appear bleak and desolate in dull weather but in sunshine there is rich variety of colour and texture.

The extensive areas of conifer woodland within the heathland date from the 1950s and 1960s. Open pastures, marshes and patches of broadleaves in and around these plantations break up their dominance of the landscape. They are nevertheless bold features which screen some of the large-scale developments in the south-east. There are also smaller clumps of trees, particularly oak and birch as well as isolated pines, many of which are wind-shaped and stunted, forming dramatic silhouettes.

JIM HALLETT/COUNTRYSIDE AGENCY

Dorset Heath on the Isle of Purbeck: reclaimed heath in the foreground contrasts with Godlingston Heath beyond. Poole Harbour is behind, with the Bournemouth-Poole conurbation visible spreading across the former heaths.

Around the edges of the heathland, and in places as pockets within it, secondary woodland and pasture form irregular and intricate mosaics. In places, open pastures are becoming overgrown, with a succession from gorse to birch and thence to mature oak. Here, the sense of enclosure is very strong, in contrast to the openness of the heath.

Surrounding the heathland, conifers, pasture and scrub at the core of the area, is a transitional landscape of rolling hills. Small blocks of woodland on the low summits increase their prominence and contrast with the surrounding Chalk.

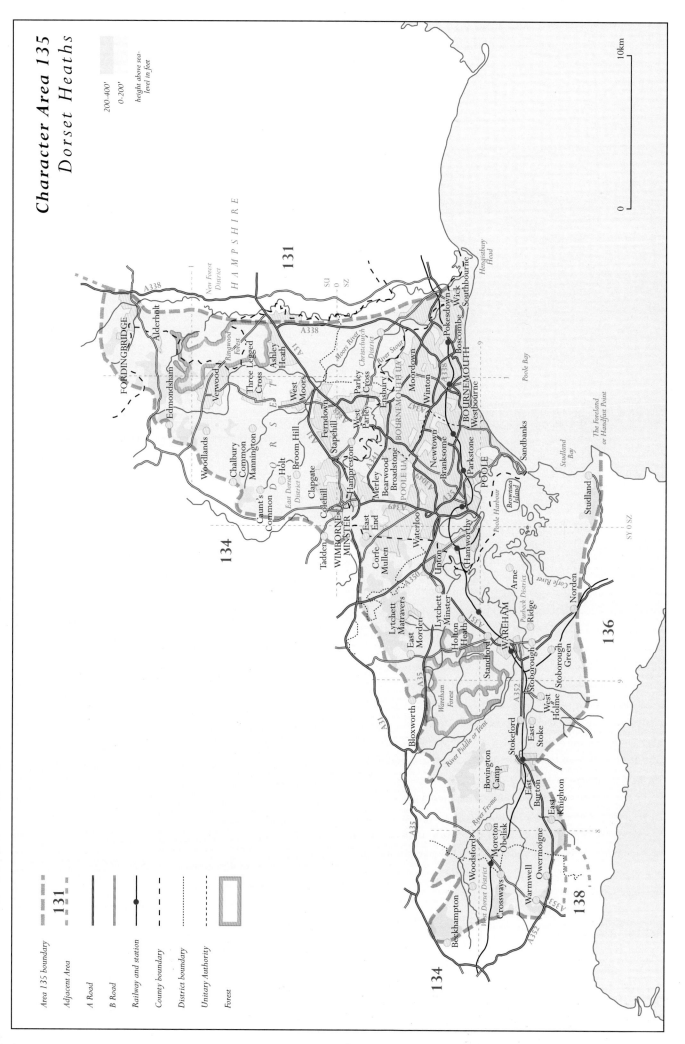

Character Area 135
Dorset Heaths

200-400'
0-200'
height above sea-
level in feet

Area 135 boundary
131 Adjacent Area
A Road
B Road
Railway and station
County boundary
District boundary
Unitary Authority
Forest

10km

Fringes of arable chalk fields extend into the hills, while to the east, the transition to the heathland is much less distinct than elsewhere. Patchworks of small fields, frequent hedgerow trees, conifers and deciduous woodlands form attractive mosaics of vegetation and the rolling landforms are broken occasionally by deeply-incised valleys.

Mineral working has taken much of the Dorset Heaths, as here at Hill View near Corfe Mullen, on the edge of the conurbation.

Broad river valleys with fertile floodplains cut through the heathlands. Large pasture fields are typical of the floated flood meadows and there are scattered riverside trees and local areas of arable farmland. Many of the older settlements, such as the small towns of Wool and Wareham as well as many villages, are sited on the low, riverside terraces.

At the coast, the valleys open out into the reed beds, marshes and mudflats of Poole Harbour with the largely 20th century conurbation of Poole-Bournemouth on its northern side. Here, urban influences dominate and the passage of commercial shipping and pleasure craft create an impression of intense activity. In contrast, the tranquil mudflats, sand dunes and saltmarshes of the southern edge grade into some of the most extensive and least disturbed heaths forming the edge of the Isle of Purbeck. The harbour itself is dotted with small islands, almost like an inland sea. The conurbation has spread across the heathland and has, in parts, an industrialised urban edge as well as satellite commuter settlements. In some cases its impact on the surrounding countryside is limited by gentle landforms and woodland but elsewhere the built edge is prominent. In the urban fringe, Bournemouth Airport, powerlines and aggregate extraction sites intermingle with tracts of heathland, emphasising its fragile character.

Physical Influences

The Heaths are largely surrounded by Chalk and the transition from Chalk to the heathland landscapes consistently follows the same pattern. The eroded dip-slope margins of the Chalk are overlain by the clays and sands of the Reading Beds and London Clay, producing a rolling and hummocky landscape along the margins. The Reading Beds and London Clay always separate the Chalk from the generally more acidic fluvially-deposited sands, gravels and clays of the Poole Formation and Branksome Sand (formerly the Bagshot Beds and the Bracklesham Beds) which occupy the middle of the Poole Basin. The bulk of the two latter deposits form the impoverished, freely-drained soils which support the heathlands. South of Poole Harbour, thick clay units within the Poole Formation give rise to the locally important 'wet' heaths.

More recent and fertile alluvial soils are present in the river valleys, covering the underlying rock to produce a flat, uniform valley floor. The rivers are commonly bordered by river terrace deposits forming extensive terrace flats. Upstream, the rivers cut through the Chalk, sands and clays in narrower, more incised, valleys.

Historical and Cultural Influences

The heathlands were originally created by clearance of woodland in or before the Bronze Age and round barrows of that period are to be seen on the more prominent sites. The internationally important Hengistbury Head, however, is the area's major archaeological site being an international port in the prehistoric period. The porous, easily-leached, sandy, heathland soils rapidly lost their nutrients as farming became more intensive and the heathlands remained as unenclosed areas of common grazing and turf cutting into the modern era. There is evidence of settlement as early as the Neolithic period in the fertile valleys. The acidic clays on the margins of the heath supported small, isolated farmsteads by medieval times. The valleys became quite densely populated and, at strategically important sites, towns such as Wimborne and Wareham were founded in the Saxon period.

The heathlands were largely unaffected until the 17th century when extensive attempts at reclamation met with limited success. Many smallholdings of this phase were subsequently amalgamated and field boundaries removed. Attempts at more intensive agriculture were largely abandoned in the period leading up to the late-19th century, with heathland reversion and encroachment by bracken, gorse and scrub.

However, although most of the area was dominated by sparsely inhabited heaths, trade and industry have had significant effects on the landscape. Poole was a major industrial centre and port in the Iron Age/Romano - British period and an important port from the Middle Ages onwards. Ball clay has been dug in the area around Wareham for the past 200 years, leaving a landscape of whitish hillocks and small pools still visible in some areas. Although clay was transported to the coast by rail, and thence across to the Bristol Channel bound for the Midlands potteries, brickmaking and Verwood pottery were significant local industries. Large areas of heathland form part of the Army firing ranges at Povington.

The Dorset Heaths, and settlements like Wimborne and Wareham, are at the core of many of Hardy's novels. The Heaths gave full rein to one of Hardy's central themes of the contrast between harsh and fruitful landscapes. Real places appear in his novels in thinly disguised form. The landscapes that Hardy created have taken on a life of their own – *Egdon Heath* for instance was written by Holst as a reference to *The Return of the Native*. The fine Woolbridge Manor, seen at its best across the attractive 17th century bridge is famous as Hardy's 'Wellbridge Manor-house' in *Tess of the d'Urbervilles*. There are many other literary figures associated with the area, especially Bournemouth, where as wide a range of authors as F.W. Rolfe, Kilvert, R.L. Stephenson and Verlane lived and worked. Kilvert wrote of 'wild sand, sweet trysts in the snow and under pine trees, among the sandhills of the East Cliff and in Boscombe Chine'.

Pristine Dorset Heath: Morden Bog National Nature Reserve.

NICK SQUIRREL/ENGLISH NATURE

Buildings and Settlement

Settlement on the infertile heaths was always sparse until recent times. It took the form of dispersed hamlets and isolated farms and cottages of red brick, commonly from clay dug from local pits, roofed in tiles or thatch. Many of these still survive, as does the denser pattern of more modern development. They are linked by narrow, winding lanes but with straighter main routes created by turnpikes and enclosure. On the rolling farmland edge, settlement is denser although screened by substantial tree cover. However, most of the older settlements and communication routes lie in the valleys. As well as the small towns of Wool, Wareham and Wimborne there are

many small villages. Wareham and Wimborne have fine cores mainly of brick buildings. Wool is an attractive historic settlement built of a variety of stones including the dark brown 'pudding stone' that locally occurs on the heaths.

BOB GIBBONS/WOODFALL WILD IMAGES

Urban expansion and afforestation have changed the open character of the Heaths.

The early settlement pattern has been overlain by the 19th and 20th century growth of Poole-Bournemouth. On the heathland areas, the urban edge is sometimes quite well-contained by landform and conifer woodland, although there are suburbanised villages beyond the main conurbation and some edges of residential areas can be very abrupt. On the more open valleys, the urban influence is strongest. For instance, industrial buildings and some residential estates extend right up to the edge of the river Stour floodplain. Major roads lie on the slightly higher land on the valley sides.

Land Cover

Outside the built up areas, there are substantial heathlands where heather is intermingled with purple moor grass and other plants of wet and dry heath. Scattered pines and naturally-regenerating woodlands are dominated by birch, but commonly with oak and Scots pine. Conifer plantations are formed of Corsican and Scots pine. Gorse scrub is also common.

The small amount of arable land is confined mainly to the river terrace deposits bordering the Frome floodplain and to a few patches on the heaths. The pasture of the heath and hilly farmland areas lies in a matrix of small woodlands and hedges which commonly comprise gorse, bracken and birch but also contain mature stag-headed oaks and occasional beech. Holly is a common, isolated hedgerow tree and the invasive rhododendron, common around Bournemouth, occurs locally in pest proportions. In the valleys, the land cover is mainly improved grassland in large irregular fields although those adjacent to the river may be smaller and have a rougher hummocky texture.

Apart from the large urban areas, there are a number of urban fringe land uses, notably golf courses, equestrian centres, garden centres and nurseries.

The Changing Countryside

- Some areas of heathland are reverting to scrub and woodland. Grazing regimes are often difficult to maintain, especially where the viability of holdings is marginal and the land is subject to urban fringe pressures.

- Heathland near urban fringes can be damaged by trespass, vandalism, fires, fly-tipping, erosion and temporary occupation by travellers.

- Urban expansion, new development and roads, aggregate and ball-clay extraction could cause loss or further fragmentation of the remaining heathland.

- Recreational pressure from the Poole-Bournemouth conurbation and from further afield is increasing, bringing with it the risk of increased traffic congestion, erosion and pressure for new facilities.

- The effect of on-shore oil exploration has, to date, had only a limited effect on the landscape.

- Some of the most unspoilt areas of heathland are those within the Army firing ranges at Povington.

The quiet waters of Poole Harbour contain many heathy islands, mud flats and reed beds: Fursey Island (with oil rig), from Brownsea Island.

Shaping the Future

- Up to 95 per cent of the remaining heathland, including all of the major tracts, are covered by protective designations and ownership. In addition, the Forestry Authority has a policy of heathland conservation, including removal of unproductive plantations and reversion to heathland. There are still opportunities for active conservation, including the promotion of better heathland management, which is particularly important in urban fringe areas.

- Objectives of the conservation bodies might include the following:

  - re-establishment of large grazing units through co-operation of landowners and co-ordination of management;

  - re-creation of heathland habitats on former agricultural and plantation land, as well as the restoration of old ball clay and sand and gravel workings, particularly where this allows links to existing heathland fragments;

  - co-ordinated management of scrub and trees to prevent encroachment of open heathland, while maintaining a balance of tree and scrub cover;

  - emphasis on the interpretation and promotion of heathlands as a valuable and irreplaceable resource.

- There is scope for the management of hedges, the replacement of ageing hedgerow trees, the reversion of arable to permanent pasture and the re-establishment of flood meadow systems in river valleys.

Selected References

Landscape Design Associates, (1993), *Dorset County Landscape Assessment*, Countryside Commission, Dorset County Council, Purbeck District Council.

Taylor, C (1970), *Dorset*, Hodder & Stoughton.

Countryside Commission (1993), *The Dorset Downs, Heaths and Coast Landscape*, Countryside Commission, Cheltenham CCP 424.

Countryside Commission (1994), *The New Map of England: A Celebration of the South Western Landscape*, Countryside Commission, Cheltenham CCP 444.